THE MINERS:
ONE UNION, ONE INDUSTRY

J. Gormley, OBE, President

THE MINERS:

ONE UNION, ONE INDUSTRY

*A History of the National Union
of Mineworkers
1939–46*

BY

R. PAGE ARNOT

London
GEORGE ALLEN & UNWIN
Boston   Sydney

GEORGE ALLEN & UNWIN LTD
40 Museum Street, London WC1A 1LU

© R. Page Arnot, 1979

British Library Cataloguing in Publication Data

Arnot, Robert Page
   The miners, one union, one industry.
   1. Coal mines and mining – Great Britain –
   History – 20th century
   I. Title
   338.2'7'20941   HD9555 1·5   78–40603

ISBN 0–04–331074–5

Typeset in 12 on 13 point Baskerville by Northampton Phototypesetters Ltd
and printed in Great Britain by Unwin Brothers Limited, Old Woking, Surrey

FOREWORD

It is with pride and pleasure that we present this volume that tells of the mineworkers during the 1939–45 War and of their subsequent achievements. These were crucial but creative times in the development of our union, as they were also the most perilous period in the whole of British history. While the governments and peoples of the British Commonwealth, together with Soviet and American and other allies, withstood the onslaught of the Berlin–Rome–Tokyo Axis, the British mineworkers played a notable part in the winning of victory. Mineworkers, while backing to the full the war effort, brought forward the necessary criticism of mistakes made by the wartime bureaucracy. As soon as the fall of the French Republic in 1940 had its disastrous effect upon the British coal trade, then in the grip of 'free private enterprise', it was the miners' leaders who saw what measures had to be undertaken, pressed for them and helped to carry them into action.

English, Scottish and Welsh coal-owners who had exploited the mineworkers for so long and whose conduct of the coal trade had proved such a source of weakness in wartime were brought under some control in 1942. But this was only possible because the mineworkers had utilised the opportunity given by the war to climb out of the Slough of Despond and the federative frustrations that had hindered all advance in the dozen dreadful years from 1927 to 1939, and in the end to bring their many associations together into one single National Union of Mineworkers.

The 'dual control' of 1942 was maintained until after the pits had been taken away from the coal-owners and made into units of public ownership under a National Coal Board set up in 1946. How this age-old demand of the mineworkers, fought for by the fathers and forefathers of the present generation, was adopted by a Labour Government and passed into law after six months' discussion in Parliament, is set forth fully in this volume.

At present, when a revival of investment in the coal-mining industry has been agreed between the government, the National Coal Board and ourselves, lessons can be learned by all from this record of past struggles.

In this latest book will be found the same high standard and grasp of essentials as in Dr Page Arnot's earlier writings. After sixty years' service to the Labour Movement, he can be justly proud, as we are, of this fourth volume of our history.

Joe Gormley   *President*

Michael McGahey   *Vice-President*

Lawrence Daly   *Secretary*

NATIONAL UNION OF MINEWORKERS

Essentially this book is a study of the approach to nationalisation, of the events and factors that immediately led to the
public ownership and control of the coal-mining industry. In
particular it is a study of how throughout the six-year war
from 1939 to 1945 the federated trade unions of the mining
industry strove to bring about its unification; and how in
the process of these contentions the various county, district
and craft associations were eventually themselves unified in one
single national body.

The first part of the book covers wartime years (the war
of the British Empire, with its Soviet, American and other
allies, against the fascist powers of the 'Berlin–Rome–Tokyo
axis') in order to specify the successive efforts of the miners'
leaders to ensure that measures deemed necessary for a victory
were actually carried out. These were struggles not only with
their mine-owners, their customary adversaries in industrial
relations, nor only with the swollen bureaucracy of the
Chamberlain and Churchill administrations, but also with
members of the Coalition Cabinet, including some hitherto
regarded as their own allies and friends within the Labour
movement. At the same time this book records how the miners'
leaders succeeded from 1939 onwards in reversing bit by bit
the onerous terms imposed by the coal-owners at the end of
the General Strike and seven-month lockout of 1926. For over
a dozen years the mineworkers had to suffer these imposed
terms including lower wages, longer hours and the conclusion of two dozen district agreements that effectively sundered
the Miners' Federation into as many separate units. In the
process of negating the owners' triumph of 1926 the national
organisation of the miners was itself re-created and was able
to shake off some of what had become federative shackles
on its advance.

In the autumn of 1939, a few weeks after Great Britain
declared war on Nazi Germany, at a meeting of the Board of
Conciliation for the Coal Trade of Monmouthshire and South
Wales the owners' President, Sir Evan Williams, Bt, made a
significant remark to his *vis-à-vis* Arthur Horner (who in turn

told me) to the effect that 'This is *your* war'. In whatever sense
the words were uttered, the coal-owners' President spoke
truly. Out of his long experience as a coal exporter from the
South African War of 1899–1902 to the War of Empires of
1914–18, and then as chosen leader for a quarter of a century
of all the exporting and inland sale colliery companies,
Sir Evan Williams had good reason to fear that the British
coal trade would prove unequal to the strain of mechanised
modern warfare. And so it proved. As had happened already
in 1916–18, so again in the midst of the 1939–45 War, the
government had to take over the coalmines and operate them
under a system of state control. But of course the malady of
the coal trade, visible for over twenty years before 1939, had
roots much deeper than could be conjectured by the foresight
of Sir Evan Williams, however fully equipped he might be
with all relevant facts and figures of the past and the
present century.

A little over a hundred years ago the drama began. At the
outset British supremacy was unrivalled in the world market.
Before 1870 the United Kingdom was producing more coal
each year than all the other countries of the world together. Output in 1865 was 100 million metric tonnes; the
United States produced only a quarter as much; Germany,
much less than a third; France and Belgium together, less
than a quarter; while Russia contributed one three-hundredth
of the British total. Then came the coal rush of the next half-
century with outputs doubling and trebling every few years
until the United Kingdom, though highest in Europe with
292 million metric tonnes in 1913, produced less than a quarter
of world output, while holding 55 per cent of all coal exports.

These commercial rivals rapidly developed a race for exports,
for protected markets and finally for the acquisition of colonies
– acquisitions pictured by geographers in 1900 as the growth
of empire, heralded and exemplified in 1877 by the proclama-
tion of the British monarch as Empress of India. By 1893
Germany and the United States had shed old forms of capital
structure that had become impediments in the race. But when
Sir George Elliott, the greatest figure in the coal trade, proposed that similar measures of combination be adopted, his
fellow coal-owners, committed from childhood to the *laissez-*

faire dogma, proved unable to follow his plan. Twenty
years later, the 'unmodernised' and increasingly backward
British coal trade proved unable to fulfil the obligations put
upon it by the European war of 1914–18 as was established by
the evidence given in 1919 to the Coal Industry Commission.
However beneficial have been the changes (of ownership and
conditions of employment), each recurring crisis since 1945
has found a shortage of skilled miners. Yet the supply
would always have been available if only the necessary
steps had been taken in time.

The research needed for this volume and the time expended
upon it proved to be much greater than was expected when
I began in 1973, greater too than the degree of continued
health and vigour that was assumed when I had the temerity
to embark upon it in my ninth decade. I conclude with
my thanks to the officials and members of the National
Union of Mineworkers for the kindness and courtesy with
which I have been met; to Sir Derek Ezra and other NCB
members for facilities given; to Lionel Murray and sundry
members of the TUC General Council; and finally to George
Jerrom, Rena Jerrom, Beulah Walker, Rosa Glading and to my
wife Olive for their continuous and critical help.

R. PAGE ARNOT

46 Byne Road, Sydenham, London, SE26 5JE
2 February 1977

CONTENTS

ACKNOWLEDGEMENTS

To Cassell & Co. for their kind permission to quote from *History of the Second World War* by Sir Basil Liddell Hart, Chapter IV, paragraph 6.

Also for their kind permission to quote from *The Second World War* by Sir Winston Churchill, Volume I, page 312.

To Frederick Muller Ltd for their kind permission to quote from *The Fateful Years* by Hugh Dalton, page 300.

To the National Coal Board for their courtesy and help in supplying photographs Nos 6 to 12 inclusive.

To the staffs of the British Museum and of the Public Record Office for their courtesy and ready assistance.

To the families of Fred Collindridge and Edward Jones for their courtesy and help in lending the photographs.

LIST OF ILLUSTRATIONS

Part One
Struggle for Unification of the Coal Trade

CHAPTER I

THE TRANSFORMING EFFECT OF WAR

I. THE FIRST IMPACT

The six-year war against the fascist powers of Europe and Asia brought in its course and in its wake a series of transformations. In the United Kingdom the changes were to be seen in each department of government; in commerce and industry; in arts and sciences; in economic policies and political situations. In the British Empire continuing transformations were more extensive and went much deeper with the sundering of century-old connections in every major continent.

When the United Kingdom declared war on Germany on 3 September 1939, the Prime Minister of the second 'National Government' was Neville Chamberlain, then supported by a large Conservative majority in Parliament. From 10 May 1940, the war was conducted by a 'Coalition Government' headed by Prime Minister Winston Churchill. From 23 May 1945, Churchill headed the 'Caretaker Government' for just nine weeks. From 26 July 1945, the war was conducted and concluded by the third 'Labour Government' with Clement Attlee as Prime Minister.

In 1939 the British coal trade, 'the life-blood of industry', was in the hands of a multitude of colliery-owners grouped in employers' associations, large and small, from the Monmouthshire and South Wales Coal Owners' Association to the South Staffordshire and East Worcestershire Coal Masters' Association, each separately conducting industrial relations within its coalfield. These in turn were linked up nationally in the Mining Association of Great Britain which had little to do with industrial relations. Those employed in the coal-mining industry were organised in trade unions, in a score of county or district associations (together with local or specialised unions to a total of nearly three score), most of them linked up in the Miners' Federation of Great Britain.

After the seven-month mining lockout (beginning with the nine-day General Strike of 1926) there had been no relations for nearly a decade between the Mining Association of Great Britain and the shaken if not shattered and disunited bodies that made up the Miners' Federation of Great Britain. A gulf yawned between the two sides. Only after spirits had been revived by a strike ballot in 1935 with a thirteen-to-one majority for industrial action (bringing tremors on the Stock Exchange); only after concessions made by multinational monopolist coal consumers under pressure from the Cabinet, did the owners on the Mining Association agree to the minimal step of setting up a National Joint Standing Consultative Committee for the Coal Trade of Great Britain.

Never had the miners' trade unions been driven so low as in the years 1930 to 1934. Even after 1935 it could be said of the MFGB that truly it had fallen upon evil days. The then Secretary of the MFGB, on whose solitary shoulders had fallen the daily task of leadership, found himself largely limited in his activities to bringing some good order into a great retreat; and then to setting forth the miners' aims and policy in a series of closely argued pamphlets: for when the MFGB approached the government it was met, not by the Prime Minister or a Cabinet committee, nor even by the Secretary for Mines, but only by one of the administrative class of the civil service. Such had been the situation at the outbreak of war.

The war and its aftermath transformed this situation out of all recognition. Within seven years from 1939 the pits had been taken away from the coal-owners and vested in the nation; the colliery proprietors' associations continued to exist for a few years but only for a sharing-out of the compensation; the county associations and the other trade union bodies had been fused into a single national union which could more effectively safeguard the mineworkers under state ownership; while the chaotic multitude of mines had been brought into order and made subject to a unified direction. .

How could this happen? How could such a massive and

complex series of changes without civil disturbance or tumult be effected in these seven short years?

The answer to questions such as these must be sought in an examination of the main factors and external compulsions, of the agencies and the episodes of the wartime years, in a word, of the deeds or failures of the actors in what can be seen as this great drama of the coalfields, played out against the back-cloth of a world cataclysm in days of utmost peril to the United Kingdom.

In the forefront of any such examination must be placed, not the persons or policies of the coal trade, but those of the government whose initiative was responsible alike for the declaration of war and for the directives given to (or withheld from) the coal-mining industry. The Chamberlain Government had made a bad start, as was shown by Winston S. Churchill himself in his six-volume history *The Second World War* when he indicted the second 'National Government' for having allowed Germany to re-arm, to build submarines, to seize Austria and Czechoslovakia, and for having spurned the Soviet proposals for joint action. Churchill wrote:

History, which, we are told, is mainly the record of the crimes, follies, and miseries of mankind, may be scoured and ransacked to find a parallel to this sudden and complete reversal of five or six years' policy of easy-going placatory appeasement,* and its transformation almost overnight into a readiness to accept an obviously imminent war on far worse conditions and on the greatest scale . . .
(Churchill, *The Second World War*, Vol. I, pp. 311–12)

A British Government so ill prepared could hardly have been expected to do well in waging a European war, still less to do the needful on matters economic. On the matter of energy resources, and particularly of coal output, they proved sadly lacking for seven crucial months – the period

*After 1933 when the seizure of power in Germany by Hitler and his National Labour Socialist Party (Nazis) had brought the danger of war in Europe, successive Prime Ministers (MacDonald, Baldwin and Chamberlain) had sought to placate the fascist powers. Chamberlain, making friendly gestures and concessions to Mussolini and Hitler, abandoned the victims of fascist aggression in Africa and Spain, submitted to the successive seizures of the Rhineland and of Austria, cold-shouldered the approaches of the USA and the definite proposals of the USSR for the maintenance of peace, and finally entered 'the Munich conspiracy' for the betrayal and handing over of Czechoslovakia.

described by the Yankee newspapers as 'the phoney war' –
from September 1939 until Hitler's unexpected offensive in
1940.*

. . . the position could only be described as one of utter chaos . . . hundreds
of thousands of people, not only in the smaller townships, but in the
largest cities, were unable to procure supplies of fuel while at the same
time many pits were working two and three days a week.
(MFGB Annual Conference 1940, Report of the Executive Committee,
pp. 335–6)

2. MINING PROTAGONISTS

The British coal trade has often been presented to newspaper
readers as an arena of disputes between capital and labour.
Whenever these industrial relations are staged in the media
there has inevitably been a reduction of the broad issues
affecting scores of thousands into differences between representative individuals, as happened most signally in the years
of the 1914–18 War and again in 1925–6 when A. J. Cook
was leading the miners.

Once again with the outbreak of war in 1939 the stage was
set: and the chief spokesmen on either side were brought to
the forefront. Between the leader of the colliery proprietors
(Sir Evan Williams) and the leader of the working colliers
(Ebby Edwards) there was a great contrast which began with
their geographical origins and extended even to their manner
of speech. Sir Evan Williams came from Llangennech on the
river Llwchwr, some four miles from the busy seaport of Llanelli,
at the extreme south-west of the great Welsh coalfield. He
was the elder son (born 1871) of Thomas Williams of Llwyn
Gwern, Pontardulais, founder of Thomas Williams & Sons

---

*Liddell Hart in his chapter 'The phoney war' wrote:
After the fall of France, the Germans captured the files of the French High Command –
and published a collection of sensational documents from them. These showed how the Allied
chiefs had spent the winter in contemplating offensive plans all round the circle – for striking
at Germany's rear flank through Norway, Sweden and Finland; for striking at the Ruhr
through Belgium; for striking at her remote eastern flank through Greece and the Balkans;
for cutting off her lone source of petrol supply by striking at Russia's great oil fields in
the Caucasus. It was a wonderful collection of fantasies – the vain imaginings of Allied
leaders, living in a dream-world until the cold douche of Hitler's own offensive awoke them.
(Liddell Hart, *History of the Second World War*, p. 36)

(Llangennech) Ltd. He went from Christ College, Brecon, an ancient foundation dating from 1541, to Clare College, Cambridge. After taking his degree he entered his father's business, a relatively small firm, owning two mines in Carmarthenshire working five seams of coal and employing 670 mineworkers in 1926.* By his early forties Evans was spreading his wings. Elected Chairman of the Monmouthshire and South Wales Coal Owners' Association in 1913, he had presided over the Conciliation Board for the Coal Trade of South Wales since 1918. In 1919 he became President of the Mining Association of Great Britain and in that same year was appointed a member of the Sankey Commission in the later stages of its sittings. From 1921 to 1925 he was President of the National Board set up for the Coal Industry and presided over the Joint Committee of Coal Owners' and Miners' Representatives appointed to inquire into the condition of the coal industry 1924–5.†

He was President of the National Confederation of Employers' Organisations, 1925–6; Chairman of the Central Council under the Coal Mines Act (1930) to 1938; Chairman of the International Conference of European Coal Owners' Organisations; Vice-President of the Federation of British Industry; Chairman of the Joint Standing Consultative Committee for the Coal Mining Industry; and President of the British Colliery Owners' Research Association, the Coal Utilisation Council and the British Coal Utilisation Research Association.

He was Chairman of Thomas Williams & Sons (Llangennech) Ltd; of Llanelly Associated Tinplate Cos Ltd; of Lime Firms Ltd; and of other industrial companies. He was a Director of Lloyds Bank; of Powell Duffryn Associated Collieries Ltd; of Welsh Associated Collieries Ltd; of Cardiff Collieries Ltd; and of other companies.

He was Deputy-Lieutenant for Carmarthen and Justice of the Peace for that county. In 1922–3 he was High Sheriff of Carmarthenshire. He was Seneschal of Priory for Wales of the

---

*A third mine, Brynlliw at Pontardulais, lying across the border in Glamorgan, was listed in 1926 as 'temporarily closed' and was still so described seventeen years later.

†For this internal inquiry, the author, together with other members of the Labour Research Department, compiled the materials on behalf of the Miners' Federation.

Order of St John of Jerusalem and a Knight of the Order. In 1935 he was created a baronet and in 1940 became a member of the Coal Production Council.

Against this towering figure of capital personified stood the miners' leader Ebby Edwards, born in the thinly populated parish of Chevington 'east-nor'-east of Morpeth' in Northumberland. But Ebby was no Johnny Raw from a remote countryside. On the contrary, as was shown repeatedly throughout his career,* Edwards was the most experienced and politically developed person to have been chief officer of the Miners' Federation.

Much earlier, in the nine-day General Strike of May 1926, Ebby Edwards had made Burt Hall (the miners' headquarters in Newcastle-upon-Tyne) the focus and centre of trade union resistance to the strike-breaking attempts of the government forces and so successfully as to baffle the Civil Commissioner, Sir Kingsley Wood, who with his general Kerr Montgomery came by night to negotiate with the Strike Committee – for which yielding to the strikers Wood had afterwards to make an abject personal statement in the House of Commons.

Ebby Edwards's studies at Ruskin College, the working men's college in Oxford, had endowed him with a grasp of political economy to which was added no small skill in writing. Deprived of responsibility for the conduct of industrial relations, Ebby Edwards devoted himself to propaganda of the miners' case. Year after year he issued pamphlets from 55 Russell Square in Bloomsbury. Already in 1933 he put out *Coal Problems: A Plea for a National Fuel Policy* in which he warned of the irruption of the multinational oil trusts and emphasised that 'Britain is a coal nation . . . If she does not make use of her own fuel resources she necessarily weakens her whole economic structure, and correspondingly depresses the standards of living of her people.' His proposals, ignored by successive Cabinets, would have made all the difference in the six-year war of 1939 to 1945 and still more in the second half of the twentieth century. In this and other pamphlets Ebby wrote with a grasp of realities superior to that shown by the statesmen in Whitehall.

*See *The Miners in Crisis and War* (Volume III of *A History of the Miners' Federation of Great Britain*), by R. Page Arnot, Allen & Unwin, 1961.

But as a public speaker Ebby could not compete with the smooth and mellifluous if somewhat hurried accents of west Wales or the flowing phraseology of Sir Evan Williams who, on one occasion for a space of nearly two hours, harangued a Cabinet committee on the grievances of the coal-owners. Ebby Edwards, after years in the metropolis, still retained in his speech the 'burr' characteristic of all from that remote shire whose inhabitants could be heard to say: 'We are no English: we are Northumbrians: we are the folk the Romans built the Wall against, to keep us out of England.'

3. NEED FOR COAL − AND FOR COLLIERS

When His Britannic Majesty's Government declared war on 3 September 1939, when on that fateful Sunday in the House of Commons the Prime Minister, faced with demands both from the Labour leader Arthur Greenwood and from Leopold Amery and others on his own Tory back benches, falteringly uttered the words that meant 'War upon Nazi Germany', there was little sign to follow of any preparedness for this step except the profusion of gas masks and the wail of sirens giving the alarm of bombing raids. There was little sign of there having been any 'War Book', with its itemised activities schemed out in advance, to be put into immediate operation as had happened a quarter of a century earlier at the outbreak of the War of Empires. In the economic sector and certainly as regards coal mining there seems to have been no sufficient preparedness by the government department responsible.

On Monday 4 September the seventy-first annual Trades Union Congress took an immediate decision to close its meeting at Bridlington in two days and so enable all delegates (108 miners amongst them) to get back to where they could most effectively do their duties in wartime. The need for more coal to meet the extra demands of a war situation naturally became a matter of extreme urgency; and so, on 12 September, at the invitation of the Secretary of Mines, the officials met him to discuss the position that was likely to arise.

In the discussion Secretary Ebby Edwards and his two

colleagues (President Will Lawther and Vice-President Jim Bowman) were startled, as upon the brink of an abyss, to find what backward notions were entertained within the Department of Mines. For the points raised were similar to those which Robert Smillie had had to combat in 1915 when there had also been a loss of mining manpower and a consequent coal shortage. The miners' officials reacted vigorously; and as appears from their Executive Committee minute of 14 September 1939 '. . . left the Secretary for Mines with no ambiguity as to where the Federation stood with regard to any increasing of hours or relaxation so far as overtime was concerned'. Moreover, as a result of that discussion, the Secretary for Mines addressed a letter to both owners and miners in which he pointed out that it would be necessary to increase the output to a figure of 260 million to 270 million tons per annum, and asked that the two sides of the industry should put forward any recommendation which could be made jointly with a view to meeting the demand.

On Thursday 14 September 1939, at the MFGB Executive Committee meeting, this letter was given lengthy and thorough consideration. Since the officials had on 12 September made it clear to the Secretary for Mines that such a joint discussion '. . . would have to provide for more than the specific question of increased production', and would have to cover the whole of the ramifications likely to arise under existing conditions, the Executive Committee found themselves already committed. They had no option but to follow the line taken by the three officials 'off their own bat'; so it was resolved finally to accept the offer of meeting on 21 September as put forward in a letter from the Secretary of the Mining Association of Great Britain. Before the end of the month the EC members were committed to very much more than that.

To understand what had happened and what had been set in train for the next few months it is necessary to realise the standpoint and the attitude of Ebby Edwards at this particular time. Acutely aware of the increasing disintegration of the MFGB into a score of separate and sometimes competing unions, Edwards saw in the outbreak of war an opportunity which he was quick to grasp; he saw that he could assert and maintain the power of the Federation and of its central elected authority over the twenty constituent unions.

After the General Strike and seven-month lockout of 1926 the coal-owners had, in effect, torn the MFGB to pieces by the setting up of so many separate coalfield agreements and by stipulating that there should be no further negotiations on a national basis but only district by district. After the 1935–6 struggle for 'the miners' two bob' on a national scale (including a thirteen-to-one ballot vote for industrial action in autumn 1935) the application of the agreement reached was remitted to each district to deal with separately. Though contact on a national scale was then resumed it was on a formula of very limited scope. In the next three years, to the dismay of Edwards and of those who had always reposed their hopes in national organisation, there was the spectacle of some district associations finding it comfortable to work along with the owners in their particular coalfield. Quarrels broke out between one district union and another, reflecting differences that had arisen between their respective owners. Edwards, knowing well that he would be faced by the opposition of several of the more important districts, was determined to take that risk and to drive through the reintegration of the Federation and the restoration of the miners' unions to the position they had held in earlier years. He drove for this all the more as it coincided with the needs of the prosecution of a successful war wherein coal was such an important factor.

The attempt had been made in the previous years to bring about a reorganisation of the Federation. One of the special four subcommittees of the Executive was devoted to this purpose and was called the Reorganisation Committee. In successive annual congresses in 1937 and 1938 some advance had been made step by step towards the desired strengthening of the Federation.

But only seven weeks earlier, at the July 1939 annual conference, the whole of the carefully worked out proposals of the Reorganisation Committee had been ruthlessly rejected by the delegates in a strong backlash of parochialism, led by Sam Watson of Durham, then the largest constituent of the MFGB. Smarting under this defeat, this rejection of the careful planning of years and devoted activity towards rebuilding the Federation, Ebby Edwards this time was taking no chances. Throughout the winter in each step taken he secured the acceptance of it or the ratification of it by the members of the Executive.

He was able to gain the adherence of the other two officers. Will Lawther, from Blaydon-upon-Tyne, Acting President up till July 1939, although never one of the leading officials of the Durham coalfield, had experience on a national scale, having been elected in 1922 to the Executive Committee of the Labour Party and having sat in Parliament as Member for Barnard Castle from 1929 to 1931. This political experience and also his preoccupation with the building up of independent working-class education predisposed Lawther to a broad outlook. This applied both to the coal-mining industry and to national and international affairs. In this last Lawther chimed in well enough with Edwards, whose international outlook, enlarged and strengthened from his position as Secretary of the Miners' International Federation, had been channelled into campaigns against fascism and against the danger of war. So it was a skilled and eager MFGB official who had hastened to meet the Secretary for Mines and to put him straight – and at the same time to prepare for a quite different sort of national conclave from what had been originally intended on the government side.

Lastly there was Vice-President Jim Bowman, successor in Northumberland both to Edwards and to old William Straker, younger than the great majority of his colleagues and of marked personal ability. It was a peculiarity in the situation that these three men from the north-east, the old Durham-Northumberland Tyne-and-Wear coalfield, should so unexpectedly be confronting all the other coalfields of Britain. The Northumberland and Durham miners' unions had been outside the Miners' Federation of Great Britain for the first twenty years of its existence and had only entered it when the hatchet had been buried over the question of the Eight Hours Act in 1909. The two districts of the north-east coast who had been in the very forefront in the beginnings of effective trade unionism a hundred years earlier were now to resume their place in the persons of these three officials as giving a lead to the whole of the disunited MFGB.

The Joint Standing Consultative Committee for the Coal Mining Industry of Great Britain, which was due to meet on 21 September 1939, had been set up in 1936 with limited functions and limited numbers – ten on each side. The miners' nine were composed of the three officials and six other members of the MFGB Executive Committee. The six appointed on 27 July 1939 had been Oliver Harris of South Wales, Harry Hicken of Derby, W. Foster of Lancashire, A. B. Clarke of Scotland, H. W. Cooper of Nottinghamshire and J. A. Hall of Yorkshire. Of these six from the workers' side the officials felt they could rely for support upon Harry Hicken and W. Foster, each of a forward-looking disposition and skilled in discussion with employers. Ebby Edwards, however, could not be certain of the other four. But at the opening of the EC meeting on 14 September the first business was a vote of sympathy with Oliver Harris who 'had unfortunately suffered a serious breakdown in health': it was agreed that 'owing to the indisposition of Mr. Oliver Harris, Mr. A. L. Horner be allowed to deputise for him as a member of the Joint Standing Consultative Committee'. This decision gave the officials not only a majority on the union's JSCC Subcommittee but also a very powerful addition in argumentative force in support of their policy. The decision had been 'that a report be given to the full Executive Committee before anything further be done'.

Despite this Ebby was now going to put forward policies without having been so instructed by any resolution of the Executive Committee.

So far Ebby, supported by his Acting President and Vice-President, had committed the Executive Committee to a policy towards others in the industry. Ebby had told the Secretary for Mines that the MFGB would not approach the owners for a meeting, as had been suggested, but that it was the business of the government to put forward that proposition to both owners and miners and to lay the first responsibility on the owners so that the miners would have the last word; and he had made it clear that when the joint meeting came it would be over a much wider field than that of increasing production.

Outside the officials, Horner was very much the maid-of-all-work on the Executive Committee where he sat already on the Safety in Mines Subcommittee and also on the Reorganisation Subcommittee. The remaining committee was that on Workmen's Compensation.

From the outset it was obvious that the chief problem facing the industry would be lack of manpower. Moreover in the first two or three weeks of the war some 27,000 men had left the industry for the military and civil defence services. The Mines Department, however, had intimated that they would do everything possible to prevent key men from being called up and would secure the return of such men wherever possible. This, clearly, could only have been a pious aspiration, and in any case applied only to 'key men'. Both sides of the industry took it as such; for everybody knew of the 1914–18 record of the recruiting sergeants, whereby coal output had been seriously endangered.

The MFGB representatives then raised the issue that 'there must necessarily be many questions, other than that of production, which were certain to arise during the war period and therefore, there should be some effective machinery to deal with such matters as they arose'. The Federation was not satisfied that the Consultative Committee, limited by the formula* under which it was set up, would be capable of dealing with such problems and the owners were asked to agree to the establishment of a body representative of the two organisations with authority to take decisions.

In his reply Sir Evan Williams stated that the owners' side would not regard the subjects which the committee might consider as limited to the terms of the formula laid down in 1936 but would be prepared to consider all the problems which the abnormal circumstances of the war made it necessary to discuss. Sir Evan said, however, that the owners could not guarantee to be able to give a decision on every question, because both sides were in a position of having to consult their constituents. But he agreed that if the cost of living increased that fact must be taken into consideration in connection with wages. The meeting then stood adjourned until

---

*'The consideration of all questions of common interest and of general application to the industry, not excluding general principles applicable to the determination of wages by district agreements.'

28 September for the owners to hold consultations on the Federation's request.

It had been obvious at the 21 September meeting of the JSCC of the Coal Industry that the question of increased production and the lack of manpower would have to be tackled in the districts. So, without any delay, Ebby Edwards sent out the following letter:

> 50 Russell Square,
> London, W.C.1
> *September* 23, 1939

Cir. No. D. S. 32/39
To Secretaries of District Organisations:
DEAR SIR,

The Federation along with the Mining Association were recently approached by the Government in relation to the question of increased coal production, it being pointed out to both organisations that it was estimated it would be necessary to increase the output up to a figure of 260 to 270 million tons per annum – an increase of 30 to 40 million tons as compared with the production figures of 1938.

The Government communication was given due consideration by the Executive Committee of the Federation at its last meeting. The Committee are fully aware that in a period of emergency such as now exists there are many problems in addition to production, viz., cost of living, working hours, wage rates, safety, etc., which will require active consideration by the owners and ourselves, and it was decided that the Federation representatives should participate in joint meetings with the Mining Association provided that any joint committee should have the fullest powers to deal with all problems that might arise in the industry during the war period.

You will appreciate that in the interests of the membership, the industry and the country, no other decision was possible, and I am sure that such decision will be welcomed by the districts.

When such a joint committee as is visualised by the Executive has been established, it may be necessary to consult the membership on certain fundamental issues, and districts can rest assured that the Committee will desire this to be done whenever necessary and practicable.

There are, however, certain guiding principles which districts are requested to note as follows:–

(a) That no extension of the working day should be agreed upon.
(b) That the Federation policy on overtime as accepted at the last Annual Conference and outlined in my circular letter to districts dated August 2, 1939, should be strictly adhered to.
(c) That any suggested reduction in the school leaving age, whether made nationally or locally, should be strenuously opposed.

(d) That there should be no extension in the employment of women.
(e) That the law relating to the employment of boys on the night-shift should continue to be enforced.

It is essential that the Executive Committee, or its representatives, shall be fully informed on the various points which may be raised in forthcoming discussions, and I should therefore be extremely obliged to receive your replies to the questions set out on the enclosed sheet at an early date.

Yours sincerely,
EBBY EDWARDS,
Secretary.

QUESTIONNAIRE
Relating to various coalmining and labour issues which are likely to arise during the present war emergency.

(1) How many unemployed men have you in your area who are ex-miners and who would be willing to return to the pits?
    If possible, divide these into three categories:
        (a) Face workers,
        (b) Other underground workers,
        (c) Surface workers.
(2) How many days per week (or fortnight) can your members work under the present District Agreement?
(3) How many days are now being worked?
(4) What would be the approximate increase in coal production if short time working was eliminated in your District?
(5) Are there any pits in your District which have been closed down in recent times and which could easily be re-opened?
    Indicate if there would be a sufficient supply of labour in the locality concerned to work the pit/s.
(6) How many compensation men, able to do light work at a colliery, are available in your District?
(7) Is the regrading of men, now employed on light work, a possibility as a means to employ compensation men capable of light work?
(8) Is unnecessary absenteeism prevalent in your District?
    If so, how do you suggest it can be reduced.
(9) What machinery, if any, exists in your District to settle grievances without resorting to strike action?

4. NATIONAL NEGOTIATIONS ACHIEVED

The German assault, the *Blitzkrieg* of air force and fast-moving tanks, bursting upon Poland on 1 September 1939, had largely

Michael McGahey, Vice-President

Lawrence Daly, Secretary

shattered all resistance within two weeks. By the fourth week of the month a large country on whose behalf the United Kingdom and the French Republic had declared war had been completely over-run.

This daunting news, and the knowledge that the rich Silesian coalfield was now in the hands of the Nazi invaders, added to the urgency of the tasks before the British coal-mining industry. Ebby Edwards, more sensitive to the European situation than many of his colleagues, immediately saw the need for a quick follow-up of what had been gained in the successive discussions on 12, 14 and 21 September. If at the forthcoming meeting of the Joint Standing Consultative Committee on 28 September a wages demand were to be put forward by the workers' side and discussed, then the deed would have been done: the old right of conducting wage negotiations on a national scale would willy-nilly have been restored to the MFGB and to its officers. So indeed the event took place.

In his own account, compiled a month later, Ebby Edwards wrote:

During the interval between the two meetings it became obvious to every-one that, in spite of the promises of the Government to take action against profiteering, the cost of living was rapidly rising and when your rep-resentatives on the Consultative Committee held a preliminary meeting to the meeting of the JSCC held on 28 September, it was decided that a claim should be made for an immediate flat rate advance in wages of 1s. per shift for those workers 18 years and over, and 6d. for those workers under 18, such advance to be adjusted in relation to the cost of living when the actual facts were published. (MFGB, 1939, p. 451)

At the adjourned JSCC meeting Sir Evan Williams intimated that the request for a much wider scope of the deliberations of the committee had been fully considered by the owners who had granted it. Thereupon the ten miners' representatives tabled their demand for a national wage increase. 'The owners were a little astonished,' reported Ebby Edwards. 'When they indicated that the scope would be widened, in went our application for an advance at the same meeting.' The owners now wanted an adjournment of two weeks to put the miners' request before their Central Council – naturally enough for those who for thirteen years had refused to discuss any such question as was now raised. As Sir Evan Williams put it, the owners could not go so far as to recommend an increase of 1s and 6d but were prepared to consult with their members and see how the position could be met.

A fortnight later, prolonged arguments brought the matter no nearer to an issue: and that lengthy meeting of the JSCC on 12 October left the ten miners' representatives feeling very dissatisfied. The next day, Friday 13 October, they had to report to the full Executive Committee of the Federation meeting at 50 Russell Square in London. There it was reported what had already taken place to get increased coal production and to carry out the EC instructions of 14 September.

Not only had the question of increased coal production been discussed, but in keeping with the instruction of the EC at its meeting held on 14 September, an undertaking had been sought and granted by the owners that the JSCC should be the body to deal with not only the question of increased coal production, but all and every question that was likely to arise during the period of the war, on an unlimited basis, with power and authority to reach decisions where possible.

The miners' representatives, who had taken upon themselves the responsibility of formulating a demand to the owners for a flat rate increase for all mineworkers, now desired 'that the Executive Committee should express their views upon what had already transpired'.

The officials, with the other six on the workers' side of the JSCC, had seized a chance and now hoped for Executive backing. They were not disappointed. Ebby's calculations were to prove justified. The record runs as follows:

After a lengthy discussion it was agreed that our representatives on the JSCC continue their negotiations with the owners' representatives on the most exhaustive scale along the lines reported by the Secretary, with a view to securing an increase in wages to meet the increase in the cost of living as shown from time to time during the period of the war. When the final offer of the owners has been received, our representatives to consider same and report back to a meeting of the Full Executive Committee in order that the committee itself will then accept the responsibility in making a recommendation to a Conference of the District representatives to be convened on the matter.

(MFGB, 1939, p. 382)

The three officials and the six Executive Committee members who made up the workers' side of the JSCC had indeed deserved well of the mineworkers. The first step had been taken to pull the mining trade unions out of the Slough of Despond and Disunity in which they had been wallowing for over a dozen years: and to restore to the Miners' Federation the functions and the powers of which it had been deprived. What would come of the claim for a flat rate war-bonus was yet to be seen.

At a further meeting of the JSCC held on 19 October Sir Evan Williams stated that the owners 'felt very strongly that the present situation would be met quite adequately by an increase of 6d. per day for adults, and 3d. per day for non-adults'. In reply the miners' representatives expressed their profound dissatisfaction, their spokesman saying that the miners were now faced with the irrefutable fact that they were paying more for their goods than prewar. For the government to have any misgivings about the miners' claim for increased wages to meet the increased cost of living was amazing when it was recognised that they themselves had failed to deal adequately with the situation. 'We were not asking to take advantage of the country because of the war; we only ask for justice.'

But the others would not budge. 'The owners', said Sir Evan, 'could not give an increase in wages unless we have the money coming in to do it.' The Federation representatives retired, considered the position and finally agreed to inform the owners: 'that the minimum figures that our representatives are prepared to recommend to the Executive Committee of the Federation for adoption should be 8d. for those workers 18 years of age and over and 4d. for those under 18 years of age.'

Sir Evan Williams then said at the full meeting of the JSCC that on the understanding the settlement would apply from 1 November to the end of the year, 'we shall take the risk of making a definite offer of 8d. and 4d.'.

Would this initiative of the Negotiating Committee, which cut across all arrangements worked out in the past dozen years, be ratified at the forthcoming Special Conference on Wages and the Cost of Living? Edwards had experience from as far back as the 1914–18 War, while in the conferences of

1925 and 1926 it had fallen to him more than once to play a leading part. As Secretary from 1932, as sole permanent official of the Federation, he had behind him seven years of conferences, both special and annual: from his point of view seven lean years. Only that summer of 1939, in July, the most carefully constructed and prepared statements on the policy of integrating the Federation had been so beset by amendments and alternative propositions that finally the matter had to be remitted once more to the districts. This time, in face of the menacing war situation and the rapidly worsening supply of manpower, Ebby was taking no chances. In his report to the Executive Committee he stated that he had prepared in pamphlet form a summary of the whole of the negotiations that had taken place to date.

The Federation's representatives on the JSCC then made their recommendation. After the MFGB Executive Committee had made a comprehensive survey of the whole of the negotiations it was decided to submit to the conference a resolution for acceptance of the settlement reached.

5. SPECIAL CONFERENCE OF 27 OCTOBER 1939

Over 200 mineworkers assembled in Conway Hall, Red Lion Square, London WC1 for the special conference. President Will Lawther called on the Secretary to report on behalf of the EC and to move the resolution. Edwards then expounded his summary of the negotiations issued that day to every delegate.

We recognised that since 1926 – thirteen years ago – the Mining Association had said not only that never again would they meet the Mineworkers' Federation, but that their constitution was such that it prevented them from taking part in national negotiations . . . Our object in securing national contact, temporarily for the war, but with the possibility of its being continued for the future, should be weighed in this Conference by every delegate as being of as much value and of as much importance as even any wage increase that is offered . . . (27 October 1939)

After questions had been asked and answered the discussion began with two speakers against the resolution. The second speaker, E. Hough of Yorkshire, said that 'Sir Evan

Williams is only meeting us because it suits him,' and ended with the words: 'I am not doubting Ebby's sincerity; I think he believes in what he said to us, but, unfortunately, I do not agree with him . . . and I shall move the rejection of the offer.'

George Spencer* of Nottingham recalled that at their July 1939 conference at Swansea, 'I did put in a caveat against the Executive assuming the right to negotiate on behalf of the district. Every district has the right to give that power and authority to the Executive if it likes, but my submission, without labouring this particular point, is that the Executive have no right to assume that authority.' Then he allowed that in the present situation there were functions which the Executive might perform 'with some advantage to the districts'. He listed two: first, that they should 'watch most carefully and closely the index figure' on the cost of living, and from time to time make known to the districts what increases in wages would meet that index figure; secondly, to agree, either with the government or with the owners, upon the figure of the increase in the price of coal.

George Spencer said, '. . . you have taken away from my district the right to express that increase either in the form of a percentage or as a flat rate . . . I do say this: the right of expression should be retained by the districts, and in so far as that has been taken out of our hands you have interfered with the district machinery.' Spencer then dealt with the differentiation of wages 'based upon the differentiation of work' and claimed, 'there are within this proposed settlement actually the elements of a reduction so far as the higher paid men are concerned . . . you are taking away some of our rights, and you are establishing a principle which is going to militate against the higher paid men in the districts. I am all for the lower paid man having his share. What I am saying is it is unfair to those men at the coal face.'

Now came support from Lancashire. Joe Tinker, MP, in 1926 a keen campaigner along with A. J. Cook, told how, at their delegate conference on Saturday 21 October, 120 delegates, with one exception, were in favour of accepting the resolution.

*See R. Page Arnot, *The Miners in Crisis and War* (Allen & Unwin, 1961), *passim*.

The next delegate to speak was J. Hibberd of Yorkshire who stated his belief that 'immediately the danger of war is removed, Sir Evan Williams will go back to the *status quo*, and we shall have no more hopes of continuing national arrangements'.

The final speech in the debate came from Arthur Horner of South Wales, who made a surprising opening statement.

I am speaking as one of the Negotiating Committee responsible for bringing about this offer, and I do it with a full appreciation that the district of which I am President has turned down the offer by 9 votes to 1. That does not make me feel that what we have done has been a mistake.

Horner then, turning to look at the districts who had been opposing the Executive Committee's recommendation, spoke as follows:

We said first, 'Let us try to solve the situation in Yorkshire. The most obvious thing to do to increase production is to utilise existing mines to their full capacity, and not two or three days a week as is the case in Nottinghamshire, Yorkshire and Derbyshire, for a great part of the year.' The first blow struck was struck for the Midland counties, and not for the export districts of the country . . . We told the owners in the first meeting – a meeting, mark you, at which we were to discuss not wages, but the raising of production by 30 million tons a year – that it was futile to hope there ever could be satisfaction in the coalfield . . . or regularity of working when prices were rising in consequence of increases in the cost of living, and the ascertainments were not giving compensation for that increase in a sufficiently rapid period of time . . . and from that moment the wages issue became the subject of the negotiations.

At the same time Horner said that they had considered the time ripe to raise the issue of a national settlement.

So we said, without disturbing the basis of wages, let us try to find a formula which will at least ensure this, that at the worst . . . the most backward district, including the Forest of Dean . . . shall have the same advantage as Yorkshire, and the same as Nottinghamshire. In fact they needed it more with an average wage of 11s. a day as against an average wage of 15s. a day . . .

There is a fundamental difference between some of us and Mr. Spencer . . . I want national organisation. I believe in national control of the wage policy. I believe in using every possible situation to unify . . . the miners of this country. I do not think it is right that the accident of geography should determine that Welsh miners should get two thirds of what the miners in the Midlands are getting. I do not even believe that the exigencies of war should produce a position where export districts such as I come from might entitle us for a period, to wages far in excess even of the inland districts. Our national policy has been to try to secure the maximum national control . . . Why don't the owners want national control? Because relatively they are weaker with national control than when they are divided into districts. What does that mean? It means that if we can establish national control for the period of the war we have gained a stronger position for the miners of this country than we will have as districts for the period of the war . . . My view is that this conference is not deciding 8d. and 4d. It is deciding whether, with the contradictions that there are in our ranks, there is the basis and the possibility for national uniform control of our wages for the course of the war . . .

Therefore, regardless of any personal consequences, I would like to say to Mr. Spencer, the issue of a flat rate versus a percentage is not a dispute between us and the owners. They asked us to take a percentage form of increase, but it is we who say that by giving a flat rate increase the labourer on 6s. 6d. would get 10 per cent of his wages, the higher paid man on 7s. 6d. would get 8.88 per cent. And ought he not to get it? Is somebody to get something in excess of the cost of living on a percentage basis at the expense of the lower paid men having something less than the increase in the cost of living? That is not a principle on which we have to split this Federation – flat rate or percentages . . . Whatever disagreement South Wales might have about the amount, they are absolutely unanimous that whatever increase there is, it must take the form of a flat rate . . .

Then, speaking with great emphasis, Horner concluded as follows:

And so I think this conference is one of the most important the Federation has ever held. You are deciding for the period of the war what you are going to do . . . Are we to go twenty times separately for the same thing, or are we going to go together to meet the one authority as one authority and say, 'This is the increase we demand; this is the increase we are entitled to; this is the increase you must make possible'? Then if the Government refuse, we should be much more effective in exercising pressure against the Government as a unified Mineworkers' Federation of Great Britain than as twenty separate districts grumbling about the dissatisfaction of the men and the frustration of their efforts to get coal prices increased.

When Horner ended his speech, there were impatient cries of 'Vote, vote'; and it was decided the vote be taken following the Vice-President's reply to the discussion. James Bowman covered the ground of the argument of the opponents; and concluded:

Let us appreciate this, that for the last thirteen years we have been a loose federation of districts without any central authority, without any central control upon the work of our industry . . . I ask this conference to appreciate the things that have been done through the efforts of the Nego-tiating Committee; you are not rejecting an offer of Sir Evan Williams; if you reject this offer you reject that which the Consultative Committee have accepted on behalf of the members.

The special conference then voted: 342,000 for the Executive Committee resolution, 253,000 against – majority 89,000. Those voting in the minority were 100 each from South Wales and Yorkshire, 51 delegates from Scotland and 2 from Forest of Dean. The arguments of the closing speakers had swept the board, except where delegates had come mandated against.

It was therefore agreed:

That this conference having received the report of the Executive Committee on the negotiations with the Mining Association in relation to advances in wages, agrees to accept the offer made by the Mining Association to apply to the whole of the coalfield.

Further, the conference authorises the Executive Committee to continue the negotiations with a view to securing wage advances which shall, at the minimum, compensate for the increased cost of living. (27 October 1939)

6. LACK OF MANPOWER

By the end of the nineteenth century the coal trade employed a greater proportion of the available labour power (males of 10 years of age and upwards) than any other industry. From three-quarters of a million in 1901 the figure rose to over a million in 1911 and nearly a million and a quarter in 1920. Thereafter, in the years between the 1914–18 and 1939–45 Wars, the contraction of the industry set in: the number dwindled from just on a million employed in the year 1929, when the world economic crisis had its beginnings, to the three-quarters of a million of 1936.

In the later thirties there was some recovery; and in 1938,

the last full year before the war, the number of wage-earners, averaged over the twelvemonth, was 871,700 with a total output of 226,993,200 tons of coal. In 1939 the sudden requirement upon the outbreak of war was for an increase of output up to a figure of 260 million to 270 million tons per annum. But how were colliery-owners and mineworkers, to whom it was obvious from the outset that the chief problem confronting the industry was a lack of manpower, to be able to cope with the steady draining away of the existing workforce? At the first meeting of the JSCC on 21 September 1939 it was pointed out that 27,000 had already left the industry for the military and civil services. At the meeting of the JSCC held on 12 October 1939 the owners had raised the question of men being called to serve in the armed forces from the mines. The position was rather alarming. The iron and steel trades had secured exemption for certain of their workers from the age of 18 years, whilst in the mining industry the lowest age was 21 years. It had been agreed on the request of the owners that joint representations be made to the Mines Department on the matter.

With each successive month of the winter of 1939–40 the position worsened. The efforts from within the industry to retain its manpower were frustrated until, in the words of the MFGB Annual Report, 'it became increasingly obvious that if production was to be even maintained, the manpower of the industry would require to be augmented while hundreds of thousands of people were unable to procure supplies of fuel'.

To what was this condition of 'utter chaos' due? In the first place the Chamberlain Government evinced a remarkable incapacity to cope with the thronging problems of wartime. The records of the previous war and of how its coal-mining problems were dealt with were all extant. But the lessons appear not to have been learned and the solutions to the problems, which should have been applied at the outset, were forgotten or ignored.

A more fundamental reason for the position of 'utter chaos' was the industry itself, with its multitude of directors with competing collieries, its anarchy of production, its antiquated economic policies and technological backwardness. It was utterly unsuitable to the conditions of twentieth-century warfare and was bound to be a drag on any national effort. This had been seen in the 1914–18 War when British industries and services such as fuel and transport had presented acute problems.

In rail transport there were 80 main lines in 1914 and also 80 railway companies that had to be put under state control – an experience that compelled their reduction to four main railway systems in the legislation that followed the War of Empires. Similarly, the many hundreds of collieries and colliery companies, having been brought under state control in 1917, were subjected to a most searching examination by the Royal Commission set up under the Coal Industry Commission Act of 1919 'to inquire into the position of and conditions prevailing in the Coal Industry'.

Apart from questions of wages and hours of labour, the main recommendations ran:

Even upon the evidence already given, the present system of ownership and working in the coal industry *stands condemned*, and some other system must be substituted for it, either nationalization or a method of unification by national purchase and/or by joint control. (Report of the Sankey Coal Commission, 1919)

Proposals for this highly necessary 'nationalization or unification' encountered in 1919 a reactionary stampede in the House of Commons and in the House of Lords, where some of the monopoly chiefs of the finance oligarchy were entrenched and trembling with a panic fear of red revolution (as witness the Cabinet minutes made available from 1950 onwards). This stampede trampled down and obliterated the solemn pledges given both by the leader of the Tory Party and by the Coalition Premier Lloyd George. The Coalition Government, unable to withstand a degree of monopolist and multinational pressure seldom or never before exerted or experienced in parliamentary annals, forsook all statesmanship and basely yielded. This British coal-mining industry, this 'condemned property', continued in private hands, and continued to be a drag on the whole economy of the country for another quarter of a century.

This was the fundamental cause of the breakdown in coal supplies and of the 'utter chaos'.

Not until March 1940 was it reported to a meeting of the JSCC that the government were considering the question of the establishment of a Coal Production Council. This was then 'discussed at great length'. Finally it was decided that the JSCC should agree to co-operate in setting up the Council and that each side would appoint three representatives. The following Notice of Appointment was issued:

I hereby appoint
The Rt Hon. Lord Portal, DSO, MVO

Mr Will Lawther	
Mr James Bowman	Representatives of Mine Workers
Mr Ebby Edwards	

Sir Evan Williams, Bart., DL, LlD	
Sir W. Benton Jones, Bart.	Representatives of Mine Owners
Mr W. A. Lee, CBE	

Mr R. H. Hill, CB	Ministry of Transport
Mr T. G. Jenkins, MC	Ministry of Shipping
Mr C. S. Hurst, CB, OBE	Mines Department

to be a COUNCIL to promote, in collaboration with representative bodies of owners and workmen in the mining industry, and with the Government Departments concerned, the greater production of coal with a view to increasing coal exports while maintaining supplies for essential home consumption.

I further appoint the Lord Portal to be Chairman of the Council, and Mr P. S. Lea to be Secretary.

Dated this 9th day of April, 1940.

GEOFFREY LLOYD,
Secretary for Mines

Mines Department, SW1

There was nothing leisurely in the behaviour of the aristocrat who had been called to be Chairman of the Council in the remaining three weeks of April. Within three weeks of its establishment, four full meetings were held. Lord Portal* as Chairman had attended joint meetings of representatives of colliery-owners and colliery workmen of fourteen districts

*Wyndham Raymond Portal (1885–1949): First Viscount Portal of Laverstoke; eldest son of Sir W. W. Portal, Bt; educated Eton, Christ Church, Oxford; late Life Guards; Lord Lieutenant of County of Hampshire; Regional Commissioner for Wales under Civil Defence Scheme, 1939; Additional Parliamentary Secretary to Ministry of Supply, 1940–2; Minister of Works and Planning and First Commissioner of Works and Public Building, 1942–4; President of Olympic Games, 1948.

including all the large districts of England and Wales. He had
still to visit Scotland and remaining English and Welsh
districts; but enough matters had emerged so clearly that the
Council thought they should make an immediate report on
them. He wrote:

Each district which I have visited has agreed to set up a District
Production Committee, and to adopt all such agreed measures of a domestic
character as may help production; and I should like to say at once that
I was most favourably impressed at every meeting by the evident goodwill which exists between the two parties in the industry and by the
sincere desire to do everything possible to provide the country with the
coal which it needs for the prosecution of the war and the maintenance
of our export markets.

Certain conditions were essential. One was that 'the manpower of the industry must be augmented'; and to this he returned at the end of his next paragraph, writing that 'if the
required output is to be achieved, it is essential that the manpower be increased'. Then he went on to say: 'Our first concern
is that the existing manpower shall not be further depleted;
and, as a first step, we have already recommended that no more
men employed in or about collieries shall be recruited for
the Services, whether from underground or from surface.'

But an even more serious factor was the continuing loss
of men from collieries to firms engaged in government work.
In some districts the loss from this cause was already as high as
10 per cent rising at some large colliery undertakings to 15
per cent. 'We consider this is a National question, and not one
for us to suggest the remedy . . . It is one which must be solved
by His Majesty's Government. We ought to say, however,
that delay will be disastrous to the Mining Industry, and
that nearly all the districts which I have visited begged us
to take this matter up urgently.'

In addition to stopping a further depletion of the manpower
already employed, it was needful to go further and augment
it. So Lord Portal put the Council's suggestion, as one measure,
'that experienced colliery workmen engaged in Civil Defence
or in Home Defence Units, such as the Searchlight and Anti-
Aircraft services, should be allowed to return to the mines as
soon as they can be replaced'.

In addition to manpower, another essential requirement 'is an adequate supply of materials and stores'; and in the case of steel, this, they were given to understand, was insufficient. So the report ended: 'if the efforts to increase coal production to the level required are not to be jeopardised from this cause, the present annual allocation should be raised by 120,000 tons, and delivery of stores expedited'.

This report, whose studiously moderate wording did not conceal the sorry plight of the coal trade, might have been expected to have stimulated the provision of immediate remedies. Another five weeks elapsed before action was taken on this 30 April report from the Coal Production Council. Then at last one of the urgent questions raised in the report reached the War Cabinet Economic Policy Committee. On 4 June 1940 the Undertakings Restrictions on Engagement Order was applied to coal mining with the object of stopping a further depletion of manpower already at work in the mines.

7. BLITZKRIEG AND NEW GOVERNMENT

In the second week of April 1940 German contingents had seized Denmark and the long seaboard of Norway from which superior British forces then failed to dislodge them. In the second week of May 1940 Hitler launched his *Blitzkrieg* upon the Netherlands and Belgium and drove towards the French frontiers – on 10 May. It was on the same day that Churchill became Prime Minister and with the backing of the Labour Party was able to form his Coalition Government.

Winston Churchill, in speeches of magnificent rhetoric, defined the aims of the new government while he warned Parliament of 'hard and heavy tidings' that they were bound to be made acquainted with all too soon. But the personnel of the new Cabinet hardly matched up to the lofty aims as put forward by the Prime Minister. Churchill's choice of ministers was restricted both by the composition of Parliament in which most of the lower house had been elected five years before in support of the Baldwin-Chamberlain Governments and by party discords and personal enmities. Neither Aneurin Bevan nor Manny Shinwell was taken into the Government; nor, from the Tory benches, was Walter Elliott. To a limited extent only had Churchill a free hand. But in two cases he took the unusual step of going outside the party circle. He chose Lord Beaverbrook, newspaper tycoon from Canada, to be the head of the new Ministry of Aircraft Production. He chose Ernest Bevin, General Secretary of the largest trade union, the Transport and General Workers' Union, to be the new Minister of Labour and National Service. One was to provide the machines, the other the men, that could withstand the onslaught of Hitler. These selections appeared to be justified within a very short period of time. Beaverbrook's feat was to deliver more aeroplanes than the German calculators had supposed to be possible to sustain the Battle of Britain in summer and autumn of 1940. He lasted in that office for just a twelvemonth before moving on.

Similar plaudits were showered in that critical year upon Ernest Bevin and it has been the custom of biographers and the tradition of the Labour Party to hail his activity as not only successful but practically flawless in the way the aims of National Service, gathering and distribution of manpower were planned and achieved. But it was not flawless, as the producers and consumers of coal were to find out in the autumn of 1940. Within a year, differences began to be voiced in the House of Commons. Although as a longstanding member of the General Council Bevin continued to have the undeviating support of the majority of the trade union movement, there is no question but that grievous errors were made.

Churchill's administration was a government of national emergency to which the people in Britain immediately responded. Ernest Bevin, made Minister on 13 May, issued that same day a call for the utmost effort. On 15 May Dai Grenfell was appointed Secretary for Mines and in two days had produced his plan for 800,000 miners to cope with the supremely urgent need for coal supplies.

Under the heading 'National Emergency' the minute of the EC meeting (held at 50 Russell Square, London WC1 on Friday 24 May) tells how Ebby Edwards 'comprehensively surveyed the position' and later tells how 'the Secretary for Mines addressed the Committee, stressing the seriousness of the present situation'.

Seven weeks later Dai Grenfell in his address to the MFGB annual conference amplified what he had told the EC about the plan for increased coal output. He recounted what had happened from the moment that he had been appointed.

I was asked if I could give an estimate of the capacity of this industry within the next few months – what quantity of production we could achieve, provided we were given the necessary conditions . . . an adequate supply of trained and skilled labour.

Asked to give a figure, he had suggested 260 million tons 'as production for the year immediately following May of this year'.

'But,' I said, 'we must get more men; to produce that quantity we must be assured of the indispensable materials, the timber and the steel for supports, the winding ropes, the cages, the sheets, the tubs, and the machines – we must be secured as to the supply of materials of all kinds, and we must also be given the right to extend pit room, bring back into production pits that may have been stopped, pits in which men could be set to work to increase production and guarantee the maintenance of our supply.'

Then he went on to tell how the matter had been discussed with the Rt Hon. Ernest Bevin who was to be put into the War Cabinet by Churchill. Dai Grenfell then said:

Ernest Bevin had more control over Labour than anybody else, and I had to go and see him. I saw him within two days of assuming office. He said, 'You have got this mining industry; you have a certain number of people working in it, I will promise you that no Recruiting Sergeant goes to those pits if you say all those men are required to produce coal.' He asked, 'Have you got enough?' I said, 'No. I want to keep every man now employed in the industry, and I must have a larger personnel if we are to carry out our programme of expansion to the limits to which I hope to reach.' Then Bevin said, and he made a public statement to the same effect within a few days of his appointment, 'I regard coal as a most vital industry, and I am giving to the Secretary for Mines the number of people he deems necessary in order that the mines may be staffed and an adequate supply of suitable labour is available at all times.'

Grenfell had then said to the Minister of Labour: 'I should be content to have 800,000 men placed in this industry made reserved and immune from further attention of the military authorities, for the duration of the war.'

Bevin said, 'All right I will give you that round figure; I will take steps to ensure the return of men to the mines – all who can be induced to come back.'

That seemed good enough so that Grenfell was able to say: 'We are proceeding with confidence, having been assured of supplies, having been assured of labour, and having been assured by the Government in regard to other matters, I was satisfied that I could go on with the programme, and we were ready.'

Such was the arrangement to cope with the coal crisis reached in mid-May 1940. By the end of May there came the 'hard and heavy tidings' of the British forces trapped and cooped up in Dunkirk, until the rescue thence of over a third of a million combatants by the British navy and British civilians.

8. THE FALL OF FRANCE

By mid-summer 1940, three short weeks since the British expeditionary force had been rescued from Dunkirk, Britain, bereft of her allies, was facing the threat of invasion. The fall of France had a calamitous effect, as was vividly recalled in mid-July at the Blackpool annual conference by the President of the South Wales Miners.

It is only a few weeks ago when all of us in every part of the country were asked to put everything we knew into the task of producing coal – any kind of coal, and for any purpose . . . At that time there was a call that France at all costs must get sufficient coal. Their northern coal-field had been taken over by Germany. France was asking for a continually increasing tonnage each month, and at that time, before France was occupied, the only safe ports to send coal from to France were the Bristol Channel Ports.

With the occupation of France, South Wales became faced with a new situation at once. We were producing 40 per cent for export. 90 per cent of the 40 per cent had become directed to France. Our normal markets in Portugal, in South America, and in Ireland, we were refusing to supply because of the paramount needs of France. In a night we lost 90 per cent of our export trade, or nearly one third of our total trade.

The fall of France revealed the historic inadequacy of the British coal trade. Coal-owners themselves were in the grip of antiquated conditions obstinately and infatuatedly maintained even after the greatest mining experts at the Sankey Commission of 1919 had exposed its deficiencies and shown its utter insufficiency especially in time of war. If there was no market and if there was no sale then from the standpoint of the colliery-owner there was no need for labour. Although there was a national need for coal and for 800,000 colliers, miners began to be turned off, thrown upon the streets in area after area, especially in the great export coalfields of South Wales and Durham.

It was from these two districts on 16 July 1940 that there came a resolution on 'Coal Trade Policy' urging that maximum coal production be maintained during the crisis, that mines be kept going 'even though short time working might be necessary for the time being', and that the load be spread from one coalfield to another 'during the period of the dislocation brought about by the loss of export trade arising from the capitulation of France – and from Italy entering the war against Britain'.

In moving the resolution (which was afterwards remitted to the Executive Committee), Ness Edwards, MP, said 'that stocks ought to be built up in the Colonies . . .' and similarly within the island, at government expense, since it was 'useless to expect the private capitalist to sink his money in large stocks of coal'.

That same morning the Secretary for Mines, Dai Grenfell, MP, in his full and detailed address, announced that the government would bear 'the expense of stocking not less than five million tons of coal in Government dumps in the next four months, the only limit being the capacity of the railways to carry.' After dealing with the problem of the 250 coal-laden ships that he had requisitioned, Grenfell made it clear no pit was to close down. He said,

There are 2,000 mines in this country . . . Jack Elks is here and he knows what pressure was brought upon himself and us to abandon the Kent coalfield. They are still working. All honour to those men. You cannot estimate the amount of moral damage that might have been done in this country even if one coalfield was abandoned because of enemy action. Would the panic spread? You are not quite sure. But the men of Kent have helped to steady us by steadying themselves . . . We must keep all the pits working, because we do not know when mines may be knocked out. Harbours may be damaged, important railway bridges, cancelling out all the efforts of distribution by the railway companies . . . We may be driven even to the transfer of our men from coalfield to coalfield in order to keep the country supplied with coal. You cannot allow a pit to close down. We must try to keep going all the pits that are going today. (17 July 1940)

The next day, 17 July 1940, there came up under the heading 'National Control' two resolutions, one of them from Lancashire, spoken to at some length by Jack McGurk.

This in effect is straight out for the Government to take over the mines; in a word, nationalise them, if that is possible at this juncture . . . while we are talking in this room about sharing out the work and the time to be made, the coal owners are on the job, doing it themselves. Our Lancashire coal owners had to go to London last week to discuss the very thing that we were talking about yesterday, each district taking a parochial view. Lancashire does not like the idea of Northumberland coming in to steal its trade . . .

We think our Lancashire owners are typical of all the owners in the British coalfield; they have still got the peacetime outlook, and that outlook is 'profits'. They cannot get away from it. If whatever profit was made in the industry was collared by the State, then the men who produce the coal and take the risk would get a proper benefit. (17 July 1940)

After McGurk had moved the Lancashire resolution Ebby Edwards rose and opposed the Midlands and the Lancashire resolutions, while he welcomed McGurk's speech. Ebby said:

I was explaining to Conference that I think both these resolutions whittle down the policy of the socialisation of the industry, which has been endorsed not only by the miners, but by the general movement. The TUC has endorsed it, the Labour Party has endorsed it, and that is what I am concerned with, as to whether you are going back on that. (17 July 1940)

Finally, on the suggestion of Chairman Lawther, it was agreed that both resolutions be submitted to the NEC. From these resolutions, two on national control and one on coal trade policy (all referred to the EC), there was gradually laid

the basis for a clear definite policy put forward by the MFGB
to solve the accumulating problems of the industry which were
not being made easier by the interventions of the Minister
of Labour.

9. A SAD AUTUMN

The resolutions on coal trade policy and on national control
referred by the MFGB annual conference to the newly elected
Executive Committee came up at the meeting of 16 August
and were deferred to the September meeting when it was
decided: 'the resolutions be relegated to the Reorganisation
Committee for their consideration and the formulating of a
policy, such policy, when propagated to be presented to the
full Executive Committee for consideration' (20 September
1940).

On the same day there was a visit to the Executive
Committee by Dai Grenfell, MP, the Secretary for Mines.
From what he told them the EC began to realise that the
steadfast attitude put forward by Grenfell at the MFGB
conference nine weeks earlier was no longer being maintained
against the pressure for other policies from inside the
government. It was a sad moment for Ebby Edwards and the
other members of the Reorganisation Committee who then
became the more determined to find a better way out than
this shortsighted policy contrived in the Ministry of Labour.
The leaders of the mineworkers were well aware of the panic
fears that had been manifest in some authoritative quarters
throughout that summer and autumn of 1940 when for a
time it was 'touch-and-go' with the air force's Battle of Britain,
preliminary to the German plan of invasion.

What may have seemed to them another example of this
shortsightedness (a Question and Answer exchange in the
House of Commons) was then cited by the Secretary for
Mines who, according to the Executive Committee minutes,
went on as follows:

from the figures he mentioned there still remained a large number of
miners who would not be able to be absorbed, and the only course
left open for them was to join the Armed Forces. This was to be made

effective by the Minister of Labour by the raising of the age of Reservation in the Mining Industry.

Whilst the Secretary for Mines wanted to avoid, as far as it was possible, losing any labour in the coalfield, the problem with which he was now confronted was to devise ways and means of satisfying the Minister of Labour that the amount of labour at present available in the coal industry was absolutely essential. He, therefore, suggested that a joint meeting of owners' representatives, Federation representatives, and representatives from his Department should be held at his Department with a view to going thoroughly into the question in order to endeavour to produce a satisfactory solution to the problem. (20 October 1940)

So it was agreed that their nine members on the National Joint Consultative Committee together with representatives from four other districts should attend a meeting at the Mines Department on Thursday 26 September to consider the whole position.

Earlier, Grenfell had informed that meeting of the Executive Committee that the proposals from the export districts of Durham and South Wales for the improvisation of some means whereby there could be a sharing of trade* throughout, so as to lessen the unemployment which those areas had come up against, had encountered 'difficulties that were absolutely insurmountable'. On the other hand he told them of the plan for maintaining the pits: where collieries were having to shut down due to enemy action, there should be instituted a levy of X pence per ton on all disposable coal produced in the coalfield, 'from which a Central Fund would be established, from which fund payments would be made to those colliery owners to compensate them for the cost of maintaining the collieries in a constant state of productivity'. It seemed that this plan, originating with the owners themselves, was not to encounter 'difficulties that were absolutely insurmountable'.

A week later, on 26 September, at the 'all-in' meeting

*On this question, in the debate at the mid-July Conference, Arthur Horner said,
We are prepared to give what guarantees are required to demonstrate that we have no intention of utilising the changing war situation to permanently steal the trade of any other district . . . I am hoping that . . . the Executive Committee will sit down and say 'Notwithstanding that we are not a national organisation in the real sense, notwithstanding our different interests, district as compared with district, it is the business of this Mineworkers' Federation to preserve the maximum equity as between its members.
It was the clearest recognition of the state of disintegration in which the mining trade unions had entered the anti-fascist war.

with Grenfell, they were told of 'the request made by the Minister of Labour to the Secretary for Mines, that the ages of Reservation of mineworkers should, owing to the present state of the industry, with its problems of unemployment plus the fact that the military authorities were pressing for further increases in the personnel of the Armed Forces, be raised'. Both owners and mineworkers were faced with the question of how best to meet the wishes of the Minister of Labour. The report given later by Ebby Edwards ran:

It was agreed by both sides that the industry did not desire to see the age of Reservation raised, therefore some other proposal must be placed before the Minister of Labour to satisfy his requirements with respect to the Armed Forces.

The suggestion was therefore made, by both sides, that the Secretary for Mines should inform the Minister of Labour of the discussion which had taken place, and, at the same time . . . express the determination of both sides to resist any raising of the Reservation ages in the industry.

On 3 October 1940 Ernest Bevin was taken into the select handful of the War Cabinet.

Twelve days later, on 15 October, a meeting of the Coal Production Council was held. They made the following recommendation:

The only men who can be spared from the coalmining industry without serious interference with supply of essential requirements are those registered by the Ministry of Labour as wholly unemployed. Such men, being no longer employed in the industry, should cease to be reserved from Military Service for that reason, and if above the age required for such service should be available for other industries.

This recommendation was put before the MFGB Executive Committee the next day. Although they had a very lengthy discussion, it was accepted. They could not do otherwise.

The result was a loss of mining manpower to the armed forces – and to other industries. The figure of the average number of wage-earners fell quarter by quarter throughout 1940 and up to the middle of 1941. There was a corresponding fall in output.*

*For detailed figures see *The Miners in Crisis and War* (Volume III of *The History of the Miners' Federation of Great Britain*), by R. Page Arnot, Allen & Unwin, 1961, p. 309.

APPENDICES TO CHAPTER I

Appendix A

A PANEGYRIC ON COAL

Early in his address to the MFGB annual conference on 16 July 1940 the Secretary for Mines claimed that the delegates represented 'the most important industry in this country – representing the men who gave the most valuable services to this community – in peace or war' and thereafter Dai Grenfell delivered the following panegyric:

Never have we realised, and never have we placed the standard high enough of the nature and the quality of the service we render day by day. This coal, this commodity found in twenty separate British coalfields, under varying conditions, sometimes lying deep in thin layers difficult to work, and difficult of access; sometimes found under most favourable conditions, is a commodity which lies at the very bottom and is the actual firm foundation upon which all the other superstructure of British industry has been built. It becomes that firm foundation as the result of the labour of men who go down the pits day by day, achieving larger results here than they achieve there, with sometimes the production – in the Midlands for example – rising to a ton and a half per person per day, or falling to well below a ton perhaps in a coalfield in South Wales. This varying production of coal is sometimes measured in terms of varying wages, but I am looking forward to the time when we shall assess the worth of coal not as a thing worth so many shillings per ton, but as an indispensable vital factor of the national life of this country. I do not want to stay too long on this aspect of the industry, but I will give you an illustration you have heard at previous Conferences.

It is vitally important that we remember this: coal is power. Coal is energy; coal is strength; coal is the highest embodiment of economic value we have in this country. I take a lump of coal weighing one pound. There it is. I could keep it in my vest pocket. It is an infinitesimal fraction of the daily output of the average miner in this country, but that one pound of coal contains, hidden in its interstices and in its component elements, matter which when placed under the process of combustion will yield energy equal to a strong man's work for a full day – one pound weight of coal equal to one horsepower for one hour, or one manpower for a full eight hours day. And the production of coal is well over one ton a day for each man going to perform his work in the mine. He sends that to the surface for the use of industry in all its varied forms in this country – an average of no less than one ton per day. That single individual whom you represent here today, and who by his day's work in the mine presents to the nation a commodity that multiplies his manpower by no less than two thousand times. That is what we have given this country from the beginning. From the early days of the industrial revolution our fathers and grandfathers have made that gift to Britain. We have maintained British industry. We have smelted and worked metals; we have reduced the hardest and most intractable of all metals to a state of softness and malleability; we have treated them as if they were putty in our hands only because of the power contained in coal. We have smelted, we have made machines, we have built railways, we have built ships, and from the wonderful mind of man have come forth the plans of the machines which should capture this motive power and employ it with mathematical strength and accuracy. The whole machine system of this country, wonderful in its manifestations, is derived from coal. We men in the mining community should therefore not be ashamed of the part we have played in building up this Britain.

That is the kind of service we are still doing, and we have come to a time when the power of the machine not only means the multiplication of effort for production in peaceful pursuits, but life and death, more than life and death, depend upon it, for we entirely depend upon the numbers and the excellence of our machines at the present time. Those machines can only be produced, and can only be applied and maintained in motion if we produce not merely the normal quantity of coal in this country, but only if we produce a larger quantity of coal for domestic use than we have ever employed before.

Appendix B

COAL RESOURCES OF THE TWO BELLIGERENTS

(from the strategic reckoning of facts and figures given by Ebby Edwards to the Mineworkers' conference on 17 July 1940)

The latest available figure of production in Germany is 229,500,000 tons. She has taken over Upper Silesia, nearly 28,500,000 tons. She has now got Alsace Lorraine with nearly 6,500,000 tons. She has control of Belgium, 29,500,000 tons. She has control of Holland, with 13,500,000 tons. She has control of Czechoslovakia, with 21,500,000 tons. She is in control of Austria, with 2,500,000 tons. She has Sudetenland, with over 6,500,000 tons. And she has the North Calais coalfields, with 28,250,000 tons. Germany, therefore, controls a production of nearly 370,000,000 tons.

Let us just look at the other side. Take 1938, and look at the markets, and see which are disposing of coal, and how the situation is going to apply. To Germany we sent 4,000,000 tons. Anybody can imagine as far as they are concerned what the situation is going to be at the end of the war. France, 6,500,000 – that has gone west. Belgium, nearly 1,000,000 – that has gone west. Holland, nearly 1,000,000 – that has gone west. Italy, 2,500,000 – that has gone west. Sweden, over 2,500,000 – that will go west. Norway, 1,500,000 – that has gone west. Denmark, 3,000,000; the Baltic States, 2,000,000; and Switzerland, 500,000.

Appendix C

ADDITIONAL RULES 1940

The adoption of these Additional Rules by the MFGB (Blackpool) annual conference on 15 July 1940 measured, in however small a degree, a definite success in the drive carried on by Ebby Edwards and his supporters to halt the disintegration of the Federation and to enable the Federation officials once more to begin to function as had been the custom, if not the rule, before the employers in 1926/7 achieved their aim of rending the Federation into separate entities.

District Documents
That each district association shall send to the Secretary of the Federation, copies of all documents, literature and balance sheets as issued to its membership.

District Negotiations
In the event of any district association entering into negotiations on important issues likely to lead to a cessation of work, or likely to result in changes affecting national policy, the Federation Officials shall be given every facility by the district to secure all the available facts for the purpose of assisting and/or advising the district direct, or for the purpose of presenting an accurate report to the Federation Executive

Committee. District associations shall also send to the Secretary of the Federation copies of all documents relating to such negotiations.

CHAPTER II

LABOUR'S PLAN FOR THE COAL INDUSTRY

I. THE BATTLE OF BRITAIN

The second year of war began in circumstances most unfavourable for the United Kingdom, battered by defeats, bereft of its allies, ill equipped with men or material. Seven countries had been invaded by the German armed forces, over-run and for the most part occupied: Poland, Denmark, Norway, Belgium, Holland, Luxembourg, France. The United Kingdom of Great Britain and Northern Ireland was left alone to face the bombing aeroplanes that in September and October were to make night hideous for the inhabitants of London and other big cities. A hundred years earlier the poet Tennyson, with strange prophetic insight,

> Heard the heavens filled with shouting,
>   and there rained a ghastly dew
> From the nation's airy navies,
>   grappling in the central blue.

For fifty-seven days in September and October 1940 the Nazi bombs rained down, nor was it known how this Battle of Britain would finally turn out. But while the earlier bombing, directed at military objectives (on shipping 3 July to 11 August; on airfields 13 August to 6 September 1940), had shifted to reprisal and night bombing of cities (the British night bombing on Berlin was on 25 August), there were few attacks on collieries or colliery junctions. Consequently production in the coal trade suffered little – nothing like so much as it suffered from the weekly deprivation of some of its most active and energetic and skilled mineworkers, taken away into the armed forces, there to abide sometimes in tents, other times in barracks, for the best part of another four years.

In the autumn the MFGB Executive Committee had been

anything but satisfied with the ministry's solution for the problems; and, while obedient to whatever was put as a wartime demand from above, could not but be sceptical of measures which they felt had been dictated in the midst of dire emergency, not to speak of a certain degree of panic.* The Minister of Labour and National Service had explained 'the need for calling up a very large number of men for the services' and, in view of the unemployment within the industry, was of the opinion 'that the present position under the Schedule could not be maintained' (22 October) and that therefore 'he had no alternative' but to call up a substantial number of young men from the coal-mining industry into the forces. Apparently, within the Ministry of Labour there was no one that autumn who thought out any alternative.

At the Joint Standing Consultative Committee on 23 October the ministry's proposals came up for consideration. There was a further discussion on 27 November and finally on 28 November the MFGB Executive Committee minute runs:

The Secretary, having completed his report, intimated, in reply to questions, that the Minister of Labour was very definite on the proposal to raise the age of reservation of all coal mining occupations to 30. The Minister had made it clear that men could not be retained for the purpose of working pits partially; also he was not prepared to take older men from other occupations while young men were retained in the coal industry. It was agreed: That the report of the Secretary in relation to the discussions in connection with the Schedule of Reserved Occupations be accepted.

*This effect of the emergency and of some degree of panic was noted in October, some ten weeks later, in the report of the TUC General Council:
the working of long hours without week-end breaks did not itself make for maximum production. It was agreed, therefore, that hours of work must be adjusted to prevent tiredness and that the continuance of an average working week of between 70 and 80 hours would quickly cause a rapid decrease in individual productivity, owing to the abnormal strain. It was therefore decided that hours should be reduced to 58 or 60 in the first place, with the aim of an eventual reduction to 55 or 56 per week . . . At the beginning of the present emergency there was more or less a complete breakdown of the control of hours of women and young persons in the industries directly affected. It was agreed that this very undesirable state of affairs should be terminated at the earliest possible moment and accordingly factory inspectors were instructed that, apart from applications for extension of hours which might be agreed to after consultation with the Trade Union officials concerned, the provisions of the Factory Acts must be enforced from August 1.
(From the Seventy-Second Annual Trades Union Congress, 7–9 October 1940)

2. COAL TRADE POLICY

The delegates at the MFGB annual conference in the summer of 1940 had instructed their Executive Committee to find a solution to the extensive breakdown of the British coal trade. Already, at that mid-July conference, Ebby Edwards, with an almost unrivalled knowledge of the coal industries in Europe as a whole, had given significant figures and added a clear prospect for the future, saying:

I am indicating those figures in the belief that we will not solve the coal problem in this country unless we have a complete socialised industry. I say that unless you can get it out of the present wreck in the contradictions of Capitalism itself you will not get it at the end of the war. With the present situation as it is, with at least a proportion of our own people in the Government, I think we should leave our socialised plan to operate without any modification, and I believe that Parliament may at least put that socialised plan in operation.

In the Roman City of Gloucester on the east bank of the river Severn, far to the west of the incessant bombing of London, the Executive Committee found a harbourage for their meeting at the end of November. Before them was a very full agenda. Under the heading 'Conscription of Wealth' the following resolution was received from the National Union of Scottish Mineworkers:

That we ask the Government to put into operation [the Emergency Powers Act of 22 May 1940, which gives the government power to conscript persons and property] that part which up till now has not been operated, viz., 'The Conscription of Wealth'.

At the Executive Committee six months earlier when Ebby Edwards had given a full survey of the situation (on 24 May) including the use of this new Act of Parliament brought forward by the Vice Prime Minister Attlee of the Labour Party and passed through Parliament in one day, great hopes were pinned upon it. So copies of their Scottish resolution were sent, by Executive Committee decision, to the TUC General Council and to the Labour Party.

At this same meeting of 21 November a letter was read from James Bowman, in his capacity as Secretary of the

Northumberland Miners' Mutual Confident Association, beginning: 'in view of the chaotic conditions prevailing in the coal industry, we call upon the TUC, the Labour Party and the MFGB to make immediate joint representation to HM Government for the introduction of Public Ownership and Control of the coal industry . . .'

This gave rise to a lengthy discussion in the course of which, while they decided that 'the letter from Northumberland be received', they also took a momentous decision: they accepted the report by Ebby Edwards of the Reorganisation Subcommittee with its recommendation 'that the Trades Union Congress and the Labour Party should be invited to implement their policy, viz., "Labour's Plan for the Coal Industry" '.

Within the Subcommittee the decision cannot have been reached or taken simply as a matter of course. The relations between the MFGB and the now enlarged bureaucracy of the TUC and the officials of the Labour Party had not been so entirely cordial and free from strife as might have been expected by outsiders. Not only the memory of 1926 but more recent causes of difference did not so readily die away from their minds. For example there was their own persistent struggle month after month in 1939 to induce the officials of the Labour Party to cancel the expulsion of Aneurin Bevan, MP for Ebbw Vale, without any imposed conditions.

Nor could miners' leaders, from Executive Committee member to lodge secretary or pit delegate, ever forget their experience of 1926 or their own unyielding standpoint, so nobly expressed in the opening words of their final manifesto.*

*FELLOW TRADE UNIONISTS!

I. After seven months of grim struggle, on a scale the like of which has not been known in Trade Union history in this or in any country of the world, the MFGB, in common with the other Trade Unions, is called to give its judgment on the events of the first fortnight of that struggle.

II. The population of these islands had never previously experienced anything resembling the situation created by the General Strike of May 4th to May 12th. Limited though it was both in number of workers affected, in the objective aimed at and in the time it lasted, the General Strike showed the working class to be possessed of qualities of courage, comradeship, and disciplined resource that had not hitherto been called forth and that gave a good omen for future solidarity.

III. If we were deserted and forced to fight a lone fight, it was not by the workers

But however little reliance on the TUC experience had taught them to feel, nevertheless 'the chaotic condition prevailing in the coal industry' (Bowman's phrase) demanded that they should take this step. So the Executive Committee, in the Guildhall of Gloucester, took their decision to request the TUC and the Labour Party (jointly making up ·the National Council of Labour) to implement their plan for the public ownership of the coal-mining industry as endorsed by the annual conference of both bodies in 1936.

3. EXCHANGE OF LETTERS AND RESOLUTIONS

In the letter of 25 November 1940 sent to J. S. Middleton, Secretary of the Labour Party, and also to the Secretary of the TUC, the operative sentences ran:

My Executive Committee are of the opinion that inasmuch as a scheme for the National control of the industry has already been accepted by the Movement, the time is now opportune for the implementation of that scheme and suggest that immediate representations should be made to the Government in this matter.

The feeling in the coalfields is naturally intense and I have to ask, therefore, that immediate attention will be given to this request.

The TUC Finance and General Purposes Committee (of which Ebby Edwards was a member) considered the request of the Mineworkers' Federation of Great Britain and decided to place it before the National Council of Labour on the morrow. The National Council of Labour resolved: 'That a Joint Committee should be set up to examine the problem and report – the General Council to appoint four members, the Parliamentary Labour Party and the National Executive Committee to appoint two each' (26 November 1940). The TUC General Council decided to appoint Messrs Allen, Harrison, Brown and Lawther; the Labour Party chose Messrs

that we were abandoned. Their hearts beat true to the end. From the workers of our country, and of the world, and especially from the Trade Unionists of Russia, we obtained unstinted aid. For the help given, whether from Union funds or from individual workers, we convey the gratitude of the miners' wives and children. (12 January 1927)

J. Walker and J. E. Swan; the Parliamentary Labour Party had appointed Messrs E. Dunn, MP, and C. Brown, MP. The Joint Committee, meeting on 11 December 1940, unanimously passed a resolution which went to the National Council of Labour, was by them approved as a recommendation on 17 December, transmitted to the Federation, and circulated to the General Council of the Trades Union Congress. It was a peculiar recommendation as it neither met the miners' request, nor gave any reason for not doing so; but offered advice to the miners' leaders to enter into talks with the government and the owners on another question, the question of national control.

No copy of this recommendation was seen by Ebby Edwards until he was actually sitting on 18 December in the meeting of the TUC General Council. Ebby was furious. For 'very obvious reasons' which he explained to his fellow members, he moved the reference back – which was carried.*

The following letters then passed between J. S. Middleton, acting as Secretary of the Council of Labour, and the Secretary of the Mineworkers' Federation of Great Britain:

December 17th, 1940.

Mr. Ebby Edwards,
6, Victoria Terrace,
Durham.

Dear Mr. Edwards,

Your letter of November 25th addressed to the General Council of the Trades Union Congress and the National Executive Committee of the Party, suggesting that the present unfortunate position in the South Wales and Durham Minefields renders the time opportune for the implementation of a scheme for the national control of the Industry was remitted to the National Council of Labour for consideration. The National Council set up a special Sub-Committee to examine the position in greater detail and at a meeting of the National Council this morning the following Resolution was presented and was unanimously approved:

'That while adhering to the general policy of Nationalisation outlined

---

*Under *Coal Trade Policy* the EC minute of 17 January records that 'owing to the fact that the recommendation contained in the report did not meet the desires of the MFGB he [the Secretary] had moved the reference back of the report and this had been agreed to'.

in the Report on Coal approved by the Trades Union Congress and the Labour Party Conference in 1936, the Committee is of the opinion that the MFGB should be advised to consider the desirability of discussing with representatives of the Government and of the Mineowners' Association the practicability of securing a scheme of national control and national pooling of profits as a war emergency measure and as a preliminary to the promotion of the machinery necessary to implement the larger and more fundamental policy of Nationalisation.'

The Council will be glad to hear in due course the views of your National Executive Council, and the result of any action they deem it desirable to take in the matter.

> With kind regards,
>   Yours very sincerely,
>   (signed) J. S. MIDDLETON,
>   Secretary.

Note: The above letter was received at Russell Square, London WC1, on 20 December 1940, whence on the same date it was forwarded to the office in Durham.

December 21st, 1940.

Mr. J. S. Middleton,
National Council of Labour,
Transport House,
Smith Square,
London, S.W.1.

Dear Mr. Middleton,

LABOUR'S PLAN FOR THE COAL INDUSTRY.

Many thanks for your letter of the 17th instant together with resolution as passed by the National Council of Labour in reply to my organisation's request that the Movement should press the Government to implement Labour's Plan for the Coal Industry.

As the General Council of the Trades Union Congress has referred this matter back to the National Council of Labour for further consideration and decision on the main issue raised in the Mineworkers' Federation request, I assume we will now await a decision of the National Council of Labour at its next meeting.

> Yours sincerely,
>   (signed) EBBY EDWARDS,
>   Secretary.

Edward Jones, Vice-President 1954–60

Fred Collindridge, Vice-President 1961–2

January 13th, 1941.

Mr. J. Middleton,
The Labour Party,
Transport House,
London, S.W.1.

Dear Mr. Middleton,

LABOUR'S PLAN FOR COAL INDUSTRY.

Following my letter to you of December 21st, 1940, re the above question, as my Executive is meeting in London this week, I shall be glad to know how the position stands.

Have your representatives met the Cabinet, and, if so, with what result?

Kindly send your reply to 50, Russell Square, in time for my meeting on Friday first.

Yours sincerely,
(signed) EBBY EDWARDS,
Secretary.

January 16th, 1941.

Mr. Ebby Edwards,
The Mineworkers' Federation of Great Britain,
50, Russell Square,
W.C.1.

Dear Mr. Edwards,

Replying to your letter of January 13th, the present position is that the recommendation of the National Council of Labour as communicated to you was, as you know, reported to the General Council of the Trades Union Congress on December 17th, and was 'referred back' to the National Council.

The matter has been under the reconsideration of the Special Sub-Committee (which was set up by the National Council of Labour) at a meeting held on January 10th in London, when the following Resolution was agreed to unanimously:

'That the Sub-Committee is of the opinion that the promotion of legislation to implement the Labour Plan for the Mining Industry is not feasible in present circumstances, and, therefore, the Sub-Committee reaffirms its view that the immediate difficulties arising from the unfortunate situation in the Durham and South Wales Coalfields, raised by the Mineworkers' Federation of Great Britain, warrant consideration by the Federation of the possibilities of securing a scheme of national control and national pooling as a War Emergency measure, and as a preliminary to the adoption of the wider and fundamental policy of nationalisation.'

This Resolution will be reported to the National Council of Labour when it meets in London on Tuesday next, and I shall be glad to inform you of the result.
With kind regards,
Yours very sincerely,
(signed) J. S. MIDDLETON,
Secretary.

Ebby's angry reaction at the TUC meeting of 18 December and his moving of the reference back of the recommendation which had so cavalierly treated the miners' request had compelled a reconsideration by the Subcommittee. Middleton's second letter had then admitted that the promotion of legislation 'was not feasible in present circumstances'.

The phrase 'not feasible' revealed to those who knew the set-up both in Parliament and in the government that there was little chance of persuading a ministry so heavily weighted with members of the Conservative Party.

As the facts on the attitude of the larger movement to the Mineworkers' Federation of Great Britain's request were now known, the Secretary asked the Committee to give direction on the course to be adopted before the next meeting of the General Council took place. The Committee refused to give any direction, and the issue was allowed to lie over until the special Executive meeting to be held on 31 January 1941.

On 24 January 1941 Ebby Edwards's account of these three months' proceedings ended as follows:

From the above report it is evident:
(1) The General Movement is not prepared to go forward to seek by legislation to embody their own plan for the mining industry as passed by National Conferences in 1936.
(2) The General Movement requests the Federation to consider the possibilities of securing a scheme of national control and national pooling as a War Emergency measure.

Ebby Edwards felt bitter about the Executive meeting of 17 January, as is clear from the sentences 'The Secretary asked the committee to give direction on the course to be adopted . . . The committee refused to give any direction, and the issue was allowed to lie over . . .' Ebby seems to have regarded this as abdication by the Executive and in particular by the President Will Lawther of their duty to fight strongly for the miners' point of view.*

On the last day of January they again discussed coal trade policy. It was a very lengthy discussion and in the end it was resolved:

That this Committee, after hearing the report of the General Council of the Trades Union Congress, and the Labour Party, on the request of the MFGB, agrees to appoint a Subcommittee to again meet in order to see how far arrangements can be made, or agreement arrived at, on the unification of the industry. (31 January 1941)

For the next three weeks the Secretary busied himself with the compilation of a memorandum on 'Coal Control during War Time'. Its ten pages, packed with much-needed information, began as follows:

The Executive Committee of the Mineworkers' Federation of Great Britain has decided to follow the advice of the Trades Union Congress and the Labour Party 'to consider the possibilities of securing a scheme of national control and national pooling as a War Emergency.' The Consultative Committee is appointed to consider and report on all issues arising from such policy to the Executive Committee before reaching any final settlement either separately or jointly, with the Government and or the Mining Association.

Equipped with this basic survey which covered very fully the facts of coal control from 1914 to 1918 and thereafter, the Consultative Committee got to work and by 19 March set forth their viewpoint in a letter to members of the Executive Committee which began as follows:

Dear Sir,
Our side of the Joint Standing Consultative Committee, acting as the Executive Subcommittee to formulate proposals for the unification of the Coal Industry, unanimously recommend the following:

---

*It may be that this incident marked the beginnings of the friction that existed between the General Secretary and Will Lawther for whom Ebby Edwards had little respect. These asperities were partly due to trade union rules which provided ever since 1921 for a full-time Secretary, who inevitably found himself on this or that issue compelled to take a leading position, and a part-time President. It was not until the war was over and a permanent President elected that this particular cause of friction could be ironed out – though not without some difficulties until the respective functions of these two officials had been definitely laid down.

(1) That we seek to have established a National Board to cover the Mining Industry. The Board to be composed of an equal number of representatives from the Mining Association of Great Britain and the Mineworkers' Federation of Great Britain.

(2) The National Board shall have power to consider and decide, either by agreement or in the event of failure to agree, by recourse to an Independent Chairman, or Board of Arbitrators, all matters which directly or indirectly affect the wages, conditions, and safety of mineworkers.

Then came a list of nine matters (eg that the Board 'shall fix a National Minimum Wage') where the miners' representatives would expect the National Board to have power to decide. Finally, the Subcommittee were 'most anxious' for substantial progress to be made 'at the next meeting of the Executive Committee'. But at that next meeting on 2 April the matter was deferred: and then at a special Executive Committee a week later, there was keen discussion and on a vote being taken, 'the opinion of the Executive was, it be resolved: "That item 3 on the agenda, viz, Coal Trade Policy, lie in abeyance and the Executive Committee proceed to consider the Essential Work (General Provisions) Order"' (8 April 1941).

4. THE ESSENTIAL WORK ORDER

When the Coalition Government realised in the spring of 1941 that there was a coal crisis, created partly by the fascist enemies and partly by acts and policies of their own making in their many ministries, they sought immediate remedies. There was no time to make a diagnosis: and so they plunged into a series of administrative measures, many of which were bound to result only in further failures.

Most of these stemmed from the Essential Work (General Provisions) Order.

It was not until nine months later that the House of Commons Select Committee on National Expenditure, in its forty-third report on 19 February 1942, revealed to the public what had gone wrong – as a preliminary to finding a more thorough-going and effective solution to a still deeper crisis. Recounting how ineffective the Undertakings (Restriction on

Engagement) Order of June 1940 had proved to be, the
Select Committee report turned to how 'the collapse of France
and the entry of Italy into the war' had resulted in the
temporary loss of exports and consequent widespread unemployment in the coal trade. Then it stated:

Repeated attempts were made by both sides of the industry, especially in
the export areas, to impress upon the Government the danger of depleting
the industry of its younger and more active men in view of the anticipated
increase in home consumption in 1941. It would appear that lack of
foresight was shown at that time by the Government in preparing for this
steadily increasing demand.

This is all the more remarkable in view of the fact that Government policy
from the beginning had been one of preparation for a long war. Inadequate
account seems to have been taken of the needs of the many new factories
which were then, and are still gradually coming into production, and of the
ever growing industrial consumption of gas and electricity.

Although the Mines Department supported the renewed representations
made to the Minister of Labour by both sides of the industry in the
autumn of 1940 the seriousness of the situation was still not appreciated
by the Government.

. . . In the spring of 1941 the depletion of stocks and the winter's experiences made it clear that a campaign for increased production would
have to be planned without further delay. By then it was realised that
well over 70,000 miners were either in the Armed Forces or in other
industries to which Essential Work Orders had since been applied. The
Essential Work (Coal Mining Industry) Order 1941 which was applied in
May came too late.

While these parliamentary broodings were to come in the
future, in April 1941 the government did the opposite of what
in common sense and in the traditional administrations of
Britain they should have done. It was a clear case of supply
and demand, of failing supply and increasing demand; that is,
the blades of the scissors were opening instead of closing to
cut out and shape the pattern of the future. This old law of
supply and demand applied. In the Select Committee report
it was said: 'Managements were unable to retain men in the
industry as they had neither inducement of regular work nor
good wages to offer them.'

The time-honoured solution – a greater incentive in the shape
of remuneration is put forward to induce the supply to increase
and cope with the increasing demand – was clearly available.

But the government did not avail themselves of it. Instead the government decided to use compulsion in order to solve an economic problem.

The Essential Work (Coal Mining Industry) Order was made by the Minister, Ernest Bevin, under the Defence Regulations, on 15 May 1941. On that day coalmines became 'scheduled undertakings' in which employment could not be terminated nor could a man leave his employment without the consent of the 'National Service Officer' – whose decisions, however, were subject to appeal. Every scheduled under-taking was bound to pay a guaranteed wage to its workers. Persistent absenteeism, if reported by the undertaking, would be dealt with by the National Service Officer who could give directions.

The effect of this compulsion upon mineworkers is described by the following passage in Court's official history:*

The Essential Work Order made very important changes in the conditions of employment at coal mines in three respects. First, it prohibited the free taking on and dismissal of men by the companies. In the name of the national interest, it bound the worker more closely to the industry than had been known since the days of the annual bond in the North of England and of mining bondage in Scotland, more than a century before. Secondly, it guaranteed the miner for the first time since the war of 1914–18 a wage, whether short-time was being worked or not, although not during an industrial dispute. Thirdly, it handed over to the State, in the form of the National Service Officer, an important part of the discipline of the mines, namely, the work of dealing in the last resort with habitual absentees. All of these changes hung together. There could be no compulsion of mining labour to stay in the mines without the guaranteed wage and freedom from dismissal; and once the unfettered right of dismissal had been taken away from the mine managements, some provision had to be made for the maintenance of discipline by State power.

These proposals for compulsion of labour first came to the notice of the miners' leaders at the Coal Production Council on 1 April 1941. The next day the Executive Committee resolved:

Coal by W. H. B. Court, Professor of Economic History, University of Birmingham (HM Stationery Office and Longmans, 1951). It is, in the words of the preface, 'one of a series of histories describing civil life in the United Kingdom during the Second World War, commissioned by the Government and may therefore be called "official"; but I, like the other historians was invited to use my critical judgment'.

That this Federation declares its opposition to the principle of compulsion as applied to the retention in, or return to the industry of mineworkers, unless satisfactory wage standards can be negotiated and some effective measure of control of the industry be extended to the workmen's representatives. (2 April 1941)

5. CONFERENCE ON ESSENTIAL WORK ORDER

There were three successive meetings of the MFGB Executive Committee in April 1941. At the last of these (held at the Mines Department, Millbank, London, where they had been meeting the minister) they considered their attitude to the Essential Work Order in the light of the deliberations that had taken place and reached the following conclusion:

That we note the decision of the Government to introduce the Essential Work (General Provisions) Order on terms arranged, and agree to inform the Minister that the Federation calls for the collaboration of the Mines Department towards the establishment of a National Board with power to consider wages or other matters affecting the industry. (10 April 1941)

Then on 1 May the Executive Committee harkened to a report from the Secretary of meetings that had taken place between the Federation officials and the Minister of Mines and the President of the Board of Trade.

From the interviews which had taken place, it was quite evident that the government had made up their minds that they would not countenance the inculcation in the Order as applying to the coal-mining industry of the questions of (a) a National Joint Board, (b) a stipulated figure of an amount for a guaranteed weekly wage (other than that the daily rate applicable to the grade or class of worker in the district concerned should be paid when entitled) and (c) the abolition of non-unionism at the mines.

The committee then considered at great length the issues involved, and it was resolved 'That a Special Conference be convened in London for Thursday, 9 May 1941'.

A week later, the morning was taken up with the Secretary's report and questions. There was then a considerable criticism made, first of the TUC and the Labour Party about their failure to go forward for nationalisation as the miners had requested and secondly of the government for their new proposal. On this the opening criticism came from Joe Hall of Yorkshire:

What is the cause of this Order? The reason is the continued complaints through the Press, and the continued prosecutions of our men for absenteeism, with no defence in Court, because we have not been allowed to defend them, or if attempt has been made to defend, little support has been granted. These continued complaints of absenteeism came to the notice of the Government, and that, in addition to the need for securing the maximum labour for the industry, was the cause of this Order.

But I say that this continued ridicule of men not attending their work has been more than astounding – it has been untruthful. Under the contract system in the mines a man must be perfectly fit when going into the pit. He cannot go like an ordinary workman to the factory or the man who goes to his office, saying he is going whether he is fit or not. He has to be fit. Ours is an industry where Nature has never been kind to us, and never will be. Ours is an industry in regard to which the finest experts and the best mining engineers have never yet been able to qualify to the fullest the facts that govern it. Impeded production can take place because of many things – bad roadways or bad ventilation – and our men have to suffer these continued abnormalities and excessive pressures.

... This Order is here, but it is not here on our bidding, and I am sure it is not here, either, at the wish of the coal owners. What do we say should be done to compensate us for the liberties we are giving away? We say there ought to be given to us an increase in wages.

On the morning of Friday 9 May, shortly before noon, all the Executive members were called to Millbank to a meeting with the Mines Secretary whom they knew well, and the President of the Board of Trade, Oliver Lyttelton, MP, whom they had never met before.* Lyttelton, who stood high in the regions of finance-capital, had been pulled out of 'his bucket-shop in the City', as Churchill scornfully called his business, to become

*Viscount Chandos of Aldershot (1954) was born Oliver Lyttelton on 15 March 1893, only son of the late Rt Hon. Alfred Lyttelton (Secretary for the Colonies in the Conservative administration of 1900 to 1905). Educated at Eton and Trinity College, Cambridge. Joined Army (Grenadier Guards) in 1914 and by 1918 was Brigade Major 4th Guards Brigade (dispatches thrice, Companion of the Distinguished Service Order, Military Cross); married in 1920 Lady Moira Godolphin Osborne, daughter of the 10th Duke of Leeds. President of the Board of Trade 1940–1; member of War Cabinet 1941–45; Secretary of State for the Colonies 1951–4; Chairman Associated Electrical Industries Ltd 1945–51 and of AEI and subsidiaries 1954–63; Director of Imperial Chemical Industries Ltd since 1954 and of Alliance Assurance Co Ltd; Trustee of the National Gallery; President of Institute of Directors October 1954.

President of the Board in 1940 and later to be taken into the War Cabinet.

Lyttelton gave the government reply: and then, in response to Ebby Edwards's request, put it in writing, as follows:

(1) The Government regard it as a matter of vital national importance that the miners' representatives should to-day recommend the acceptance of the Essential Work Order.

(2) The Government regard the subject of rates of wages as a matter for negotiation under the existing machinery, and could therefore not agree to introduce legislation which would compel the establishment of a National Board.

(3) The Government understands that if so requested the owners are prepared to enter at once into these negotiations, and the Government undertakes to do all possible to ensure that they are carried through speedily.

The Executive Committee then made the following recommendation to the adjourned conference:

That the Conference strongly protests against the owners and the Government failing to appreciate the need for increased wages in the operation of the Essential Work Order, but in view of the serious war situation the Conference recommends the Consultative Committee be given power to examine, seek to amend, and apply the Order in terms applicable to the mining industry. Further, the Conference recommends the Executive Committee to press for fundamental changes in the industry having regard to the wages position. (9 May 1941)

6. EWO IN PARLIAMENT

Twenty days later when the President of the Board of Trade, Oliver Lyttelton, opened a debate in the House of Commons on the Essential Work Order it had anything but a favourable reception from either the Labour benches or the miners' MPs. Of these the clearest statement was made by Alexander Sloan, MP for South Ayrshire, who was also Secretary of the National Union of Scottish Mineworkers.

When I listened to the speech of the President of the Board of Trade, I was anything but impressed at his statement. I think that the Government are making a fatal blunder in introducing this Essential Work Order. If any proof were needed that we are moving down the slippery slope towards totalitarian government, we have it in the introduction of these Orders. It is curious that during wars we have always suffered in this country from retrogression. The worst acts of aggression have been carried out against the common people when their sons were fighting on foreign battlefields. We are so often told that we are fighting for freedom, liberty and democracy, and we are so prone to gaze across the seas, that we may discover that the freedom, liberty and democracy for which we are fighting elsewhere will disappear from before our very eyes. If there is any trade or industry in the country that has no need for an Essential Work Order, it is the mining industry. There is no more loyal, patriotic, industrious, painstaking and hardworking people than the mining community. There is no body of men with a greater sense of responsibility than the miners. They require no Essential Work Order to compel them to do their work. They require no conscription or compulsion. They require no big stick. They are perfectly willing and able to give their services without any pressure at all.

Sloan recalled the history of the mining industry, which made 'bitter reading' as the 'cock-pit of industrial strife and the scene of internecine warfare'. He said:

It interests me to hear people on the other side of the House having a good word to say for the miners, because in the history of industrial warfare miners have always been classed, not as patriotic people, as the suggestion is now, but, as on one stirring occasion, as the enemies of our country. I remember what nice things were said about the miners in 1914–18. I remember when the Right Hon. Gentleman the Member for Caernarvon Boroughs [Mr Lloyd George] said we were the salt of the earth. You could, he said, stand gazing out to sea and see the German mercantile marine banished from the sea, and he knew that this was due to the British miner in conjunction with the British sailor. Time moved on, and we found ourselves in the midst of industrial strife. Instead of being the salt of the earth, we were the scum of the earth. Instead of heroes, we were Huns. A Noble Lord who was going to ring us round with the economic blockade said, 'We did not feed the Germans when they were our enemies, so why should we feed the miners when they are our enemies?' The picture can change, and the war heroes of to-day may be the Huns of tomorrow.

   In dealing with this Question, let us not merely aim for the things of to-day. In the course of events the war will come to an end, and it will be a disastrous thing for us if nothing has been done for the mining industry save the introduction of this Essential Work Order, a measure of conscription and compulsion, with the industry still in the hands of private enterprise. This Essential Work Order will fail. It will not bring a ton more coal. (28 May 1941)

Members of Parliament were not satisfied and in Question and

Answer of 20 May there had been a series of points made under the heading 'Coal Supplies' as follows:

Mr Hannah asked the Secretary for Mines whether he is aware that the shortage of coal in the Midlands is steadily growing more acute; and will he take steps to get released from the Army men needed in the mines?

The Secretary for Mines [Mr David Grenfell]: I am aware of the shortage in several areas. Steps are being taken in order to increase the production as rapidly as possible.

Mr Hannah: Will the Minister carefully consider cases where skilled miners now in the Army would probably be better employed in the national interest in coal mining?

Mr Grenfell: I hope the remarks of my Hon. Friend will be read by other Departments too. (20 May 1941)

Members of Parliament were still not satisfied and on 19 June under the heading 'Coal Industry' the Minister of Labour was asked a series of questions.

Mr Gordon Macdonald asked the Minister of Labour whether in view of the need for increased production of coal, he will give further consideration to the releasing of men from the Army for the coal industry?

Mr Bevin: I am not prepared to recommend the release of men from the Army for this purpose, but I am taking other steps in conjunction with my Hon. Friend the Secretary for Mines with the object of meeting the requirements of the industry.

Mr Macdonald: In view of the fact that a number have been taken in the last few weeks whose training has not commenced, will my Right Hon. Friend consider releasing them, and will he give instructions that no further men are to be called-up from the mining industry?

Mr Bevin: The numbers taken into the Army in the last few weeks must be very small, because the instruction to call up people was limited to young persons working on the surface only, and if they are employed below ground in their proper capacity, they are automatically reserved. I have taken steps to prevent any calling-up of underground miners, and also taken steps, in conjunction with the Secretary of State for War, to stop recruiting from this industry, with one exception, that is, young men volunteering to become pilots in the Air Force. (19 June 1941)

Ernest Bevin's answer in which, a year too late, he gave the assurance that he had already given (and afterwards broken) to Dai Grenfell in mid-May 1940 was taken up by James Griffiths and other Members in the following questions:

Mr James Griffiths: Is the Minister aware of the desirability of keeping an even balance of age in the mining industry, in view of the fact that so many thousands of young, virile men have gone into the Army that unless younger men come back production will be affected, and will he seriously reconsider this matter?

Mr Levy: Is my Right Hon. Friend aware of the chaotic position of the coal industry and that it cannot be very long before some of our munition works may have to close down for lack of coal; and what is he going to do about it?

Mr Ness Edwards: Is the Minister aware that men are being called up this week from the mining industry?

Mr Bevin: Coal seems to be a burning subject.

Mr Levy: It is, but the difficulty is that we have no coal to burn.

In response to these last questions Mr Bevin startled the House of Commons by the attempt to shuffle off responsibility and to put it on to the shoulders of the Secretary for Mines who was merely carrying out the instructions of Ernest Bevin. Bevin made an unfavourable impression on the House of Commons at the time.

Mr Bevin: Most of the questions that have been put to me ought to have been put to the Secretary for Mines. With regard to the calling-up, I would like to have particulars of people called up recently. It is not in accordance with the facts except in the limited sense that I have indicated; and with regard to the chaotic position in the coal industry, I can hardly be held responsible for that. It is not my Department.

When the delegates assembled at Edinburgh for the seventy-third annual Trades Union Congress they found in the General Council's report: 'The question of the adequate supplies of coal for industrial and domestic purposes during the coming winter has been a subject of discussion by the National Council of Labour and the ministers concerned for some considerable time.'

The upshot had been a letter to the Prime Minister 'pointing out the grave danger of a shortage of coal during the coming winter and strongly urging that the temporary release of ex-miners from the Armed Forces should be ordered forth-with'. 'The Prime Minister has replied regretting that the serious needs of the army for manpower are such that he cannot take the responsibility of agreeing to release from the army the large number of men contemplated by us.' Churchill had given the stock reply, such as any Prime Minister of the last two centuries would have given to shield the War Office. Churchill, a man of outstanding capacity, was very much in his proper place as Minister of Defence. But his notorious lack of interest in economics enabled him to shuffle off responsibility for a serious domestic situation and to leave it to be dealt with by other members of the War Cabinet.

Members of the House of Commons found they could get very little change out of the unfortunate Dai Grenfell who was very much in the position of a subordinate and had been frustrated in several ways by Labour Minister Ernest Bevin. Parliamentarians now turned on this urgent question to the War Office itself. On 30 September 1941 under the heading 'Coal Miners (Release)' the following took place:

Mr Purbrick asked the Secretary of State for War how many skilled miners have been temporarily released from the Army for that work during the months of May, June, July and August and up to date in September, respectively, and how many more are available temporarily?

Mr Keeling asked the Secretary of State for War whether he has given further consideration to the urgent national need for the return to the mines of coal miners in the Army.

Major-General Sir Alfred Knox asked the Secretary of State for War whether, owing to the serious danger of shortage of coal in the coming winter, he will release skilled miners on temporary leave from the Armed Forces?

Captain Margesson: The Government's policy with regard to the release of coalminers from the Armed Forces was explained by my Hon. Friend the Secretary for Mines in answer to Questions on 9th September. He stated that it had not been found necessary to ask for the return of more men from the Fighting Forces, and I have nothing to add to that statement.

Sir A. Knox: Does the Right Hon. and gallant Gentleman not consider that as these men have now no doubt been fully trained, they might be allowed out on leave, in order to get more coal and to increase the war effort?

Captain Margesson: It is not a question of their having leave for a short time. My Hon. and gallant Friend, who has been a soldier himself, knows that you cannot just train a man and then let him go. Training is a continuous process.

Sir A. Knox: Shortage of coal is the governing factor.

Captain Margesson: I can only answer that by repeating what my Hon. Friend the Minister of Mines said in his answer of 9th September. (30 September 1941)

It was at this point, if not earlier, that the miners' leaders began to realise the nature of coalition; and that a parliamentary party has least influence when its leaders are functioning as junior partners in a coalition government.

7. THE AYR CONFERENCE

The two hundred miners' representatives (182 delegates with two dozen members of the Executive Committee and officials) received a warm welcome to the Burns country in Ayrshire and its capital,

> Auld Ayr, wham ne'er a toun surpasses
> For honest men and bonnie lasses

but discovered its accommodation was largely taken up by evacuees from recent heavy bombing raids in nearby parts of Scotland. On their agenda they found a resolution on 'Nationalisation' submitted from Lancashire, beginning: 'This Conference of the Mineworkers' Federation of Great Britain strongly resents the action of the Labour Party and the Trades Union Congress General Council in refusing to implement the resolutions relating to the Nationalisation of the Mining Industry . . .'

On the morning of Monday 15 July the Chairman of the Business Committee, A. L. Horner, reported that both Lancashire and Scotland had refused to withdraw the words 'strongly resents the action of the Labour Party'. The Executive Committee therefore would oppose it, not because of 'any opposition to the principle of nationalisation but on the grounds that it 'cannot be a party to a condemnation of itself'. On the Wednesday morning a considerably toned down resolution was moved by J. T. Brown of Lancashire, formally seconded by J. McKendrick of Scotland and carried unanimously:

This Conference of the Mineworkers' Federation of Great Britain regrets the action of the Labour Party and Trades Union Congress General Council in failing to implement the resolutions relating to the Nationalisation of the Mining Industry and reiterates its demands for the Nationalisation of the coal mining and ancillary industries, with effective workers' control. Having regard to the international situation, the precarious state of the country, the importance of producing a considerably increased output of coal in the present emergency and the need for an increased rate of wages for the workpeople employed in the industry, it instructs the National Executive Committee to make an early approach to the Government in connection with this matter.

The nationalisation resolution of the 16 July annual conference at Ayr was remitted to the Reorganisation Sub-committee which on 20 August recommended:

That under the terms of this resolution we ask the General Movement, through the National Council of Labour, along with ourselves to jointly approach the Government with a view to the implementing of 'Labour's Plan for the Coal Industry'.

This had resulted, a month later, in a meeting at Transport House between the MFGB Reorganisation Subcommittee and the National Council of Labour. It was not an easy meeting, arising as it did from the miners' conference's unanimous 'regrets' at the National Council's 'failure' the previous winter. But 'after very lengthy deliberations the following resolution was carried by the National Council of Labour:

That a Subcommittee be constituted of three representatives of the National bodies represented on the Council, together with the Mine-workers' Federation, to examine and report upon the proposal submitted by the Federation: to examine the Movement's Plan for Nationalisation, together with possible alternatives that might be considered as competent to meet the immediate difficulties of the industry, with a view to discussions with Labour Ministers in the Cabinet, prior to official representations being made to the Government. (23 September 1941)

At the Executive Committee meeting, held at the Doncaster Rural District Council Chambers on 20 November 1941, the Secretary gave 'a résumé of the negotiations that had taken place up to the moment' by the Subcommittee of the National Council of Labour 'which comprises our own representatives'.

How would nationalisation beneficially assist in the war effort by increasing production? On this question further details had been asked for from the three officers of the Federation. So Ebby Edwards once more prepared a comprehensive and closely argued memorandum. It was exactly fifty-two weeks since the miners had first made their request to the TUC and the Labour Party, as an urgent wartime measure, and had suffered a rebuff. The decision was: 'That the memo presented by the Secretary be approved and our representatives on the Joint Subcommittee proceed to complete the further details required by the Joint Subcommittee'. (20 November 1941).

8. EBBY EDWARDS'S MEMORANDUM

The urgency with which the National Council of Labour besought the Miners' officials to let them have within eight days a memorandum of further details was symptomatic of the growing anxiety as the various remedies, such as the Registration of Mines Scheme, failed to produce enough coal. It reflected also anxiety about Asia. The Japanese blow on 7 December 1941 at Pearl Harbour, the chief United States naval base in the Pacific, was followed by their invasion of all the European empires in South-East Asia, to complete their aims, that had begun ten years earlier with their seizure of the three north-eastern provinces of China and their setting up in that vast region of their puppet empire called Manchukuo. Then from the Marco Polo Bridge incident of 1937 in Peking they had invaded all the great plains of China up to the mountains and southwards to the frontier of the British Crown Colony of Hong Kong. From 8 December 1941 their attack was launched simultaneously upon the Philippines, on Hong Kong, on Malaya, across Indochina into Burma, on to Borneo, Celebes and Java in the archipelago of Indonesia.

Within a matter of weeks these vast and populous territories were over-run and their defenders, including the hastily dispatched fleet of British battleships, had been outwitted, outmanoeuvred, sunk by bombing aeroplanes and signally defeated. Finally, the surrender of the great naval base of Singapore on 15 February described by Churchill as the greatest disaster to British arms in history, had a shattering effect on the British Empire with repercussions in Great Britain that affected Parliament, government and the armed forces.

It was at the beginning of this tense situation in the winter of 1941–2, continuing into the spring and summer of

1943, that further steps were taken along the road to 'unification' of the coal-mining industry, this time by an intervention of the War Cabinet. First, however, came the requested Memorandum, written at 6 Victoria Terrace, Durham (a temporary office headquarters of the MFGB) by Ebby Edwards on 18 November 1941. The Memorandum was prepared to form the basis of an inquiry by the Subcommittee into the following issues:

A. How far can Labour's Plan for the Coal Industry in total, or in part, be immediately implemented by legislation in present circumstances having regard to the composition of the Parties in the Government and the existing situation of the country at war?
B. Failing to secure agreement by the Cabinet as to the implementing of Labour's Plan by legislation either as a whole, or in part, should the Movement (1) use its machinery politically and industrially to force the issue, or (2) propose a compromise (a) by means of suggested legislation to limit the free play of coal capitalism without a change of ownership, or (b) by assisting the Mineworkers' Federation of Great Britain to secure changes and improvements in the existing system by industrial or political negotiations?'

There followed ten brief paragraphs with the following headings: An Examination of Labour's Plan; Establishment of Coal Corporation; Members of Corporation; Transfer of Mines, etc; Compensation Commission; Compensation for Mines and Minerals; Coal Marketing Board; Supply of Fuel; Regional Boards and Pit Councils; Fuel Consumers' Council.*

In a second series of paragraphs headed 'An Examination of the Request of the Mineworkers' Federation of Great Britain' there occurred a significant sentence: 'To press for reforms even when it is known that Labour's opponents will successfully resist clearly brings into the open the distinction of the Parties in the House and may mean further converts to secure Labour's political majority.'

There followed words of warning both to the Labour Party parliamentarians and to the Labour men who held posts in the Coalition Government.

---

*At this point Ebby Edwards wrote: 'The foregoing has given but a brief outline of the general principles. See Scheme endorsed in 1936 and Nationalisation Bill, October, 1937, for detailed proposals.'

In consideration of the composition of the Political Parties in the Government at present, the question arises, should it really count? Unless the Labour Movement's representatives, industrial and political, had been in the Cabinet and other Government positions, the measures which have shackled the industrial workers could not, and would not, have been passed on to the Statute Book without industrial and political conflict. Labour members in the Government represent not themselves, but the whole of Labour power, and should act accordingly. We are not entitled to measure Labour's power merely by the pre-war strength of political parties in the House of Commons.

The next warning was both to capitalist interests in general and in particular to those of the coal trade.

In a period of war, when under Defence Acts and Regulations, provision is made to commandeer persons, their services, *and their property*, without political upsets from the House of Commons, the chance might come to test the real capitalist interests for economic changes. In addition to the efficient prosecution of any war, the Order (May 22nd, 1940) provides power to take over property '*for maintaining supplies or services essential to the life of the community.*' On this issue of supplies, politicians of every Party have been very critical of the coal industry.

Then came two paragraphs in which the contrast was pointed out between the position in wartime of the mine-owner who was given compensation, and that of the miners whose lives, in thousands, had been 'confiscated to fight for the country'.

While life is owned and controlled by the State, what of property? The Colliery Companies carry on as in normal times; where they are called upon by the Government to adjust their control for the necessities of war, a compensation is granted by allowing increased revenue, which comes out of the consumers. The only penalty of limitation by Excess Profits Duty disturbs the owners nil. Accountancy is now a fine art for capitalist evasion.

What of the miners, in thousands, whose lives have been confiscated to fight for the country; upon their return should they depend on a privately owned industry for an existence? Following the last war, no industrial workers suffered more at the hands of private ownership than the mine-workers.

Then Ebby voiced a feeling very prevalent among face-workers, who were working so hard and were being urged all the time to increase output.

Public Ownership of the mining industry was adopted by the Movement as being in the interests of the country as a whole. Does the position still hold? The Mineworkers' Federation believe that it does and that the issue of Labour's Plan, as a whole, should be pressed. We cannot accept the conception that after all the sacrifices that are being made in this war *it should end with coal capitalism supreme* as against ownership by the nation.

Under the heading 'If We Abandon Labour's Plan' Ebby Edwards brought forward what must surely have been in his mind for many months if not for years. This was the stipulation in the Labour movement's 1936 plan for nationalisation that if the coal industry were to be transformed by unification, so also must its trade unions be transformed both in policy and in organisation. To Ebby the best policy in wartime, and for the purpose of winning the war, was to get rid of private ownership of the coalmines. For this he had driven forward from the moment in mid-July 1941 when the conference resolutions on 'Coal Trade Policy' and 'National Control' had been remitted to the Executive Committee; and now that an intensified coal crisis was to come up before the War Cabinet, the opportunity opened out of solving at the same time the previously intractable problem of the disunity and disintegration of the Miners' Federation of Great Britain. 'If Labour's Plan for the Mining Industry is rejected, either by the Movement or the Government, alternative plans for greater unification of the industry will bring keen controversy and divisions within the Miners' organisation itself.'

The Memorandum then made a significant quotation of Section 109 of Labour's Plan:

The Trade Unions, however, must realise their own responsibilities if they are to play an adequate part in socialised industry. Obvious steps in that direction must be the proper unification of trade union policy, and of trade union organisation which must conform to that of the industry.'

The mining organisation awaits legislation on Labour's Plan to impose a change from district to national organisation. I see no hope of a voluntary change.

Ebby's personal statement above ('I see no hope of a voluntary change') was a very significant utterance. It was based on the experience of twelve years since 1927 when successively most admirable plans for integration of the trade union side of the industry had been worked upon, voted on, carried in conference and then never carried into effect – so strong was the resistance of habitual procedures within the districts, so great the resistance to change. In the next paragraph Ebby gave his reasons.

At the moment, all of our twenty-two districts have local district autonomy. They have separate wage agreements. Their wages are determined by the economic capacity of the district. The average wage varies from district to district as between a few pence to shillings difference per shift. Districts are very jealous of their district position, and are only prepared for national unity on condition it does not materially affect their district wages. Regulations as to safety and hours of work are national by legislation. The flat rate wage increase is national by agreement.

In the foregoing Memorandum there is revealed the whole strategy which Ebby Edwards had conceived, especially after the fall of France had showed up the utter inadequacy for war purposes of the British coal trade.

9. HATCHING THE CHICKEN

The Ebby Edwards Memorandum of 18 November, after going through stages of discussion, was adopted by a resolution, significantly headed 'Nationalisation', of the miners' Executive Committee, which decided that 'our side of the Joint Sub-committee' be empowered to take 'immediate steps to formulate a Scheme'.

The scheme, embodied in a memorandum headed 'The Position of the Coal Mining Industry', was finally accepted on 24 February 1942 by the National Council of Labour which 'agreed to place same before the Labour Members in the Cabinet'. The chaotic condition of the industry with '1,135 colliery companies producing coal from approximately 1,900 coal mines' was set out. The remedy put forward was '*a National Authority to deal with its affairs on a national basis*'.*

---

*This was spelled out as follows:
1. The establishment of a Coal Board, composed of representatives of the Government, the Mineowners' Association, and the Mineworkers' Federation of Great Britain, who should devote the whole of their time to the business of the Board.
2. The functions of the Board would be to plan and organise the industry; to decide on

The month of February 1942 had opened in gloom with the cumulative effect of the disasters to British arms on all fronts, and with a gradual realisation that on the home front plans for coal had failed. There was a reconstruction of the Cabinet. Churchill on 22 February conceded one of the Tory-prized ministries, the Board of Trade, to Hugh Dalton.

Three weeks later Dalton, on 11 March, having the agreement of the miners' leaders, undertook to explore with the Mining Association of Great Britain the proposals embodied in the National Council of Labour's Scheme. What took place at an exchange of views between the coal-owners and the new President of the Board of Trade is related in Hugh Dalton's autobiography as follows:

On March 19th I met a whole roomful of coal-owners. Their spokesman, Evan Williams, looking like a Galsworthy character, was seventy-one years old. He denied that there had ever been any trouble in the industry, except when there had been 'political interference'; this had been the sole cause of bad relations between the owners and the men; the owners would, of course, like to pay more wages, but the money wasn't there; they were opposed to a National Board on which both sides would sit; this was put forward with a political motive; it could only do harm. He spoke for an hour and a half, with much historical detail. He had been the owners' spokesman since 1919. No others spoke, except a few, very briefly, to say that they agreed with him. He then asked for higher coal prices. At this they all brightened up and several became quite talkative . . . I hinted that we might consider coal prices and improved organisation together at another meeting. They did not like this, protesting that the two questions were quite separate. They seemed to me to be a body of men – except, perhaps, a few of the younger ones – who could be dealt with only by orders, not by persuasion; and finally only by liquidation. (H. Dalton, *The Fateful Years*, p. 300)

The Plan to overcome the coal crisis, in a number of variants, kept being discussed between the various ministries. Time was being lost. Meanwhile, as Dalton records, 'there was increasing evidence of a seething discontent in the mines'.

Then the pace of events (or the reflection of these events in Whitehall) quickened. A letter from the Privy Council

matters which directly or indirectly affect it, including coal production, the allocation of supplies, prices, wages, mining conditions, safety, pensions and welfare; and to settle all matters affecting the financial and labour aspects of the industry irrespective of pre-War interests or post-War prospects.

Office, Whitehall, 20 April 1942, on behalf of the Lord President of the Council, invited six leading miners and six leading coal-owners on the next Friday. The government were represented by the Lord President (Sir John Anderson, MP)* and six ministers concerned with coal production. It was a general talk on issues of manpower and coal production as part of the war effort. The miners emphasised the need for the government to adopt the Scheme as endorsed at the National Council of Labour. The government were more concerned to know how coal production could be increased than as to the form or suggested organisation of the industry as a means towards that. Copies of this Scheme were then sent to all Cabinet members. This Coal Plan of the National Council of Labour came before the annual conference of the Labour Party on 25 May and received a unanimous vote.

The government, however, looked at it in a different way and had their own methods and ways of making a very much needed change in the coal industry. The leading part (under Sir John Anderson) was played by Hugh Dalton. Dalton, with the backing of Bevin, wanted to requisition the pits for the duration of the war and proposed this to the Cabinet, both being sure that if the owners lost control of the pits they would never get it back. 'But we met great resistance, some from most surprising quarters, and had to fall back on a second-rate compromise' (Dalton's autobiography). This 'second-rate compromise' was the famous White Paper agreed by the Cabinet on 1 June: *Coal*, 'presented by the President of the Board of Trade to Parliament by Command of His Majesty, 3rd June 1942'.. The Department of Mines was taken out of the Board of Trade and became the most important part of a new

---

*Viscount Waverley of Westdean; John Anderson was born 8 July 1882, son of D. A. P. Anderson of Westland House, Eskbank, Midlothian. After his education at Edinburgh and Leipzig Universities he entered the Colonial Office in 1905; it was the first stepping stone in a career through the Civil Service. From Secretary to the Ministry of Shipping (1917–19) he became Chairman of the Board of Inland Revenue 1919–22 and then got a Permanent Under-Secretaryship of State at the Home Office 1922–32. There he proved himself so well as a sort of super-jailer that he was made Governor of Bengal 1932–7. On retirement he became MP for Scottish Universities 1938–50 as a staunch Conservative. His reputation had preceded him and immediately on his arrival in Parliament he was pulled into the Cabinet as Lord Privy Seal 1938–9; Home Secretary and Minister of Home Security 1939–40. On 3 October 1940 he became Lord President of the Council and so remained until in 1943 he moved to be Chancellor of the Exchequer. His honours began with a knighthood in 1919; Fellow of the Royal Society 1945; Order of Merit 1957.

ministry, the Ministry of Fuel and Power. The new minister
(Gwilym Lloyd George having taken the place of Dai Grenfell
– much to the displeasure of the miners' leaders) was to 'take full
control over the operation of all coal mines'.

In order to ensure that all practicable means of increasing output are
adopted without delay and pressed forward vigorously, private interests
being subordinated to the over-riding needs of increased production, the
Government have decided to assume full control over the operation of the
mines, and to organise the industry on the basis of national service, with
the intention that the organisation now to be established will continue
pending a final decision by Parliament on the future of the industry.

The minister would preside over a National Coal Board,
representing the different interests within and around the
industry: but this and the regional boards were advisory. The
minister would·have under him controllers and regional controllers, who gave what orders and instructions were needed.
Nothing was left to the mine-owners – except ownership and
finance.

CHAPTER III

THE END OF THE WAR AGAINST FASCISM

I. MID-SUMMER DAYS

It was in the first days of June 1942 that the coal crisis, inherent in the British economy since autumn 1939, was at last dealt with, if not finally solved, by the White Paper (Cmd 6364) and the accompanying government measures and decisions. To the miners' leaders, sick at heart with hope deferred some twenty months, it seemed to happen all at once. The Mineworkers' Federation of Great Britain Executive Committee, which at their meeting on 22 May had decided for an immediate increase in wages,* were suddenly convened for 5 June to hear a report of negotiations in a new and urgent situation. They were then told by the President that on the previous day the Federation representatives on the JSCC had presented to the owners their request. The owners' side was 'not able to accede to our request'.

On Tuesday 2 June, the Secretary had received a telephone message from Sir John Anderson's office 'asking that our representatives attend a meeting' of the Cabinet Coal Sub-committee to be held on 3 June, to hear proposals the government were to enunciate in the form of a White Paper on organisation of the industry and their proposals to deal with wages. Sir John Anderson said it was the intention of the Government as outlined in its White Paper to set up a Board of Investigation to begin its task on the following Monday 8 June. This Board would first of all deal with the immediate

---

*(1) That we seek to secure a minimum weekly wage of not less than £4.5s. per week for all adult mineworkers.

(2) That we seek to secure an immediate flat rate advance of 4s. per shift for adult workers and 2s. for others per shift.

(3) That our representatives on the N.F.C.C. raise these points with the Owners' representatives at the meeting to be held on May 28th, and following such meeting our representatives take such steps as they may think necessary, even to the extent of convening a Special Conference. In the event of a Special Conference being convened, the Executive Committee be called to meet the day previous to the Conference being held. (22 May 1942)

application for a wages increase and hear evidence from both sides: at a later stage it would hear further evidence in regard to the setting up of a permanent Wages Board for the industry. It was intended that the government would take 'full control of the Coal Mining Industry in order to secure an increase in coal production'.

Having taken those decisions on their own wages demand and the prospective investigation, the miners' leaders then sat down to examine the White Paper because of forthcoming meetings of the National Council of Labour and of the Parliamentary Labour Party, each anxious to know the views of the Federation. That day there was a second prolonged discussion, at the end of which it was agreed:

This Executive Committee of the Mineworkers' Federation of Great Britain, having considered the Government's White Paper on Coal Mines, reaffirms its view that ownership and control of the Mines is essential to efficient organisation.

Whilst acknowledging that the Government's Plan will give an increased measure of control and organisation in the Coal Mining Industry, the Federation is of the opinion that such Plan does not provide for a complete solution of the coal production problem.

The Federation declares, however, that having regard to the urgency of the question of coal production, it will, as hitherto, do all that lies in its power to meet the needs of the Government in relation to increased production . . .

They concluded with listing eight questions* on which they urged the need to amend and strengthen the Plan.

After additional points had been raised by members of the Executive Committee it was decided that the whole matter be relegated to the JSCC Subcommittee to prepare amendments to the White Paper, and 'if it is considered necessary, assistance be secured in the preparation of documentary evidence for presentation to the Board of Investigation, and the resolution adopted be the text of the report to be given to the Press of the Committee's policy, and that we also inform the Mining Members of Parliament of our decision' (5 June 1942).

*(a) Ownership; (b) Managerial control; (c) Financial structure; (d) Absenteeism; (e) Pit production committees; (f) Direct representation of Federation on the National Board; (g) Nomination of single persons; (h) Determination of regions.

That same 5 June Hugh Dalton and Ernest Bevin, in immediate implementation of the White Paper, set up a Board of Investigation of five headed by the Rt Hon. Lord Greene, Master of the Rolls. The Greene Board, as it came to be called, moved fast. 'Nine times the space that measures day and night' sufficed for them to settle the wage claim. They were much assisted by the speed with which Ebby Edwards, given authority, had engaged the services of the Labour Research Department with a resultant big array of facts, figures and appendices available for the first meeting of the Board.

At this point the mine-owners' chairman and his associates made a tactical error. Accustomed for nearly twenty years to dealing only with an ill-equipped and deferential Secretariat for Mines, and not as yet fully realising the impact of the White Paper upon the owners', present and future, Sir Evan Williams did not prepare detailed material for the Board of Investigation. He turned up as in duty bound but had not done anything to prepare a case. Sir Evan Williams seems to have underestimated the mandatory nature of the White Paper as a war measure. After the Executive Committee of 5 June, the next meeting decided:

This Executive Committee resolves that a full report of proceedings re the Wages Claim now being considered by the Government Board of Investigation be presented to the National Conference of the Mineworkers' Federation of Great Britain to be held on June 11, 1942.

The Executive Committee further resolves that the Conference, having received the report, be recommended to endorse the decisions of the Executive Committee in accepting the Government procedure for the settlement of the wages claim and that the Conference stand adjourned to a date to be decided upon by the Executive Committee following the Government decision. (10 June 1942)

This resolution was unanimously carried the next day. Arthur Horner then proceeded to report on the White Paper and discussions with the Anderson Committee.

We said that there are three things wrong with the industry. First, the men in it are dissatisfied with the treatment they are receiving in relation to other workers in war industries. Secondly, we said that we have not enough men. And, thirdly, that we never will be able to improve the mood of the men so long as their efforts can be connected to profits to mine owners, whom they hate and detest over a long period of years. In short, we put forward before the Anderson Committee arguments in favour of the Coal Plan adopted by the National Consultative Committee.

At the special conference called to hear a report of the Executive Committee on the findings of the Greene Board of Investigation, the delegates accepted unanimously the resolution moved by Ebby Edwards:

This Conference having received the report of the Recommendations of the Investigation Board on Wage Increases and the establishment of National Minimum Wage Rates for Underground and Surface Workers respectively, notes that they have now been accepted by the Government.

The Executive Committee whilst reaffirming the miners' claim to equality with workers in other War industries recommends acceptance of the findings.

The Conference further notes the proposals to introduce a Bonus Output Scheme, and instructs the Executive Committee to examine this proposal or alternative proposals calculated to improve coal production. (23 June 1942)

The Greene Board had been very speedy in dealing with the immediate wage demand but on the question of the new kind of conciliation machinery to be set up they were as careful as they could be, no matter how much time might be spent. Their object was to get something that would settle the matter not only for a few months during the war period and afterwards. The stages by which this discussion was carried on by the Board of Investigation and the two sides of industry resulted finally in the setting up both of the National Negotiating Committee and of a National Reference Tribunal.

The miners were only partially satisfied. They had asked for nationalisation not only as the best remedy for the troubles of the coal trade, but also because, in the consciousness of the three officers at any rate, it entailed a single national union for mineworkers. Their determination to work for nationalisation remained unaltered, and was expressed at the annual conferences of 1942 and 1943.

2. THE BLACKPOOL ANNUAL CONFERENCE
(20–22 JULY 1942)

At the Executive Committee on 23 June there was a prolonged discussion and then it was resolved:

In view of the resolution on 'Coal Production and Reorganisation of the MFGB', the Reorganisation Sub-Committee meet and prepare a scheme on the Reorganisation of the Federation for presentation to the Conference, and, due to the exceptional amount of work at present facing the Secretary, the Vice-President act as Secretary to the Reorganisation Subcommittee. (23 June 1942)

The importance of this decision is brought out in a subsequently compiled appendix setting forth 'the objective' of the resolution.*

At Blackpool on 20 July the Executive Committee's resolution on 'Coal Production and Reorganisation of MFGB' was moved by Vice-President James Bowman. He asked:

What do you visualise when you speak of national wage machinery? Do you see a conglomeration of districts pulling twenty-two different directions each trying to further its own opinion or bringing forward its own point of view, irrespective of the good or bad effect that may have upon other districts?

. . . Do you see the parent body – the Mineworkers' Federation of Great Britain – regarded as an outsider or an interloper, or do you see one national directing force through the medium of one Miners' Union speaking for the miners of the country as a whole, directing, fighting and acting in the name of the miners of Great Britain, but with overriding unity impossible in the basis of our existing formation? Can there be two opinions on that?

The Objective of Resolution 11

1. To merge all the individual district and sectional miners' unions into one national organisation covering all mineworkers employed in or around the collieries of Great Britain.
2. For the purpose of union administration the areas shall be the same as the districts covered by the separate district organisations at present affiliated to the Mineworkers' Federation of Great Britain, always providing that this shall not prevent any two or more adjoining districts voluntarily agreeing to become one area.
3. The terms of the amalgamation shall be agreed to after full consideration with the district unions, it being understood procedure will be adopted in order to reach finality and practical application within a specific period to be determined.
4. Each individual union shall on a date to be decided transfer to the National Union a proportion (to be later determined) of its assets and liabilities.
5. A uniform amount of contributions shall be paid from every full member (half-members to pay half such amount) to the National Miners' Organisation. (11 June 1942)

As soon as James Bowman had finished, George Spencer, MP from Nottingham, said:

I take this opportunity of rising to state the opposition of my district to this proposal . . .

In that very admirable speech which we listened to this morning emphasis was laid upon our great value of liberty and freedom. Whose liberty? Whose freedom? There is one definite outcry. That outcry is against Hitlerism. What is Hitlerism? It is purely over-centralisation of government – purely a method of government which is being suggested by this very resolution, depriving the districts of a right to govern themselves, and, if I may say so, without even any slight adumbration as to what the new form of government will be, over and above the Executive.

Sam Watson of Durham, in his contribution to the debate, said:

One question he poses (which is the pivot upon which this discussion may revolve) is: What is Hitlerism? Hitlerism, said Mr. Spencer, is the centralisation of government. I want to suggest from this platform that Hitlerism is not so much the centralisation of government as it is the destruction of the workers' movements, those movements not having been sufficiently alive to the inherent ruthlessness inside Fascism and the policy of Fascism to destroy its enemies inside their own country one by one.

The debate concluded with speeches from Fred Swift of Somerset and J. Elks of Kent. The resolution was carried with only two delegates against out of the two hundred miners' representatives present.

This did not end the opposition. At the EC meeting of 24 September it was suggested that 'Prior to any meeting of the Subcommittee to deal with the question of reorganisation of the Federation, there should be a ballot vote of the membership on the principle involved in the annual conference resolution.' After discussion it was agreed: 'That a meeting of the Reorganisation Subcommittee be held within the next fortnight to examine the whole problem and report back on its findings to the Executive Committee' (24 September 1942).

Three weeks later Vice-President James Bowman reported on that meeting of the Reorganisation Subcommittee. Before a scheme could be drafted for consideration by the Committee it would be necessary to collect information from the districts as well as discuss with the district representatives their views in relation to the principles involved in the proposed changes and in this connection the Subcommittee proposed that three representatives from each district should meet the officials of the Federation in London. This was 'endorsed'.

Nine months later the report of the Executive to the annual conference contained a section (afterwards distributed to districts as a twenty-page pamphlet) on 'Reorganisation of the Federation'. The matter was not debated but tabled so that in the ensuing months it could be discussed and dealt with in each of the districts. It was essentially the argument for a single union concluding with a complete draft of rules.

3. WINSTON CHURCHILL INTERVENES

The plan of dual control established with the White Paper of June 1942 was functioning fifteen months later, but less and less effectively. A proposal on 23 September 1943 by the Ministry of Fuel and Power that there be an extension of the working week was clearly a desperate measure. In response to it the Executive Committee of 7 October 1943 published a 'Statement of the Mineworkers' Federation in Respect of the Proposals of the Ministry of Fuel and Power for Increasing Coal Production and the Counter-Proposals of the Federation'. Their series of proposals were: immediate legislation governing hours of work after the war; government control of the disposal and price of coal, both inland and export; guaranteed week and national minima; pit-head baths and canteens or snack bars at all collieries; comprehensive Workmen's Compensation Scheme; safety measures including dust suppression; extension of scientific research on coal utilisation.

In conclusion, the Federation submits that the industry is suffering from a number of accumulating factors that cannot be wholly solved so long as the ownership of the industry remains in private hands. The responses that are required by the Nation from the men cannot be forthcoming unless the workmen can be assured that the benefits of those responses do not accrue to the colliery companies.

Five days later a debate was about to take place in the House of Commons on what was now the very vexed question of coal production. It was being argued that the system of dual control, though better than that of the unrestricted owners, was nevertheless in many ways a failure. In Parliament and also in the ranks of the government itself there was very considerable difference of opinion. The cry from many sections in the country was for something much more to be done, something in the nature of the nationalisation of the coalmines. The War Cabinet found they had to bring forward their biggest gun, Churchill himself, to quieten the very strong feeling aroused by some of the most effective speakers – Aneurin Bevan, for instance, who had said on a point of procedure: 'It is not good enough for the House that the Minister should be called upon to defend a policy for which the War Cabinet itself was responsible.'

When the Prime Minister came into the House of Commons to speak on that 12 October he was in much better shape than in the spring of 1942, when he had been weighed down by the disasters in South-East Asia in mid-February culminating in the fall of Singapore; and when he had had to reconstruct his Cabinet. He was now supported by a twelve-month record of British and Allied successes in the field (El Alamein and the victorious onward sweep of the Eighth Army led by Montgomery; Stalingrad and the victory of the Kursk Salient planned by Marshal Zhukov; a series of successful US actions in the Pacific; and finally, only five weeks before, the surrender on 7 September of the Italian Government.)

Surely the Premier and Minister of Defence had only to appear on the Treasury Bench and the mutineers, mining members and their various supporters would immediately hoist signals of submission. But Churchill had behind him a very long record of relations with the Miners' Federation and its districts. While yet in his thirties, Winston Churchill, youngest member of the Liberal Cabinet, was invited by Lib.-Lab. mining MPs to come to South Wales where he gratified his hosts by denouncing the beer barons, crusading for temperance and against the demon alcohol. But two years later, in 1910, when he had become Home Secretary, there was the unpleasant business of his Metropolitan Police being sent to deal with the miners at Ton-y-Pandy and given backing by both cavalry and infantry.

By the mid-twenties, as a turncoat, Churchill took a post with the Tories and as Chancellor of the Exchequer in Baldwin's Cabinet (1924–9) brought economic disaster to the country by his budget of spring 1925 nailing the pound to the gold standard. British goods would be unsaleable abroad unless costs were cut, by a 10 per cent lowering of wages. J. M. Keynes, the already famous economist, made himself more famous by his pamphlet *The Economic Consequences of Mr. Churchill* in which he foretold that the miners, attacked in this way, would be bound to resist. When on 31 July 1925 (Red Friday) the TUC General Council compelled the government to give a subsidy in aid of wages of the miners,* Churchill resolved never again to be caught napping. Nine months later he got his chance. In a Cabinet cabal with Joynson-Hicks and others he used the pretext on 2 May 1926 of a printers' strike on the Daily Mail to break off negotiations and precipitate the General Strike. Thereafter he was hand-in-glove with the mine-owners until his wavering in the autumn of the long-drawn-out seven-month lockout.

From 1910 onwards Churchill, however undeservedly, bore an unsavoury reputation amongst the British miners.

In Derbyshire after the war a BBC reporter, finding that miners had defaced a public house that had taken the name The Winston Churchill, also found the reason 'that Churchill had tried to starve the miners telling them to eat grass'.

But now, whatever his record had been, was the opportunity for him at one and the same moment to promise an immediate repeal of the Trade Disputes and Trade Union Act of 1927

---

*When, before midnight of Thursday 30 July 1925, Stanley Baldwin with Churchill in tow met the mine-owners and broke the news of the decision to yield and to pay a subsidy, there were some moments of silence. Then Sir Evan Williams spoke:

As I understand it, Mr. Prime Minister, the Government have decided to buy off the Danes. It is an experiment which was tried in this country a thousand years ago and failed. It will fail again as surely as it failed then. In naming the date of the end of the subsidy the Government will be naming the date of the commencement of the strike. It will then be an immensely more difficult situation to face than it would be if the Government held to their decision today to face it. (W. A. Lee, *30 Years in Coal*, The Mining Association of Great Britain, 1954)

Churchill had to hear his chief, and himself, rated like schoolboys: and his ducal blood boiled at the humiliation.

Main conveyer (Sutcliffe) at Fernhill

Miner moving forward power supports by push button control at the
coalface (Daw Mill Colliery, Warwick)

and cancellation of all the grievances and difficulties of the coal trade. But, half genius and half mountebank, as a great Marxist once said of him, Churchill proved unequal to the occasion. In Parliament he fell back on rhetoric, on his old skill of using honeyed words. He sought to show that the miners personally were wonderful and that the situation was by no means as serious as supposed.

It was a dreadful speech. Jim Bowman said Churchill's speech was one of 'the greatest disservice to the mining industry'.* 'The capitalists', said Bowman, 'are now crawling out of their funk holes and claiming their position for the post-war world.'

To these activities of the mining capitalists, or some of these activities, we must now turn.

4. THE PRIVATE OWNERS

The White Paper of June 1942, the Greene Board of Investigation, a new and powerful Ministry of Fuel and Power – all these had given a severe shock to the coal-owners. It disturbed all their assumptions, all their four-centuries-old way of living. They brooded over it for many months. Then at a meeting of the Joint Standing Consultative Committee in the Spring of 1943, Sir Evan Williams said that the owners, who had initiated a study of postwar policy in September 1942, felt it necessary to begin to give attention to what might be called in general terms the future of the industry. The owners felt that 'great credit was due to both sides for their cooperation in handling the industrial problem with which they had to deal; and in order to develop that understanding and a sense of partnership in the industry that was necessary, they suggested that the two sides should sit down together and consider jointly all questions of future policy which had a bearing on the prosperity of the industry.' After a very full discussion it was agreed that a subcommittee, consisting of

*Within a very little while after the war Churchill was to realise that his attitude to the mining industry had been a blot and a disaster. On a trans-Atlantic vessel he confessed to Sir Will Lawther, 'The mineowners were the millstone that sunk the Conservative Party.'

six representatives from each side, should be established to examine the 'whole question of post-war policy, and that the Joint Secretaries should be instructed to inform the Government of the decision, who should be requested not to commit itself to any views in this connection until there has been an opportunity of consulting the industry upon it'.

The following letter was then addressed by the Joint Secretaries to the Minister of Fuel and Power in the spring of 1943:

At a meeting of the Joint Standing Consultative Committee for the Coal Industry yesterday we were desired to inform you that we are giving consideration to the post-war problems of the coal industry. The Committee are certain the Government will appreciate our keen interest in the post-war problems of the industry and our joint endeavour to overcome any difficulties that may arise. One important part of these problems is that of the coal export trade and it is hoped that a joint statement of the industry's views on the subject will shortly be presented to you. Meantime the Committee expressed the hope that the Government will not commit itself to any view in this connection until there has been an opportunity of consulting the industry upon it. (26 March 1943)

Before the second meeting of this subcommittee could take place, there was a discussion of the whole matter at the Federation Executive Committee of 8 April which agreed to endorse the action of the Joint Standing Consultative Committee and to authorise continuation of the discussion on postwar policy but that prior to any agreement on policy being reached with the owners' representatives a full report be made to the Federation.

When they came to the meeting on 24 June, the employers found a difference in the attitude of the Federation representatives.

What was the reason for this apparent change of attitude?* In fact the discussion on after-war policy of the Federation Executive on 30 June 1943 in the North British Hotel,

*In his book *30 Years in Coal*, The Mining Association of Great Britain, 1954, W. A. Lee, Secretary for long of the Mining Association, states:
Alas, the explanation was quite simple. I was informed that shortly after the meeting of the Joint Standing Consultative Committee the political side had objected strongly to joint consultation on post-war policy on the ground that it would prejudice the case for nationalisation.

Edinburgh, had made it clear. The owners would have to go it alone with the minister.

The owners, and in particular the committee to deal with postwar policy set up in September 1942, were not unduly discouraged by the decision of the Miners' Federation no longer to co-operate in the process of formulating plans for after the war. Several of their members had weathered a difficult situation similar to this at the end of the war of 1914-18. Though the White Paper of 3 June 1942 spoke of government control continuing 'until Parliament took the decision on the future of the industry', they could remember clearly how a similar uncertainty about the future had been settled by the government's sudden de-control of the industry in 1921. Something not so different might happen again, when the war was over, as had happened in 1918 when a strongly Conservative House of Commons had been elected. So they decided to go ahead with postwar plans. In November 1943 they addressed a letter to all the district colliery owners' associations asking that each association should prepare a statement 'showing the units into which the undertakings in the district best be combined for the purpose of constituting them into the smallest number of units consistently with proper regard to practical considerations'.

In less than six months every district had accepted the recommendation of that special committee that they should agree to formulate schemes to secure maximum efficiency of production in the district as a whole 'and in that connection to facilitate the concentration of control in such smaller number of undertakings as might best conduce to that end'.

It was at this point, in the spring of 1944, after the October 1943 discussions in Parliament, and the unmistakable attitude of the Prime Minister against any change in the mining industry, that a significant public statement was made, namely, Sir Evan Williams, Bt, announced that in view of his age he wished to retire from the presidency of the owners' organisation to which from 1919 to the spring of 1944 he had been each year re-elected. He was early recognised by his peers as the leading statesman of private enterprise in the mining industry.

It was after the 1914–18 War ended and in the troublous times of the Sankey Commission that the feeling had grown up amongst the owners that Evan Williams, so successful as Chairman, from 1915 onwards, of the Monmouthshire and South Wales Coal Owners' Association, was the fittest person to lead them through the storms which they saw looming ahead in the third and fourth decades of the twentieth century. Now Sir Evan Williams, with all his responsibilities and all his honours thick upon him, thought that under the burden of advancing years he should retire. His retirement was accepted and the post of Honorary Life President was created for him. This he held from 1944 for ten years during the remainder of the lifetime of the Mining Association of Great Britain.

Andrew K. McCosh became President from 1944 to 1945 when the Rt Hon. Earl of Crawford and Balcarres, GBE, son of a previous president, took over throughout the period 1945 to 1947. Robert Foot,* who had been made Independent Chairman from 1944 to 1947, became President from 1947 to 1952 when he left Britain and the British coal-mining industry. To the special activities of Mr Foot in the post created for him the coal-owners now looked forward with the liveliest anticipation.

5. FOOT ON COAL

On 23 January 1945 there was published, and the Mining Association received, the independent report of its new full-time Chairman, Robert Foot, on his plan for the coal-mining industry. He proposed that the industry should be organised into a single cartel, i.e. an association of companies in which their separate identities are retained but which imposes a common policy on prices, output, and so on. He proposed that a central Coal Board should be set up consisting of

---

*Robert William Foot, born 7 June 1889, educated at Winchester, had from 1929 to 1941 been General Manager of the Gas Light and Coke Company which employed about 25,000 persons and purchased annually 3.5 million tons of coal. He was one of the founders of the South Eastern Gas Corporation controlling twenty-nine gas undertakings in outer London and in Kent. Invited by the government in 1941 to review the organisation of the British Broadcasting Corporation, he was, on the acceptance of his plan for reorganisation, given the post of Director-General. This post he occupied at the time of the invitation to him to undertake the independent chairmanship of the Mining Association. He was without previous direct experience of the coal-mining industry.

fifteen men drawn entirely from within the industry, that is to say, the mine-owners, with a chairman appointed and paid by the Mining Association. Neither the government nor the employees through their trade unions should be represented. To enable this Board to function, every colliery undertaking in the country employing over thirty employees should bind itself irrevocably to operate every decision made by the Board, which would not be under any control, but would submit an annual report 'for the information of the Government, of Parliament and the general public'.

From a source usually friendly there came a deadly comment:

It is difficult to resist the conclusion that Mr. Foot's scheme would result in almost precisely the present state of affairs. There would be no effective movement towards closer integration – for at this time of the day it is simply impossible to believe that voluntary methods plus an appeal to the Coal Commission would achieve anything. There would be no drastic re-equipment – because the capital does not exist within the industry and cannot be raised on market terms. There would be no improvement in the labour position – because the men would regard the scheme as reactionary. All that would exist would be a certain amount of subsidising poor pits, the subsidy to be derived in part from the good pits, but mainly from the consumer by means of monopolistic selling organisation. (*The Economist*, 27 January 1945, pp. 104–5)

What were the results of Mr Foot's scheme? The first result was that two weeks later Ebby Edwards presented to the miners' National Committee a draft reply and a subcommittee (three officials plus A. Moffatt, J. A. Hall and A. Horner) were to meet the next week to complete the reply.

Two weeks later the Executive Committee were not yet satisfied with the draft of the subcommittee which was told to meet in the following week 'for the purpose of amending the document'.

That following on the publication of the Union's reply to the 'Foot Plan' the Labour Party and Trades Union Congress be requested to establish a Joint Committee for the purpose of drafting a detailed plan in respect of Nationalisation of the Coalmining Industry. (8 March 1945)

Three weeks later the reply appeared: 'The Miners' Case. An Answer to the Foot Plan, 1st March, 1945.' It was issued by Ebby Edwards from new offices in 5 Westminster Bridge

Road, SW1. This brief, well-reasoned pamphlet, militant in tone, had the following conclusion:

In advancing our own proposals in respect of public ownership and control of the mines, we are deeply conscious of the fact that only in this way can an industry be created which will protect the public interest and at the same time give to the men engaged in it a sense of dignity in their calling.

In 1943, Lord Sankey made a speech in the House of Lords in which he said:

'We shall never have peace or prosperity in the coalfields until we have public ownership of the mines. We shall never have efficiency in the production and distribution of coal until we have nationalisation and unification of the industry.'

Our experience fully confirms the views put forward by Lord Sankey, who was Chairman of the Royal Commission on the Coal Industry which in 1919 declared that the 'present system of ownership and working . . . stands condemned, and some other system must be substituted for it.'

6. THE REID REPORT

While the Foot Plan for Coal issued at the end of January was being discussed amongst both mine-owners and miners, while 'The Miners' Case: An Answer to the Foot Plan' was being circulated from 1 March onwards, there was maturing a government Blue Book which was to have an effect on the main domestic problems of Britain. This was the Reid Report.* In September 1944, the Minister of Fuel and Power had appointed a committee 'to examine the present technique of coal production from coal-face to wagon, and to advise what technical changes are necessary in order to bring the Industry to a state of full technical efficiency'. It was composed of seven outstanding mining engineers who had been, or were, directors of colliery companies.†

*Cmd 6610. Coal Mining: Report of the Technical Advisory Committee Presented by the Minister of Fuel and Power to Parliament by Command of His Majesty March 1945.

†The members of the committee were:

CHARLES CARLOW REID, Esq., JP, M.I.Min.E. (Chairman), Director of Production, Ministry of Fuel and Power, formerly General Manager and Director, Fife Coal Company Ltd.

HERBERT JOSEPH CROFTS, Esq., M.I.Min.E., M.Inst.C.E., FGS, Group Production Director, Midland Region, Ministry of Fuel and Power; formerly Joint Managing Director, Chatterley-Whitfield Collieries Ltd.

DOUGLAS ALFRED HANN, Esq., Director of Production, Powell Duffryn Ltd.

For well over a century there had been numerous parliamentary inquiries and governmental examinations of the British coal trade. There had been select committees of the House of Commons, royal commissions, departmental committees, courts of inquiry. Not only Sir Humphrey Davy at the beginning of the nineteenth century, but thereafter and right into the twentieth century, leading men of science had given their skilled help or their testimony. To most of the recommendations of these bodies, even when enacted in Acts of Parliament, coal-owners throughout and with few exceptions had maintained an attitude of aloofness, and sometimes of open hostility. In the repeatedly voiced opinion of the Chairman of the Mining Association of Great Britain, it was all interference, if not with natural rights, at any rate with private enterprise in an industry that had never known any other than the capitalist social-economic formation. Although in the twentieth century, and to some extent before it, coal-owners had participated in such investigatory bodies, neither the procedures nor the recommendations had been entirely to their liking.

The Technical Advisory Committee made a clean break with this. It was composed solely of capitalists, coal-owners who were also outstanding engineers and thus could bespeak a favourable hearing. No questions were to be brought into their inquiry save those appertaining to technology. The opening sentence of their report to Major the Rt Hon. Gwilym Lloyd-George, MP, Minister of Fuel and Power, ran: 'We should like to make it clear that we have undertaken this task in our capacity as mining engineers, and that all our conclusions and recommendations have been formulated from our professional viewpoint.'

They did not take evidence in public but they had witnesses to give the benefit of expert knowledge. In addition they

JOHN HUNTER, Esq., M.I.Min.E., Managing Director, Doncaster Amalgamated Collieries Ltd.

AUSTIN KIRKUP, Esq., M.I.Min.E., Joint Managing Director, Lambton, Hetton and Joicey Collieries Ltd.

JAMES ADAM NIMMO, Esq., BA, B.Sc., M.I.Min.E., Regional Production Director, Northern 'A' Region – Cumberland, Ministry of Fuel and Power; formerly General Manager (Mining), Workington Branch, The United Steel Companies Ltd.

HARRY WATSON SMITH, Esq., JP, M.I.Min.E., M.I.Amer.Min.E., M.Inst.C.E., FGS, Managing Director, Hardwick Colliery Company Ltd.

said: 'We have studied a mass of information and statistics
specially prepared for us (and sometimes specially collected
from the colliery undertakings) by the Headquarters and
Regional Staff of the Ministry, together with charts, abstracts,
development plans and descriptive material relating to the
coal industries of the Continent of Europe and of the United
States of America, as well as of our own country.'

Thus they were fully equipped for their task. The report
they made fell into two parts with a final chapter. Part I
was historical. It dealt with the technical developments of
British mining up to 1914–18; then up to 1926; and thereafter in the period 1927 to 1939. Dealing with employers,
managers and workmen before the War of Empires 1914–18,
they noted that with the widely dispersed ownership of the
undertakings, the average output per mine was small: 'In
1900 there had been 3,089 coal mines at work with an
average annual output per mine of 73,000 tons against 2,734
mines with an average output per mine of 97,000 tons in
1914. The individualism of a large number of self-contained
units was unlikely to encourage major developments in the
science of mining.'

In short, progress was slow. 'The thriving industries of the
biggest exporting country of the world needed coal, and yet
more coal; and a large coal export trade was built up which
contributed greatly to the national wealth and well-being.'

After a mention of some of the accumulating defects of this
early period, they piously paid tribute to their forefathers:
'When we come, therefore, as we must, to point out the
mistakes which were made in these early years of the coal-
mining industry, let us beware of merely being wise after the
event, or of withholding the meed of praise due to a great
race of men, employers, mining engineers, workmen and
machinery makers alike.'

This century saw the beginnings of machine mining as shown
in the Report of the Royal Commission on Coal Supplies
and Resources of 1905. 'Between 1908 and 1913 the percentage of the coal output mechanically cut rose from 5 per
cent to 8 per cent . . . In 1913 there were about 2,900
coalcutters against about 360 conveyors.'

With war in 1914 came an insistent demand by the military

authorities for the raising of great new armies. Rather more than one-fifth of the total mining manpower was induced to enlist. By the beginning of February 1915, after six months of war, the coalfields were being denuded of the younger portions of their labour force. So there was a sudden belated increase in the number of coal-cutting machines, 'from 2,897 in 1913 to 5,071 in 1920'. Thereafter the number of coal-cutters 'rose from 5,071 in 1920 to 6,650 in 1925'. The number of conveyers rose 'from about 800 to 1,513'.

But as the seven of the Reid Committee pointed out, suggestions for 'intensive mining' fell short 'for a variety of reasons', and 'failed to develop at a crucial stage in the history of the industry'.

Another point was 'the failure to appreciate that machine mining requires properly trained men and officials to get the best results'.

Effect of Machine Mining on the Miner

Before the system of Longwall mining with face conveyors became common, the coal had been gotten by small self-reliant teams of men, able and accustomed to perform all the operations required in their working places for keeping themselves secure and for getting the coal.

When conveyor faces were first started, it gradually came home to the miner that, though he was spared on these faces the severe physical toil of hand getting, he was still involved in considerable effort with little scope for the exercise of the skill he had acquired through the old system.

Unfortunately it was not appreciated that machine mining was resulting in an impairment of his status, and that the effect of this upon his outlook and behaviour would be likely to reduce the advantages in productivity expected from the change of method.

A brief and sombre paragraph on the 'Background to the Stoppage of 1926' pointed to the transience of the boom in coal after the 1914–18 War.

OMS [output per man shift of saleable coal] in 1925 was only 88.7 per cent of the pre-war figure. Prices were high and profits negligible. Wage costs constituted 71 per cent of total costs, and the employers could see no hope of a substantial restoration of the export trade (upon which several important coalfields depended for their existence) except in a decrease in costs. The most obvious ways of securing this were by a reduction in wages and/or an increase in the hours of work.

Technical Developments 1927–39

After the seven-month stoppage of 1926, when the Conservative Cabinet had put itself in pawn for a claim by the coal-owners that longer hours and lower wages would achieve prosperity for the coal trade, a dozen lean years followed. They were a sorry story, as recounted in Chapter III of the Reid Report. Increased competition in the export trade from such countries of Europe as Germany and Poland spurred on further mechanisation. But the industry in these countries was already in process of a reorganisation that carried them far ahead 'of our OMS before the present war broke out in 1939'.

Comparison of Britain and Other Countries

Before the 1914–18 War the OMS in Britain compared favourably with that of practically all the major coal-producing countries other than the United States. In particular it was higher than in the Ruhr which was Britain's only important rival. This fact, combined with relatively cheap rail hauls from mine to port enabled Britain to dominate the seaborne coal trade of the world. The Report continued:

By 1925/1927 the three European countries and Britain had recovered their 1913 level of OMS. Taking the OMS in the year in which each country regained its pre-war level as an appropriate basis for the measurement of subsequent progress we find that, by 1936, which was the peak year in every country, the increases had been as follows:

Country	Basic Year	OMS in Basic Year cwt	OMS in 1936 cwt	Percentage Increase per cent
Poland	1927	23.44	36.20	54
Holland	1925	16.48	35.94	118
The Ruhr	1925	18.62	33.66	81
Britain	1927	20.62	23.54	14

In Britain, the main roads were formed in the seams. These roads had proved generally incapable of accommodating anything but rope haulages, or conveyors, and the adoption of the former had become standard British practice. Mechanisation should have been started at the shaft-bottom instead of at the face. The underground roads and haulage systems should first have been remodelled before any extensive introduction of conveyors took place, and a proper basis would thus have been provided for the efficient removal of the larger tonnages of coal to be brought by the conveyors from more intensively worked faces. British haulage systems had failed 'to solve our problems in principle', let alone in practice, and their failure had become progressively greater with the spread of intensive mining, and the increasing distances from the shaft-bottom. The figures . . . already given of the average tonnage of saleable coal handled by each haulage worker per shift in Britain, the United States and Holland gave startling proof of this fact. 'One haulage worker for every 50 tons of coal produced in the United States. One haulage worker for every 20–25 tons of coal produced in Holland. One haulage worker for every 5 tons of coal produced in Britain.'

Conclusions were: (1) no justification whatever in the future (even if there ever was any) for haphazard, wasteful or un-co-ordinated exploitation of our coal resources; (2) an intensive and nationally co-ordinated programme of searching and boring for coal, so that the wide gaps in the present knowledge could be filled as completely and quickly as possible. Their detailed analysis showed that the position could not be righted merely by putting more machinery into the workings on the lines adopted between the wars (described as 'New Wine in Old Bottles') but required large-scale reconstruction of existing pits and sinking of new ones. This, they recognised, 'cannot be satisfactorily carried through by the industry organised as it is today'.

Because of this 'a vast programme of reconstruction of existing mines and the sinking of a number of new ones is now required, and the importance of avoiding the mistakes of the past, and of providing for the efficient layout of the underground workings and the orderly position of the surface buildings, should need no emphasis'.

Some of the main technical changes suggested as urgent were as follows:

(1) Where possible room-and-pillar working (as practised in the USA) or long wall retreating (i.e. driving main roadways to the boundary of the colliery and then working

back) are preferable to the present usual system of long wall advancing (ie working outwards from shaft-bottom), which results in wasting labour especially on repair work for the sake of quick profits in the early stages of development.

(2) Development of machinery, especially mechanical loaders suitable for British conditions, which may require financial assistance to machine manufacturers.

(3) New roadways: making possible the use of locomotive haulage with large mine-cars of 2/10 tons, in place of obsolete British tubs holding under 1 ton and sometimes as little as 3 cwt, dating from the time when they wer᷄ manipulated by hand.

(4) Men should be enabled to ride to work. In 1943, of 650 collieries employing over 250 men underground, 407 were working faces over 2,000 yards from the shaft-bottom without provision for men riding.

(5) More coal should be mechanically cleaned than the 47 per cent of output so treated in 1938, and handpicking of house coal, which was wasteful of labour, should be cut out.

(6) Training systems, much less developed here than on the Continent, should be provided for all new entrants, with specialised training for machine work.

After dealing with these six examples and others of the main technical changes which they regarded as urgent, they outlined further modern methods which would also provide a higher standard of safety and of healthy working conditions as well as higher production. Their findings on this matter may be put under five headings: ventilation, lighting, electricity, working hours and training.

The Reid Report favoured double shift working and considered that there were strong technical grounds for a working week of five eight-hour days.

The Reid Committee recognised problems bound up with the structure of the industry. 'In Britain the effect that ownership of the mineral has been in private hands has often resulted in unduly small or awkwardly shaped leaseholds; in the development of an excessive number of mines of insufficient capacity for the requirements of the best mining practice; and an inadequate attention to the conservation of the national resources.'

The conditions attaching to the transfer of the ownership of the mineral to the Coal Commission had left most of these difficulties unsolved. On the Continent, the mineral was owned by the state, and both concessions and individual mines had generally been large. The grouping of a number of mines under the same ownership on the Continent has facilitated the closing down, or merging, of uneconomic mines, and the concentration of operations to the remaining shafts.

The Reid Report seemed to draw an immediate moral, namely, the necessity of nationalisation. This, however, was not the moral drawn by the seven experts. Their proposal was for compulsory amalgamation covering large areas or districts, which fitted in both with what was desired by the Tory Reform Committee and also with the plan put forward by Mr Foot. *The Economist*, for over a century the organ of private enterprise, stated:

If it can be proved that some form of public ownership is technically necessary for efficient production, then the opposition to it in this pragmatic land, will melt away. And the proof is now very nearly complete. It might conceivably be possible, though only with great difficulty, to bring about the necessary amalgamations by private negotiation; but the provision of the additional capital is a task for the state alone. (7 April 1945)

Sir William Beveridge, a member of the Samuel Commission which twenty years before had reported against nationalisation and in favour of compulsory amalgamations, was converted by the Reid Report to nationalisation.

Within months, other Liberal spokesmen had taken up a similar standpoint, to rid the British coal trade of the palsied grasp of private enterprise. In sum, the Reid Report, willy-nilly, confirmed the demand the miners and the Labour movement had been pressing for well over twenty-five years.

Indeed the mining engineers had done their share of the work only too well. The Reid Report was an example of overkill. The intention was to prove the need for a complete overhaul and reorganisation of the coal trade. In the early summer of 1945 they found that they had proved much more, that they had convinced the general public that private enterprise in coal must be swept out of existence. They had done no more as technological experts than complete what Sir Reginald Redmayne, HM Chief Inspector of Mines, had done in 1919 in his evidence to the Sankey Commission. He had shown that the coal trade then was ripe, rotten-ripe, for unification. Twenty-five years afterwards the Reid Report disclosed to the public a coal trade in an advanced state of putrefaction.

7. FOOT PLAN BECOMES TORY PLAN

'Twenty Principles' set forth in Part 1 of the Foot Plan had been preceded by a statement: 'I would say that I believe very deeply in the value of private enterprise in industry.' Drastic and far-reaching as it seemed on the surface, the Foot Plan, published in January 1945, had been given the general support of the coal-owners on 22 February at a meeting of the Central Committee of the Mining Association. They requested their independent chairman to draft the constitution of the Central Board and the district boards and of the covenant to be entered into by each colliery undertaking; and in the meantime Foot attended meetings in the various districts where he met the chairman, managing director and principal technical executives of every undertaking of any size or importance.

By the beginning of April 1945, these draft constitutions were published and Foot was able to claim that the owners 'to the extent of 95 per cent of British output' had given approval to the principles and to the structure recommended in his proposals. He was then in a position to make an addition, '. . . in view of the special importance of the coal trade to the national wellbeing and prosperity and in view also of the existing public uneasiness with regard to it and its future'. He proposed that a statutory arbitral tribunal should be established.

Meanwhile in the international field there had been a most rapid advance at the end of March and throughout the whole of April on every war front. On the eastern front Marshal Zhukov by the beginning of March had been attacking westwards in the basin of the river Oder; Soviet troops were nearing Stettin and Danzig. United States troops crossed the Rhine at Remagen and established a bridgehead. Montgomery's forces were across the lower Rhine on a 30-mile front. The main German defence line had been broken. In Asia Indian troops were nearing Mandalay in Burma. In the Pacific, organised Japanese resistance island by island had ended. In Italy Bologna was captured and the Allies crossed the river Po. On 29 April Mussolini and twelve members of his Cabinet, captured by Italian partisans, were put to death and Milan was entered.

On 1 May the death of Hitler was announced. On 2 May the Red Army captured Berlin: in Italy the German forces unconditionally surrendered. On 9 May the final act of Germany's unconditional surrender was signed in Berlin before Marshal Zhukov and Air Chief Marshal Tedder. It was victory in Europe.

At home in May the Labour Party conference at Blackpool decided not to remain in the Coalition Government. On 23 May Winston Churchill resigned and, rid of his Labour colleagues, formed a new government. Parliament was to be dissolved. Polling day for a general election would be 5 July: and the results thereof would be counted three weeks later. This gave the Caretaker Cabinet a scant nine weeks of power ahead. It also gave the coal-owners and their independent chairman the chance to move fast, and to get their schemes accepted and so put down an obstacle in the path of nationalisation.

Four days after he had been confirmed as Minister of Fuel and Power in the Caretaker Government, Gwylim Lloyd George made the following declaration of policy on coal in the House of Commons:

The Government consider that the working, treatment, and disposal of coal should continue to be conducted by private enterprise provided these are planned in accordance with the national need and conducted with the maximum efficiency.

The Government have decided that a Central Authority, appointed by the Minister of Fuel and Power and subject to his general directions, should be set up to insist that the necessary measures are taken and to provide such help and guidance as are useful.

The measures to which I refer centre upon the proper development and efficient conduct of operations in each coalfield, according to the best modern practice.

In so far as the grouping or amalgamating of collieries is necessary for this object, it will be carried through, voluntarily if possible, but otherwise by compulsion.

We do not propose amalgamation for amalgamation's sake, for in this diversified Industry, where conditions vary widely, there are often to be found highly efficient undertakings which are sometimes not large. In such cases amalgamation would only be proposed if there were clear advantages to the nation and to the Industry.

The making and carrying out of these plans will be undertaken by the Industry itself. The duty of the Central Authority will be to satisfy itself that the scope and the effect of the plans conform to the national requirements, and it will have powers of enforcement in reserve.

The policy will preserve the incentives of free enterprise while safeguarding the Industry from political interference in its day-to-day management. It will also provide the necessary sanctions for making sure that the essential improvements recommended in the Reid Report are carried through. (29 May 1945)

In the second paragraph above the central authority to be appointed by the minister removed the need for the statutory arbitral tribunal contemplated in the supplementary plan issued by Robert Foot in April. Foot therefore abandoned the arbitral tribunal and modified his plan for the functions and powers of the central board. At the same time it was decided to get from the owners an approval of the proposed modifications of the plan. Meantime the progress continued with the practical work of organisation in various departments. The Mining Association appointed a Director of Education and Training on lines set out in a Report of a Joint Committee of Representatives of Colliery Owners, Institution of Mining Engineers and National Association of Colliery Managers. On 14 June the Central Committee of the Mining Association of Great Britain passed a resolution, published subsequently, recording:

(a) The Association supported the policy announced by the Government and would would do all in its power to make it effective.

(b) The structure to be established within the industry would now be worked out in relation to the Government's proposal for the setting up of a Statutory Authority, taking fully into regard the Foot Plan.

(c) In accordance with its resolution of 17 May and in conformity with the terms of the Government's announcement of policy the Technical Survey Committee would proceed immediately in conjunction with the District Panel and District Associations with all necessary arrangements for a detailed technical survey of the industry which would take fully into regard the Reid Report and the Foot Plan and should proceed on the firm understanding that it was the policy of the industry to ensure that all technical impediments to achieving maximum efficiency in mining operations were removed. (W. A. Lee, *30 Years in Coal*, The Mining Association of Great Britain, 1954, p. 199)

It is not recorded how far these plans and activities had proceeded; nor is it important to find out and set down what steps were taken within the Ministry of Fuel and Power to implement the government's declaration of policy of 29 May. For on 15 June Parliament was dissolved.

8. THE GENERAL ELECTION

Twelve days after 9 May, Victory Day in Europe, the annual conference of the Labour Party met at Blackpool to decide future policy. They knew that Prime Minister Churchill had wanted coalition to continue till the end of the war against Japan. If Attlee and his party were not prepared to agree to this, then he would declare a general election. This was a threat. Churchill apparently believed that he could repeat the Lloyd George victory of 1918 on the slogan 'The Man Who Won the War'. The Executive Committee of the Labour Party were opposed to any more coalition. The delegates unanimously decided to reject the Churchill offer. Thereupon Churchill handed in his seals of office as head of the wartime Coalition Government and immediately took office again as head of a 'Caretaker' administration, pending a general election. Parliament was to be dissolved on 15 June; it had lasted nearly ten years. Polling day in the general election for a new Parliament was to be 5 July.

The results were not to be announced until three weeks later to allow for the counting of the votes of the armed forces overseas.

The National Executive Committee of the National Union of Mineworkers, meeting on 1 June, approved a list of thirty-nine parliamentary candidates.* The NUM Executive Committee also instructed the three officials together with W. E. Jones, A. L. Horner and G. H. Jones, to prepare an election manifesto, which would have as a prominent feature the union's programme for the nationalisation of the coal-mining industry. The manifesto, of which over half a million copies were issued, ran as follows:

General Election, 1945
MANIFESTO
of the
National Union of Mineworkers

A Vital General Election
This election is of such great importance to every mineworker and his family that they must vote Labour and persuade every other elector to do the same. Politics affect the life and livelihood of every man, woman and child. War and Peace, Food, Health, Safety, Wages, Labour Conditions, Education, Recreation, Compensation, Pensions, Housing, and hundreds of other economic and social issues are influenced or decided by those whom YOU elect to Parliament. If you have an interest in your individual or social life it is vital to send your Labour candidate to Parliament.

Why Vote Labour?
You should vote Labour because the Labour Party fights this election on a programme of progress. It is the party for those who labour by hand or brain, and comprises the mass of the people who live by wages and salaries, as opposed to the Tory Party of vested interests. This election gives you the opportunity of determining your progress and putting an end to unemployment and poverty by voting Labour. To VOTE LABOUR is YOUR opportunity and YOUR responsibility.

Coal a Basic Industry
Coal is the basic industry of Britain. The nation's industrial life and social progress depend upon it.
THE FUTURE OF THE MINING INDUSTRY IS ONE OF THE MAIN ISSUES IN THIS ELECTION.

*See Appendix to this chapter.

It is in a dangerous state, and as at present owned and organised cannot recover. The future of coal-mining, therefore, must be the responsibility of the nation and not of any financial or sectional interest. LABOUR STANDS FOR A NATIONALLY-OWNED AND CONTROLLED MINING INDUSTRY.

The Churchill Tory Government is against all forms of effective control and national ownership. It admits that such controls and ownership enabled this country to win the war against Germany. Whilst national organisation has won the war, the Tory Party is not prepared to organise and plan in a similar way to win the peace. It prefers to put private interests before national needs.

Progress – Not Reaction

We have bitter memories of the period between the two wars.

The deliberate depression of the purchasing power of the millions, directly and indirectly connected with the mining industry, had its repercussions on every other industry and business in the country. These conditions must never return. The industry must be organised to ensure full employment and economic security for those who depend upon coalmining for a livelihood and to attract new entrants into it without compulsion.

An uneconomic industry, as we have learned to our disadvantage in the past, means sweated conditions for the employees. COAL is now owned by the nation, and to enable it to be produced and distributed at an economic price it is essential that the industry shall be reorganised. The capital required to enable this to be done can only come from Government sources; such expenditure of the taxpayers' money cannot be left to private enterprise.

It is admitted by Mr Robert Foot, Chairman of the Mining Association of Great Britain, and in the recent technical Report of the Reid Committee, that the industry needs reorganising on the basis of national service. National service can only be effective if it rests on Public Ownership. Any other form of reorganisation will inevitably lead to a dangerous monopoly.

Churchill Is Not an Issue in This Election

The issue in this election is not one of personalities – it is a choice between the LABOUR policy of planned and efficient industry and the policy of the so-called National Government which represents 'Unconditional Surrender' to vested interests.

The Tories, led by Churchill, have said that private ownership of the coal mines shall continue. This is a question of great principle; it is a fundamental issue which will determine your standard of existence in the post-war years. To nationalise the mining industry needs legislation; to secure legislation requires a majority in Parliament. A vote for Labour is a vote for the public ownership of the industry for the benefit of the Nation.

Inquiry after inquiry on the running of this industry has reported on its inefficiency; every verdict has gone against the colliery owners. For generations the coal industry has been mismanaged under the direction of profit and free enterprise; this industry has never served the people's needs.

A vote for Labour will determine a change.

**GIVE LABOUR THE MANDATE
TO MAKE THE COAL MINES
PUBLIC PROPERTY
VOTE FOR LABOUR CANDIDATES**

On behalf of the National Executive Committee

WILL LAWTHER, *President*
JAMES BOWMAN, *Vice-President*
EBBY EDWARDS, *Secretary*

APPENDIX TO CHAPTER III

GENERAL ELECTION CANDIDATES
(SUMMER 1945)

Area	Number of Seats Contested	Name of Candidate	Constituency
Derbyshire	2	White, H.	North-Eastern
		Neal, H.	Clay Cross
Durham	6	Lawson, J. J.	Chester-le-Street
		Grey, C. F.	Durham
		Blyton, W. L.	Houghton-le-Spring
		Murray, J. D.	Spennymoor
		Glanville, J. E.	Consett
		Whiteley, W.	Blaydon
Lancashire	2	Brown, T. J.	Ince
		Foster, W.	Wigan
Northumberland	2	Taylor, R. J.	Morpeth
		McKay, J.	Wallsend
Nottingham	1	Taylor, H. B.	Mansfield

Scotland	5	Sloan, A.	S. Ayrshire
		Watson, W. M.	Dunfermline
		Timmins, J.	Bothwell
		Fraser, T.	Hamilton
		Pryde, D.	Peebles and S. Midlothian

South Wales	13	Mainwaring, W. H.	Rhondda E.
		Edwards, Ness	Caerphilly
		Williams, E.	Ogmore
		Dagger, G.	Abertillery
		Edwards, C.	Bedwelty
		Bevan, A.	Ebbw Vale
		Jenkins, A.	Pontypool
		Griffiths, J.	Llanelly
		Grenfell, D. R.	Gower
		Davies, S. O.	Merthyr Tydfil
		John, W.	Rhondda West
		Hall, G. H.	Aberdare
		Williams, D. J.	Neath

Yorkshire	8	Brookes, T. J.	Rothwell
		Williams, T.	Don Valley
		Smith, T.	Normanton
		Griffiths, D.	Rother Valley
		Griffiths, G. A.	Hemsworth
		Paling, W.	Wentworth
		Collindridge, F.	Barnsley
		Paling, W. T.	Dewsbury

Part Two
The Legislative Process

CHAPTER IV

PARLIAMENTARY BILLS FOR NATIONALISATION

1. THE FIRST PROPOSALS: KEIR HARDIE'S BILL

From the formation of the Miners' Federation in November 1889, resolutions for taking the pits out of the hands of the coal-masters by measures of nationalisation had been frequently brought up at conferences or put forward to an annual meeting of the Trades Union Congress. For example, at the Glasgow 1892 Trades Union Congress, at which J. Keir Hardie, MP, was present as delegate from the Ayrshire Miners' Union, W. Small of Blantyre, seconded by Robert Smillie of the Larkhall Miners' Association, moved a resolution:

This Congress, recognising the fact that well-nigh three-quarters of a million workers are engaged in winning from the bowels of the earth produce that is national property, is of opinion that the enterprise should also be, like the Post-Office, a State department, and accordingly instructs the Parliamentary Committee to prepare a bill embodying the foregoing facts and opinions. (10 September 1892)

Fourteen months later a parliamentary Bill to nationalise the 'Mines and Minerals of Great Britain and Ireland, and to provide for the working of the same', prepared and brought in by 'Mr Keir Hardie, Dr Clark, Mr Murray MacDonald, Mr David Randell, Mr John Burns, Mr William Allen, Mr Michael McCarton', was ordered by the House of Commons to be printed on 17 November 1893. Of the seven sponsors only three (Keir Hardie, Dr Clark, John Burns) could be classed as socialists. A preamble began with a reference to the current strike in the Federated Area.*

*WHEREAS coal having become an essential factor in the manufacturing industries and transport service of the nation, any interference with a regular and continuous supply is fraught with gravest dangers to our commercial supremacy . . .

And whereas the present system of working mines as private concerns leads to great waste of our mineral supplies, and to strikes and lock-outs thereby imposing great hardship on the mining community and trades dependent on a mineral supply for their continuance . . .

Though a measure heard only on First Reading (which orders its printing) Keir Hardie's five-clause Bill was of signal importance. This noble fragment, being in due parliamentary form, brought an aspect of reality for the miners who from the first had combined their own industrial democracy with a persistent reliance upon Parliament to find remedy for the ills with which they were afflicted. Their combination of industrial action with political agitation had brought many democratic advances such as the Master and Servant Act of 1867 or the return to Parliament from 1874 onwards of their own mining members; and it was in this tradition within the confines of bourgeois democracy (and not as a socialist transformation)* that their parliamentary Bills were conceived.

The Bill, transferring mines and minerals to the Crown, met the claims of ownership by an issue of mining bonds, the interest on which (together with a sinking fund) was to form 'a first charge upon the working of the mines'. The government were to create a Mining Department which would pay such wages as would ensure 'a healthy and comfortable existence'. There was to be an eight-hour day in the pits, from descent to ascent; and in the Schedule to the Bill it was provided that 'during the continuance of incapacity, the result of an accident sustained while at work or of sickness, the workman shall receive his full weekly wages, and free medical and other attendance'.

2. THE BILL OF JULY 1913

Thereafter for some twenty years of resolutions and debates on nationalisation there was no parliamentary Bill until the minimum wage dispute. The minimum wage strike of over a million miners for six weeks in March and April 1912 dwarfed all other issues and aroused the keenest interest in the working-class movement of Europe and overseas. The strike and the Coal Mines (Minimum Wage) Act, 1912 which concluded it gave impetus to a parliamentary Bill on nationalisation.

*Socialism then, stipulated in the Fabian Basis, signified that 'the vesting of land and industrial capital in the community would be carried out *without compensation*'.

Robert Smillie, the socialist President, seized the opportunity to get a Bill drafted. The Bill, prepared by H. H. Slesser,* then parliamentary draftsman of the Labour Party, was examined at the Federation annual conference which took a unanimous decision that 'the principles contained in the Mines Nationalisation Bill as drafted by the Committee be and are hereby approved, also it be an instruction to the executive to carry on the agitation' (3 October 1912).

The instruction to the Executive Committee to 'carry on the agitation' was in part fulfilled when in July 1913 the Fabian Society published the Bill with explanatory notes.† Simultaneously, the Bill to nationalise the mines and minerals of the United Kingdom and 'to provide for the national distribution and sale of coal' was brought in by a dozen Labour Members headed by Mr Steven Walsh** and ordered, by the House of Commons, to be printed on 9 July 1913. In Clauses 1 and 2 there was created a Minister for Mines in whom would be vested all mines and minerals acquired by purchase. By Clause 3, however, owners of minerals, mineral rights and mineral weighleaves were precluded from receiving the compensation awarded to the proprietors of the coalmine. Purchase price was to be based in the main on the annual output of each colliery, and 10s or 12s per ton of such output was named as the maximum price which would amount to about £135 million. Payment was to be made in 3 per cent government coal stock at par. Clause 8 provided for the Minister of Mines working the mines with his own staff. Clause 15 specifically preserved the right of the state coalmine officials to form trade unions, strike and generally

---

*Slesser, Rt Hon. Sir Henry (Lord Justice of Appeal 1929–40), was born in London, 1883, and from St Paul's School went to London University. He became the Labour Member of Parliament for South-East Leeds 1924–9 and was HM Solicitor-General in 1924. From 1946 he sat on the Devon County Council (as alderman in 1956) and was Chairman of Dartmoor National Park Committee. He entered the Order of St Benedict as oblate. .

He wrote *Trade Union Law*, 1922 (3rd edn 1928); *Religio Laici*, 1929; *The Pastured Shire and Other Verses*, 1935; and many other books, including *The Anglican Dilemma*, 1952, and *Art of Judgment*, 1962.

†Fabian Tract No. 171 in which it was made clear that the Fabian Society, with its socialist tenet of 'No Compensation', took no responsibility for the Bill which it put out 'for public information'.

**The others were 'Mr Tyson Wilson, Mr William Edwin Harvey, Mr James Parker, Mr Pointer, Mr Keir Hardie, Mr George Roberts, Mr Thomas Richardson, Mr Sutton, Mr John Taylor, Mr Goldstone and Mr Hancock'.

to join in industrial and political activities. Otherwise everything was in the hands of the new Minister for Mines.

3. NATIONALISATION WITH JOINT CONTROL

The reign of King Edward VII, ending quietly in 1910, was succeeded by a decade of tempestuous and turbulent changes at home and abroad. With great strikes in 1911 and 1912 there came a spring-tide of the trade unions, a tide that mounted higher amid the following years of war and revolution. Total trade union membership, which stood in 1910 at $2\frac{1}{2}$ million, had risen by the end of 1913 to 4 million: by the end of 1920 it was to be 8 million. This doubling and more than trebling of the number of British trade unionists within an only slightly increased population of the United Kingdom had significant effects, not least in the mining unions. There came a new democratic impetus and many signs of a new outlook in the coalfields.*

In 1918 the MFGB annual conference passed with unanimity a comprehensive resolution for nationalisation 'with joint control and administration by the workmen and the State'. Once more they secured the services of H. H. Slesser in whose chambers the elaboration of these momentous new provisions was completed in December 1918. These provisions in Sections 1, 2 and 3 of the new Bill of 1919 established a Mining Council to consist of a President (who should be the Minister of Mines) and twenty full-time members 'ten of whom shall be appointed by His Majesty and ten by the Association known as the Miners' Federation of Great Britain'. The twenty members were to be appointed for five years, but were to be eligible for reappointment with power for the Crown and the Miners' Federation respectively to remove members appointed by them and appoint others to fill vacancies for the unexpired term of office.

*In the report on Monmouthshire and South Wales, the Commission of Inquiry into Industrial Unrest, set up on 12 June 1917, distinguishes 'Collectivists or advocates of State Socialism' (instancing the Coal Mines Bill of 1913) from 'those who believe in direct action and industrial unionism' – amongst whom were two sections, the Syndicalists and the Guild Socialists.

A further significant change came in Section 12 wherein the Mining Council were to set up District Mining Councils each of ten members (with a term of three years), 'half of which shall be appointed by the Miners' Federation of Great Britain'. The Mining Council might delegate to any district mining council or pit council such of their 'powers under this Act as may conveniently be exercised locally'. Similarly a district mining council would have power within its area to appoint annually pit councils for each mine or group of miners, 'composed of ten members, half of which shall be members of the Miners' Federation of Great Britain, and nominated by the workers of the mine or groups of mines aforesaid'.

Of the remaining sections the most important was that headed 'Regulations'.

19.(2) The Mining Council, before making or altering any regulations or conditions of employment, including wages, as affect workmen engaged in the mining industry, shall consult with the association known as the Miners' Federation of Great Britain, and, in the event of such representatives and the Mining Council failing to agree, the matter in dispute may be referred to arbitration on such terms as may be mutually agreed.

Section 23 contained seven words, namely, 'This Act shall not apply to Ireland.'

The first Schedule enumerated nine minerals such as chalk, flint, igneous rocks, which were excluded from the Act. The Second Schedule listed enactments repealed of the Parliaments of England and Scotland.*

*Enactments Repealed

Session and Chapter	Title or Short Title	Extent of Repeal
1 William and Mary, ch. 30	An Act to repeal the statute made in the fifth year of King Henry IV against multiplying gold and silver	The Whole Act
5 William and Mary, ch.6	An Act to prevent disputes and controversies concerning Royal Mines	The Whole Act
55 George III, ch. 134	An Act for altering the rate at which the Crown may exercise its right of pre-emption of Ore in which there is lead	The Whole Act
1 James I of Scotland, ch. 12	Mines of Gold and Silver pertains to the King	The Whole Act
12 James IV of Scotland, ch. 31	Anent the Tenth Part of Mynis	The Whole Act

4. THE BILLS OF 1923 AND 1924

Consequently, four years later, in very similar terms to the draft Bill of 1919, a Bill to nationalise the mines and minerals of Great Britain, 'and to provide for the national winning, distribution, and sale of coal and other minerals, and for other purposes connected therewith', was presented by Mr Lunn supported by other members* and was ordered, by the House of Commons, to be printed 5 March 1923.

After the general election of December 1923, a Bill in almost identical language to that of ten months earlier was presented on 18 January 1924 by George Hall who was supported by other mining members. † Once again, after the exordium ('WHEREAS . . . Be it therefore enacted . . . as follows') came the historic words 'for the purpose of winning, distributing, selling and searching for coal and other minerals, there shall be established by His Majesty by warrant under the sign manual, a Mining Council, consisting of a President and twenty members, ten of whom shall be appointed by His Majesty and ten by the Association known as the Miners' Federation of Great Britain'.

During the Tory administration of 1924–9, there was little opportunity or likelihood of socialisation measures being debated in Parliament. So the miners reverted to passing resolutions at their annual conferences. For example at Llandudno: 'That as a National Federation of Mineworkers, we continue our propaganda for the nationalisation of the coal mining industry, believing that nationalisation is the first most important step in the reorganisation of the British Coal Trade' (17 July 1928).

Then after the general election of 30 May 1929 when there was once more a minority Labour administration, the resolutions passed at the MFGB annual conference in Blackpool included the following, moved by Straker of Northumberland: 'That as a Federation we continue to urge the national Labour Party to take the earliest opportunity to introduce a par-

---

*These were Messrs Hartshorn, Adamson, Duncan, Graham, Lawson, Steven Walsh and Guest.

†These were Messrs Tom Smith, John, William Jenkins, David Grenfell, Smillie, Barker and Charles Edwards.

liamentary measure for the Nationalisation of the mining industry' (25 July 1929).

Before the resolution was put to the vote a speech by Arthur Horner of South Wales concluded:

I realise that the demand for nationalisation of the mines with workers' control, without compensation, is something you cannot get by discussion or talks in Parliament. When we ask for that, and that is the least that will satisfy our people, then we have got to be prepared to challenge capitalism fundamentally, because you are confiscating capital, and not compensating it at a higher value. I am satisfied that advocacy of nationalisation of mines without compensation but with workers' control, cannot be realised in this country unless we have a revolutionary workers' Government.

Amid the bleak climate that followed on the 1926 lockout and with the impending threat of a world economic crisis which might be as great as that of 1879 and the ten lean years of the 1880s, Horner had reverted to the standpoint of the late nineteenth-century socialists.

At the annual conference held at Weston-Super-Mare, in the second week of August 1930, with the Rt Hon. Thomas Richards in the chair, there was no resolution whatever about nationalisation on the agenda. Meantime in this second Labour Government from 5 June 1929 to 24 August 1931, when a series of changes were contemplated in the traffic of the metropolis, Herbert Morrison was Minister of Transport. Finally, after many negotiations with Lord Ashfield, the monopolist controller of much of London's transport, arrangement was made by which 'a public corporation' was set up, a very different form of public ownership from that favoured by the Miners' Federation: the more democratic features, as found in the miners' Bills, were to be removed. Throughout the thirties Morrison busied himself in reshaping the policies of the Labour Party; and this in turn had an effect also upon the TUC General Council. Ernest Bevin with other union leaders* had no liking for the new Gospel according to Morrison but did not find an effective means by which it could be opposed.

*To some of them Morrison's plan 'simply perpetuated bosses in the form of an uncontrolled bureaucracy' (Donoughue and Jones, *Herbert Morrison – Portrait of a Politician*, p. 185).

5. TUC PLANS AND PUBLIC CORPORATION

Amongst a series of TUC plans was Labour's Plan for the Coal Industry passed in 1936 at the Plymouth Congress. Two months later a Bill for nationalisation of mines and minerals was presented by Mr Batey, supported by eight other members,* and was ordered, by the House of Commons, to be printed 6 November 1936. This Bill, while retaining the routine preamble of nationalisation measures ('Whereas it is expedient for coal mines to be taken into the possession of the State . . .') had a new rubric, 'Establishment of Coal Corporation', and began: '1.(1) For the purpose of this Act there shall be established a body, to be called "the Coal Corporation," which shall be a body corporate with power to purchase and hold land without licence in mortmain.'

In subsequent sections it was laid down that the Chairman and ten other members of the Corporation would be appointed by the minister, being persons of experience in industrial, commercial or financial matters or in the conduct of public affairs, including representatives of consumers' organisations and (after consultation with the General Council of the Trades Union Congress) of those employed in the coal-mining industry. The Chairman and members of the Corporation were to be disqualified from being elected to and from sitting in the House of Commons. Neither the Chairman nor any member of the Corporation was to own or hold any stock or financial interest in any mine or in the production, distribution or export of any minerals or to occupy any official position in any trade union.

After Sections 5 and 6 (Transfer of Mines, etc) (Compensation for Mines and Minerals) there came a special short Section 7 which reversed the provisions of previous Bills. With the rubric 'Compensation for Rights' it was stated: '7. There shall be paid out of moneys provided by Parliament to the owners (other than the Crown) of rights transferred to the Corporation by this Act such compensation as is assessed by the Commissioners.'

---

*The eight were 'Mr George Hall, Mr Tom Smith, Sir William Jenkins, Mr Grenfell, Sir Charles Edwards, Mr Ritson, Mr Tinker and Mr Ellis Smith'.

Clearing up after the disaster showing the prehistoric slime (Knockshinnoch, Ayrshire)

Hand-getting at the coalface with Dowty hydraulic props and Vandwerch bars at Bates Colliery, Northumberland

In the regional boards of ten members each (persons having experience of the coal-mining industry) half were to be appointed 'on the nomination of the General Council of the Trades Union Congress'. Similarly pit councils were to be composed of ten members 'half of whom shall be nominated by the workmen of the mine or group of mines aforesaid'.

Thus by 1936 'joint control and administration' by the workers in the industry (through their trade unions) had been eliminated. But in its place certain rights of nomination were reserved to the General Council of the Trades Union Congress.

6. THE BILL OF 1945

By the spring of 1945 when the miners' leaders had alerted the Labour movement to the menace of the coal-owners' schemes for after the war (the Foot Plan), the Morrisonian device of 'the public corporation' had already for some years been dominant within the counsels of the Labour Party. So, as we have seen, the miners resolved to call upon the two national bodies for their assistance. The Labour Party Policy Sub-committee, of which the Rt Hon. Herbert Morrison, MP, was Chairman, accepted the invitation from the NUM to participate with the TUC to prepare such a plan. The Labour Party representatives on this joint committee included Emanuel Shinwell who had been Secretary for Mines in the brief Labour Governments of 1924 and 1929. Shinwell was not only equipped to play a leading part but was fully conscious of the significance this might have for the future of the Labour Party – and of the Mineworkers' Union. He plunged with great energy into the work and was made Chairman of the joint committee. He was thus in the position to jog on some of the more sluggish-minded of his colleagues and to press for coal nationalisation to become a legislative first priority after the general election.

Neither the stages of this discussion, nor the report of the joint committee, was made public. But the story was told in successive reports to the Trades Union Congress in 1945 and 1946:

In a letter dated 13 March 1945 the Executive Committee of the National Union of Mineworkers suggested to the General Council that a Joint Committee consisting of representatives of the General Council, the Labour Party Executive Committee and the National Union of Mineworkers should be set up to prepare a detailed plan for the public ownership of the coalmining industry. (TUC Report 1945, p. 182)

At that time the work of the General Council's Economic Committee on a plan for the public corporation of the fuel and power industries was well advanced, but since any report on the coal-mining industry separately prepared by the TUC would normally be submitted to the Labour Party Executive Committee and to the National Union of Mineworkers before adoption, the General Council readily agreed with this suggestion. The joint committee met on five occasions. Its report, being a scheme for the public operation of coal-mining, was in an advanced state of preparation, when the general election took place on 5 July 1945. But the report was completed shortly after the election resulted (on 26 July) in the return of a Labour Government.

The original Chairman of this joint committee, Emanuel Shinwell, MP, became the new Minister of Fuel and Power. Thereupon, 'in view of the changed political circumstances it was agreed that no useful purpose would be served by publishing the final report'. Instead, it was forwarded to the new minister for his information and guidance in the preparation of the Coal Industry Nationalisation Bill. The detailed elaboration of the dozens of clauses of the new measure now fell into the hands of civil servants in the Ministry of Fuel and Power, and their parliamentary draftsmen. Not for over four months was the measure (whose progress through Parliament in the next year is narrated in Chapters V and VI of this volume) ready for presentation.

Then on 19 December 1945 came the First Reading of a Bill 'to establish public ownership and control of the coal-mining industry and certain allied activities; and for purposes connected therewith'. The rubric to the first clause ran 'Establishment of National Coal Board and Functions Thereof'. Clause 1 ran as follows: '1.(1) There shall be a National Coal Board which shall, on and after the primary vesting date, be charged with the duties of . . .'

In the second clause under 'Constitution of the Board' the chairman plus eight other members were to be appointed by the Minister of Fuel and Power 'from amongst persons appearing to him to be qualified as having had experience of, and having shown capacity in, industrial, commercial or financial matters, applied science, administration, or the organisation of workers'.

There were fifty-eight clauses in all and three schedules. It was a large and comprehensive Bill, to be larger still when it emerged from the parliamentary process with sixty-five clauses and an additional schedule of enactments repealed. The short amending Act of 1949 was to be limited to thirteen clauses.

7. FUEL AND POWER ADVISORY COMMITTEE

Meanwhile in October 1945 the Minister of Fuel and Power invited the TUC to set up a small committee to advise informally on any questions relating to the fuel and power industries. The General Council, accepting the invitation, appointed the following committee of seven members: W. Lawther (Chairman), E. W. Bussey, G. Chester, A. Deacon, C. Duke, L. Evans, C. M. Galley. At the first meeting of the Fuel and Power Advisory Committee on 4 January 1946 the Minister's Coal Industry Nationalisation Bill was the principal subject for discussion. The TUC representatives welcomed the Bill and assured the minister of their broad agreement with all its many provisions, but raised a number of points of detail in which apparently it diverged from the proposals of the joint report and the TUC report 'on post-war construction'.

In the report of the General Council to the 1946 Congress it is stated:

The Minister gave us an assurance, however, which has subsequently been carried out, that two members of the Board would be appointed on account of their experience in the Trade Union Movement, and that as regards one of these appointments he would seek the views of the TUC and as regards the other he would seek the views of the National Union of Mineworkers. Sir Walter Citrine and Mr Ebby Edwards were subsequently appointed.

The minister was also asked why there was no provision in the original Bill for the setting up of consultative machinery on matters other than wages, hours etc. between representatives of workpeople in the industry and the Coal Board. To this Shinwell replied that such consultation was implied in the Bill and in the fact of public ownership, and that it was certain that the Board would in fact set up appropriate machinery in consultation with the trade unions, since this was an essential condition of its efficient working. If, however, any difficulties arose he would be able to issue a direction to the Board to ensure that suitable consultative machinery was established.

A further subject discussed at this meeting was the absence of any clause which provided for the payment of compensation to workpeople whose remuneration or prospects might be affected or whose jobs might become redundant as a result of the public acquisition of the industry by the National Coal Board. The minister expressed his fear that general legislative provisions to meet this problem might be exploited by interests without a genuine claim for benefit but promised to examine any proposals submitted to the TUC.

As a result of these discussions, but without further consultation with the General Council, the Bill was amended by the government to make it obligatory on the minister to issue appropriate Regulations. The General Council accordingly asked the minister that they should have an opportunity of examining the draft of the Regulations before they were issued. To this request the minister replied that he thought it was premature and that consultation should be with the National Union of Mineworkers rather than with the TUC. At the second meeting of the Committee on 11 July 1946 the matter was pursued with the minister, when it was pointed out that consultation with the TUC would not conflict with consultation with separate unions. TUC policy had required that precise provisions for compensation should be included in the Bill, and a considerable concession had been made in the interests of flexibility by approving a Bill which only contained a requirement that the minister should make appropriate Regulations. These Regulations would actually be the legislation to which the TUC had always attached considerable importance. The minister agreed to give further consideration to the matter.

As this Report goes to press the TUC has received from the Minister a letter in which he reiterates and amplifies his original view. The broad policy would be laid down by the Government following consultation with the TUC. In the Coal Industry discussions on detail would take place between the Board and the Unions concerned. The Unions would, no doubt, consult the TUC. The Minister would make the actual Regulations and would need further consultation with the TUC only if a question arose as to whether the broad principles laid down by the Government were being observed. The letter will be considered at the next meeting of the TUC Committee. (TUC Report, 1946)

CHAPTER V

THE NATIONALISATION BILL

1. SHAPING THE WORLD ANEW

The month of July 1945 marked the end of the old order in more ways than one, and widespread hope of a new epoch. Throughout the United Kingdom and also throughout the British Empire, then covering a quarter of mankind, there was rejoicing. Fascism in Germany, in Italy and in lesser countries of Europe had been defeated and was about to be extirpated. In Great Britain and Northern Ireland members of a new Parliament were being chosen by a process of general election, the first for ten years.

But the war was not yet over. In East Asia the Japanese forces, though hard pressed, still held in their grasp the countries of the French Empire in Indochina, the Dutch Empire in the vast archipelago of Indonesia and the British possessions beyond the Indian Empire in South-East Asia; and in the first weeks of July Prime Minister Winston Churchill had given British consent to the use of the atomic bomb. Polling day in the general election was 5 July: and on 17 July Churchill and Foreign Secretary Eden, taking with them Clement Attlee and Ernest Bevin as observers, set off for Berlin, there on the ruins of Hitler's Third Reich to meet Generalissimo Joseph Stalin and Harry Truman, elevated by the untimely death of Roosevelt in April to be President of the United States of America. The Tripartite Conference of Berlin, lasting from 17 July to 2 August 1945, laid down the principles and detailed plans for a settlement for Europe and a guarantee against revival of German fascism.

After a week in Berlin the Tripartite Conference was broken off to enable Prime Minister Churchill to return to London for the counting of the votes on 25 July. The count was decisive. The Tories were defeated: and next day Churchill, whose Caretaker Government had lasted nine weeks, went to the king to submit his resignation. The same evening Attlee was summoned to the Palace and undertook to form a govern-

ment. On 27 July the new Prime Minister chose Ernest Bevin
as Foreign Secretary, Hugh Dalton as Chancellor of the
Exchequer, Herbert Morrison as Lord President of the Council,
Arthur Greenwood as Lord Privy Seal, Lord Jowitt as Lord
Chancellor; and, leaving this skeleton Cabinet, dashed back
to Berlin to resume discussion and to reach final agreement
with Stalin and Truman on 2 August.

The result of the general election had been the return of a
Labour Party majority in overwhelming numbers. The Labour
Party held 393 seats, the Conservative Party 189. The vote
for the government in a division included also, it was reckoned,
12 Liberals, 3 Independent Labour Party, 2 Communists,
1 Commonwealth and 2 Irish Nationalists, making 413 in all.
Similarly the Conservatives with 13 National Liberals, 9
Ulster Unionists and 2 National MPs mustered 213 votes.
There were also 16 Independents making a total of 640.

The aggregate vote for the Labour Party, which had sunk
to 6.6 million in the 1931 rout and risen to 8.3 million
in 1935, now sprang up to 12 million, an increase of nearly
50 per cent. The Conservatives, with their 'National Government' allies, had topped 14.5 million in 1931, fallen to 11.8
million in 1935 and now sank to 9.9 million.

The Liberal Party polling 1,400,000 votes in 1935 now rose
by over 50 per cent to 2,200,000: but did not receive a
corresponding representation in the House of Commons.
Proportional Representation, advocated and adopted by
many advanced trade unions, had passed the House of
Commons in 1918 but had been taken out of the Representation of the People Act by the House of Lords: and without
it the House of Commons was to that extent not fully
representative.

Such a sweeping change in parliamentary representation
brought great hopes for the future to the Labour Party
supporters in general and to none more than the mineworkers. For never before in the history of the House of
Commons had there been such an atmosphere, such a feeling
expressed by large numbers of Labour Party members that a
mandate had been given them for the march forward to
socialism. Demonstrative applause of a most enthusiastic nature
was a feature of support for every speech that gave the

slightest indication that the Labour Party had before its eyes the goal of socialism. Labour Members of Parliament on the first evening rose and sang 'The Red Flag': the strains of its music, for the first time in the history of Parliament, rang through the Chamber.

> Though cowards flinch and traitors sneer
> We'll keep the Red Flag flying here.

On the other side of the House there was what the meteorologists call 'a deep depression'.

2. THE NEW LABOUR GOVERNMENT

In forming his administration, the Leader of the Labour Party, C. R. Attlee, drew largely upon the mineworkers' representatives. Though they numbered less than a tenth of the Parliamentary Labour Party, over a third of them entered the Labour Government, while inside the Cabinet of twenty, miners were given the following five posts:

Secretary for War	J. J. Lawson (Chester-le-Street)
Secretary for the Colonies	G. H. Hall (Aberdare)
Minister of Health	Aneurin Bevan (Ebbw Vale)
Minister of Agriculture & Fisheries	Tom Williams (Don Valley)
Secretary for Scotland	Joe Westwood (Stirling)

Other ministers (but outside the Cabinet) were National Insurance, James Griffiths (Llanelly); Information, E. J. Williams (Ogmore); and Pensions, Wilfred Paling (Wentworth). With a quarter of the thirty-two ministries held by their parliamentary representatives, the National Union of Mineworkers had good reason to be well content with the composition of the Attlee administration.

Before settling on their legislative programme, however, and even before the state opening of the new Parliament, the Labour Government had many other urgents tasks before

them, both at home and abroad. There was the war still going
on in the Pacific, the gigantic problems in Europe following
the German surrender and the acute problem of the British
economy, short of manpower and overstrained by six years of
war. At the Tripartite Conference of Berlin ending 2 August,
President Truman, Premier Stalin and Prime Minister Attlee
reached agreement and signed a document (usually called the
Potsdam Decisions) in the confidence that their governments
and peoples 'together with the other United Nations' would
'ensure the creation of a just and lasting peace'. A council
of five foreign ministers was to meet and draw up treaties of
peace with the former enemies in Europe (Italy, Finland,
Hungary, Bulgaria and Romania). But the main purpose was
to carry out the Declaration of the Crimean Conference on
Germany signed at Yalta in February 1945 by Churchill,
Roosevelt and Stalin. Divided into four zones of occupation,
Germany was to be completely disarmed and demilitarised, its
National Socialist Party destroyed, its Nazi institutions dissolved and not to be revived in any form, while steps were to
be taken to foster 'democratic ideas'. All Nazi laws which
established 'discrimination on grounds of race, creed or political opinion [were to] be abolished'. In order to eliminate
Germany's war potential, 'the production of arms, ammuni-
tion and implements of war, as well as all types of aircraft
and sea-going ships, [was to] be prohibited and prevented'.
A series of other questions and other countries were discussed;
in particular, on Article Ten, which dealt with the conclusion
of peace treaties and admission to the United Nations, 'the
Three Governments', while supporting the application of
'peace-loving States', declared that they '. . . would not favour
any application for membership put forward by the present
Spanish Government, which, having been founded with the
support of the Axis Powers, does not, in view of its origins,
its nature, its record and its close association with the aggressor
States, possess the qualifications necessary to justify such membership (2 August 1945).*

*To the NUM Executive Committee Arthur Horner gave a report of a meeting con-
vened on 7 August by the International Miners' Federation in Paris.
    Discussions had taken place with the representatives of the French Miners as to the
future of the Home in the South of France which had been established in 1939 to

In the new Parliament the King's Speech on 15 August made the necessary references to these Potsdam Decisions, and laid down the first session's programme. It included repeal of the Trade Union and Trade Disputes Act of 1927 and nationalisation of the coal-mining industry.

3. END OF THE WAR — AND OF LEASE-LEND

The end of the world war came sooner than expected. On 8 August the Soviet Union, at the request of her allies, declared war on Japan, inflicted heavy defeats on her armies on the mainland of China and drove them out of the islands of the North Pacific coast. Three days earlier on 5 August the first atomic bomb had been dropped on Hiroshima by a US aeroplane killing some 60,000 outright; on 9 August a second atomic bomb hit Nagasaki.

On 16 August Emperor Hirohito issued orders for all Japanese troops to cease fire: it was unconditional surrender. The whole world could now turn to the works of peace: or so it seemed then.

The problems of peace, however, were manifold and immense in every country of Europe and Asia. Alone, the economy of the United States had received a gigantic impetus: its reserves had been brought into play, its productive capacity had shot ahead; and it had been immune from the destruction by enemy bombs, or enemy occupation, to which its European and Asian allies had been subjected for so many years. It came therefore as a considerable shock, all the greater by force of contrast, when President Truman, five days after the surrender of Japan, abruptly announced the ending of Lease-Lend, the financial device by which the resources of the United States

---

shelter Spanish orphans. The representatives present had agreed to recommend the national association to agree that the Home should be placed at the disposal of the French miners and that immediately they were in a position to do so, they would make an offer to the British miners with a view to purchasing the Home.

The NUM thereupon decided on 17 August 1945 that the French miners be informed that 'we desire to hand over to them our interest in the Spanish Home and to have no claim upon the Home' nor had they any demand to make in this respect upon the French organisation.

were cast into the common pool of the Allied effort. It was said at the time that the United States administration, which had lost much of its relative generosity of outlook with the sudden death of President Roosevelt in April 1945 (and was thereafter to lose more with the successive dismissals of most members of Roosevelt's Cabinet) was shocked by the emergence of a Labour Government in Britain: and that its anti-socialist and anti-communist standpoint was responsible both for the abrupt stoppage of Lease-Lend and for much else that was to follow in its relations with the United Kingdom. Even Churchill, who had better cause than the anti-socialists of the USA to rue the emergence of the Labour Government, called it, 'this harsh decision'. The effect was that the Labour Government found itself in a dilemma before it had been four weeks in office: either it must ask the people of Britain to endure greater hardships and privations for years ahead; or it must beg for a loan from the allied power which had so abruptly cut off supplies and which could hardly be expected to grant one except on onerous terms. The decision was to ask for a loan; but the negotiations were long-drawn-out and difficult; and when the loan was granted it proved to be loaded with unusual conditions. The Conservative Party evaded responsibility, when the matter came before the House of Commons early in 1946, by a massive abstention from voting. The loan eased the situation; but the working out of its terms showed Britain's economy in a position of inferiority in relation to the United States. This in turn was to affect the relations of the mineworkers with the Labour Government for many years ahead.

But apart from all this, the outlook in that early autumn of 1945 was in no way rose-coloured. Victory had been won. But now the time had come to realise the wounds the war had inflicted not only on human bodies but on the human society that made up the United Kingdom. Thus when the new Minister of Fuel and Power had a discussion with the NUM Executive Committee on 17 August, on the day after Japan's surrender, it was on the administrative problems of the ministry, and the prospect for the whole of Britain's industry and people of manifold shortages, in particular a shortage of coal supplies.

4. SHINWELL CALLS FOR HELP FROM THE NUM

Emanuel Shinwell* as Minister of Fuel and Power had been given a task which on the one hand called forth his administrative abilities, his experience in negotiations, and on the other gave full play to his debating powers and parliamentary skill. In administration, his quick apprehension and his scorn of the hesitations that beset slower mentalities stood him in good stead, so long as that ready scorn was not too openly expressed. In the House of Commons, on the other hand, it was precisely the display of his talents for invective which had brought him to the front.

At his first meeting with the National Executive Committee of the National Union of Mineworkers the minister besought them to bring about an additional coal output during the winter months of 1945–6 of 8 million tons. That same afternoon the National Executive Committee instructed their most experienced members † to examine the question of production and report within fourteen days. The result was a very detailed report and proposals, including one (for which there was no precedent) that each area should appoint a production officer for six months, to be full-time in the case of Northumberland, Durham, Lancashire and Cheshire, Yorkshire, South Wales, Scotland and Nottinghamshire.

The National Executive endorsed these recommendations and endorsed also the further recommendation to appoint Arthur Horner as National Production Officer for six months, retaining 'his full status as an Area Officer'. The campaign for additional output was to begin from Sunday 16 September.

The NUM special conference at Blackpool on Model Rules, after full debate, passsed the following resolution unanimously:

That this Conference of the National Union of Mineworkers, having

---

*Emanuel Shinwell, born in London in 1884, a tailer by trade, had played a prominent part in stormy Clydeside; in January 1919 he was convicted when the Riot Act was read in George Square, Glasgow, at the time of the forty-hour strike. Afterwards he was a stormy petrel of trade unionism amongst seamen and, with the backing of the TUC General Council, headed the Maritime Workers' Union.

†'That a special subcommittee consisting of Messrs A. Moffat, W. E. Jones, A. L. Horner, S. Watson, E. Jones, J. Hammond and the Officials be instructed', etc; minute of Friday 17 August 1945.

considered a Report of the National Executive Committee in regard to the present situation in the coalmining industry, appreciates the pledge of the Labour Government to nationalise the mines forthwith and pledges itself to assist by all the means in its power to achieve that standard of coal production which will meet the needs of the country. (10 October 1945)

As Will Lawther said nine months later in his presidential address to the 1946 annual conference:

We were the first Trade Union to seek to increase our production by engaging in a campaign financed with our own money! . . . The mine-workers, during the six months since the campaign started, were able to provide the country with two million tons above the estimate which had been prepared by the Minister of Fuel and Power before the Labour Government took over.

5. THE MINERS' CHARTER

In the last months of 1945 it came home to Shinwell that his recruitment campaign was not succeeding: and that numbers in the coal industry, despite the weeks and months of demobilisation, were continuing to fall. Once more he appealed for help to the miners' leaders, who on the same day (18 December 1945) decided that 'we associate ourselves with the recruitment campaign' and that their union's representatives on the Joint National Negotiating Committee prepare a charter of the demand of the union in respect of the working conditions of the members.

By 8 January the workers' side of the JNNC considered and accepted a memorandum prepared by Ebby Edwards, and this on 10 January 1946 was adopted by the National Executive Committee. The claims of the union as set out therein in their view would 'determine the rate of entry of new recruits to the industry'.

THE MINERS' CHARTER

(1) The modernisation of existing pits and the sinking of new ones as rapidly as possible, whilst strictly observing as a minimum the standards laid down in the Reid Committee Report; the provision of adequate compensation for those who become redundant; and at the same time aiming at the general application of the day-wage system.

(2) The adequate and careful training of youth in the various phases of mining operations, and the establishment of a clearly defined scheme of promotion; the provision of further training and tuition required in cases where workers desire to enter for a colliery technician's career.

(3) The introduction of new safety laws to meet the conditions of modern mining and especially to suppress the development of industrial disease.

(4) The payment of compensation rates to meet incapacity due to industrial injury or disease which shall guarantee the injured person from financial loss and the provision of an adequate income for the dependants of those killed as a result of injury or who died from an industrial disease . . .

(5) The average wage standards shall not be permitted to fall below those of any other British industry.

(6) The restoration of the 7-hour day for underground workers; the introduction of the 40-hour week for surface workers; and the establishment of the 5-day week without loss of pay.

(7) The continuation of the principles of the guaranteed weekly wage when the Essential Work Order is withdrawn.

(8) Payment to be made for two consecutive weeks' holiday and six statutory holiday days in each year.

(9) The provision of pensions for mineworkers who cease to be able to follow their employment after 55 years of age and the payment of a subsidiary pension from the industry in addition to pensions provided from other legal enactments.

(10) The building of new towns and villages of a high standard and situate at places calculated to enable miners to have increased opportunities for social facilities and to break down the segregation of mineworkers and their families from the rest of the community, accompanied by the provision of adequate transport services at reasonable rates.

(11) The complete re-organisation of health and welfare services so as to put a brake upon the wastage of manpower due to ill-health.

(12) Compulsory medical examination with training arrangements at full wages pending employment as a skilled workman in another industry if withdrawn from the coal mining industry on medical grounds.

A note was added to the effect that the NUM, having in mind the manpower crises and recognising the complete dependence of the country's economy upon coal production, 'calls upon the Government through the Minister of Fuel and Power to give guarantees that effect will be given to the foregoing measures in accordance with a time-table and a progressive plan'.

To this missive of 10 January 1946 there came a reply on 11 March from 'Yours sincerely, E. Shinwell', saying that following their meeting of 21 February he gave them 'a considered statement of my views'. This was that 'one of the principal objects of Government policy' in nationalising the coal-mining industry was to achieve 'the kind of far-reaching reforms and improvements contained in the Charter'. He said that objectives could only be 'brought to fruition' by consultation between the National Coal Board and the National Union of Mineworkers – and to them he remitted the carrying out of the reforms, with his blessing. In an annex to his letter Shinwell added a number of comments on items in the Charter, such as 'my intention to introduce legislation' to give effect to the recommendations of the Royal Commission on Safety in Coal Mines 'as soon as parliamentary time permits'.

6. THE BILL – FIRST READING

Meanwhile, from the day of the King's Speech announcing the policy of nationalisation, the Ministry of Fuel and Power, then preoccupied with the shortage of coal supplies, had to prepare and elaborate the provisions of a parliamentary measure that had no precedent to give them guidance. Not only had the National Union of Mineworkers to be consulted but the experience of every aspect of the coal industry had to be drawn upon.

Of all the interests concerned, the coal-owners were the first off the mark. Their Chairman Robert Foot was quick to appreciate the new situation resulting from the general election which had jettisoned his Plan for Coal together with all the schemes of the Tory Reform Committee. In his view the coal-owners should spend no time or energy in 'crying over spilled milk' but would be well advised to make the best of the new situation. Following Foot's proverbial wisdom, the Central Committee of the Mining Association of Great Britain came together on 16 August (the day after the King's Speech) for a general discussion on what should be their policy. There were three dozen members in all, each democratically elected from one of the two dozen big or small local colliery-owners' associations which varied in title from the Lanarkshire Coalmasters' Association to the Monmouthshire and South Wales Coal Owners' Association.

At a second meeting on 30 August, following upon full discussion in each locality, their policy was decided by a unanimous vote. Their resolution was made public the next day:

(i) The Colliery Owners believe that private enterprise is the right basis for the efficient conduct of the Coal Mining Industry in the national interest.

(ii) But in view of the fact that legislation for the transfer of the Industry from private enterprise to public ownership is to be proceeded with, and having regard to the statement made on behalf of the Government that the Industry would be fairly treated as far as compensation is concerned, the Colliery Owners, through the Mining Association, place themselves at the disposal of the Government, in connection both with the working out of the necessary organisations to be created on the basis of public ownership and with the arrangements which will be necessary to facilitate the transfer from private ownership to the new organisation.

(iii) In the interim period it is of vital national importance that the output of coal should be increased and the colliery owners will co-operate with the Government in the fullest possible manner with this object in view. (W. A. Lee, *30 Years in Coal*, The Mining Association of Great Britain, 1954, p. 248)

Six days later the Central Committee went in a body to meet the Ministry of Fuel and Power; then Chairman Robert Foot addressed Shinwell in honeyed words:

Mr Shinwell expressed his appreciation of this approach on the part of the colliery owners. He made it clear that the Government were not going to consult anyone on questions of policy and on the legislative provisions for bringing nationalisation into effect, but that there must be consultation both on the question of compensation and on that of the organisation' that it was necessary to maintain in the transitional period; and in this connection he proposed that a small committee might be appointed to consider the owners' suggestions as to carrying on without interruption the work in connection with the technical survey, the plans for recruitment and training, and the arrangements for the expansion of research work. (W. A. Lee, *30 Years in Coal*, p. 206)

While many members of the Labour Party at that time looked

upon the nationalisation of the coal-mining industry as but the
first step in a continuing series of similar measures that would
lead to a socialist goal (and some of them were already in a
flush of enthusiasm talking of 'our social revolution'), their
more sophisticated leaders knew well enough that coal nationalisation was essential for the national economy, and for the
rescue of the industry from nearly a half-century of obso-
lescence. Both Ebby Edwards and the man who was to be
the miners' Secretary for the first dozen years of the new
regime saw clearly enough the distinction between nationalisation as a democratic advance and nationalisation as part of a
social revolution. But if it was clear enough to Arthur
Horner, at that time the union's National Production Officer,
it was not so clear to all engaged in the industry.

By mid-December a Bill to 'Establish public ownership and
control of the coal-mining industry and certain allied activities;
and for purposes connected therewith' was presented 'by Mr
Shinwell, supported by the Prime Minister, Mr Herbert
Morrison, Mr Chancellor of the Exchequer and Sir Stafford
Cripps' in what is known as 'First Reading'. It was ordered,
by the House of Commons, to be printed 19 December 1945.
The purpose of the Bill, as shown in an attached explanatory
and financial memorandum, was: '. . . to nationalise the coal
industry in Great Britain including not only the working, getting
and supplying of coal but certain allied activities, in particular
colliery coke ovens, manufactured fuel plants, colliery electricity
plants, colliery transportation works, colliery merchanting
property and colliery welfare activities.'

Secondly, a monopoly was to be established, a National
Coal Board 'to have exclusive right of working and getting
the coal in Great Britain'.

Thirdly, the running of the industry was to be broadly
subject to control by the minister, as to both performance
and future plans.

Fourthly, there would be an Industrial Coal Consumers'
Council and a Domestic Coal Consumers' Council established
to consider, within their respective spheres, matters affecting
the sale or supply of coal.

Fifthly, the Bill arranged for transfer to the National
Coal Board (as from a date to be fixed called Vesting

Day) of the assets of the colliery companies. For assets so transferred compensation was to be paid.*

7. THE BILL – SECOND READING

The Minister of Fuel and Power, on 29 January 1946, rose at 3.32 pm in the House of Commons and said: 'I beg to move, "That the Bill be now read a second time".' In his opening remarks, Shinwell taunted the Opposition by an assertion that both the Leader of the Conservative Party and the representatives of the coal-owners 'have accepted the principle of nationalisation'. When this was greeted from the Tory back benches by cries of 'No' he went on to say:

On the 13 October, 1945, the Rt Hon. Gentleman the Member for Woodford [Mr Churchill] declared: 'The principle of nationalisation is accepted by all, provided proper compensation is paid.' And on 5 September, 1945, the Mining Association stated that: 'while they preferred private rather than public ownership nevertheless because of the result of the General Election and the acceptance by Parliament of the contents of the Gracious Speech they did not propose to continue their opposition to the principle of nationalisation of the coal industry.'

Then, still in a bantering tone, he sketched in the background to the Bill. He stressed the fall since 1924 in the number of pits operating from 2,718 to 1,634 in 1945; of output from 267 million tons to 174 million; in numbers employed from 1,172,000 to 694,000. The serious reduction in output had a profound bearing on the price of coal; it reduced 'our capacity for export'. Therefore he gave a warning of industrial disaster, saying: 'The drift from the industry is appalling.'

The remedy was the 'change of ownership' which 'the

---

*The fruit of the owners' appearance before Shinwell as willing sellers ('What this means is that we are out to help you' quoth Robert Foot) was set out in the Bill under 'Compensation for Transfer of Assets'.

(3) The aggregate amount of the compensation to be made in respect of the coal industry value of all the transferred interests shall be a sum fixed, in accordance with the terms of reference specified in the agreement made in that behalf before the passing of this Act between the Minister and the Mining Association of Great Britain, by a tribunal constituted as therein specified.

Labour Movement has placed on the forefront of its programme for nearly half a century'. Shinwell then interrupted
the flow of his argument to turn on those 'who would prefer
a country where private profit is the sole criterion, where
the State never interferes'. For whilst the sort of dual control
as exercised during the war was 'as far removed from nationalisation as private enterprise itself', what would have happened,
he asked, suppose there had been no control at all? 'Prices
would have soared. Thousands of miners would have left the
industry seeking more remunerative employment. We might
easily have lost the war.' Those who disliked control and
intervention by the state were on their knees begging for
state assistance whenever they got into trouble, he remarked;
and having flung a few further taunts at his opponents,
Shinwell for the rest of his speech expounded the contents
of the Bill.

The withdrawal by the Mining Association from its opposition to nationalisation and its acceptance of the global figure
of compensation had left the Conservative Party in rather an
awkward pass.* It was therefore not an easy task for Anthony
Eden, deputising for the conspicuously absent Winston
Churchill, to oppose the Second Reading. So he criticised the
Bill not so much for its contents (in fifty-eight Clauses and
three Schedules) as for what it left out: '. . . nothing here
to show how the industry is to be run when it is thus transferred . . . The Bill does not tell us, and the Rt Hon.
Gentleman has not told us, how the proposals of the Reid
Committee . . . are to be brought any nearer fruition by
the transfer of ownership, which is all that this Bill does.'

He then raised a series of points about the organisation of
the industry 'so far as it has been revealed to us today', about the
finance of re-equipment, about output, about the price of
coal and the way it was to be fixed. He gibed particularly at
the Consumers' Councils; and ended by saying:

The Rt Hon. Gentleman said the other day, perhaps in a jovial mood – I do
not know, it was before Christmas – that after a 40 years' study of nationalisation he had never realised the complexity of compensation. Let me tell

---

*'The Mining Association has "sold out" on the Tory Party' (Hugh Dalton, Chancellor
of the Exchequer, later in the same debate in the Commons).

him that this is going to be the least of his complexities. If he failed to foresee the minor difficulties of acquiring ownership of the mines, what assurance is there that he has foreseen the major difficulties of running them?

Clement Davies, Leader of the Liberal Party, came forward to bless the Bill and at the same time to curse the colliery companies. He reminded the House that the Sankey Commission had condemned in 1919 'the very system we are operating today' and had declared national ownership and control the only solution. The owners had only one thought, to lower prices and 'in order to lower prices, they again had only one remedy – to lower wages'. Through all the difficulties up to 1926, when real wages 'were far lower than they had been for half a century', he asserted that 'no other idea had occurred to the mine-owners except that of lower wages and lengthened hours'.

Transferring his attack to the Conservative Party, Clement Davies said:

This attitude of the mineowners was the very fact that led to the general strike in 1926 when the miners were ultimately beaten but not in argument. They were beaten by starvation. The only measure that the Right Hon. Gentleman the Member for Warwick and Leamington [Anthony Eden] and his friends introduced into this House – and this ought to be said about them – was a measure for increased hours for men working underground. It was introduced by them in 1926, and increased the hours to eight per day.

He was eloquent on why 'the miner has left, or wants to leave the coal mine'. It was, pronounced the Liberal Leader, because of 'the whole history of tragedy of private enterprise'.

It destroys the beauties of the countryside. A hundred years ago the county of Glamorgan was one of the most beautiful in my lovely Wales. The bards sang about the beauties of its valleys. Today, after 50 years, it is a black and desolate waste. There are no amenities for the miner or his children. It is a long history of sheer neglect of the most vital industry of the whole of the country. The other reason is low wages.

Lastly, Clement Davies gave his full blessing to the Bill, saying that it would be one of the most epoch-making Acts of Parliament in our history.

After these three opening speeches it might seem that the case for private ownership of the coalmines had gone by default. But the debate went on in the form not so much of a dialogue as of a parliamentary free-for-all. There now came to the surface a distinction between Labour representatives telling in their several vernaculars of their early years, of their toil and danger underground, and on the other hand some Opposition speakers nurtured until their early twenties in preparatory school, in public school and university. To mine-workers, eagerly following the debates as their forbears had followed the long-drawn-out parliamentary proceedings over the Eight-Hours Bill, there was thus presented a class contrast that in essence was still of the same nature as when Disraeli, father of the Conservative Party, had written his *Sybil (or The Two Nations)* in the previous century.

But in the course of the two-day debate on the Second Reading the government encountered a real opposition within the speeches of their own supporters. This emerged when the deal that Shinwell had made with Robert Foot and other representatives of the coal-owners came under varying degrees of sharp criticism.

The Commons debate 'on the floor of the House' began with Frank Fairhurst, Member for Oldham, late President of the National Association of Power Loom Overlookers at Wigan. Making his maiden speech, he immediately went back to the great lockout of 1926 saying:

For seven months after the General Strike was over, the miners fought again, and again starvation drove the miners back, beaten, but not de-feated. The owners and the Government won a complete victory. What was left to national agreements the owners destroyed and forced the district agreements; the seven hours' day went; they almost destroyed the Miners' Federation in some areas and crippled it in others . . . Did they increase output? They did not. Output fell from 267 million tons to 237 million tons.

He spoke with the knowledge of what a miner's life means, his father a miner, with four brothers working as miners, himself born in the year of the 1892 strike:

I have seen my father brought home in a trap – ambulances in those days were very scarce – with a hole in his leg you could put your fist into, to spend weeks at home trying to get fit to go back, while there were five of us to be kept, and he received compensation of about 23s per week. I had a brother brought home in an ambulance, as black as a nigger, and placed on the bed where he lay for two days without speaking or moving – he had been crushed and injured in the head . . .

The year 1926 hurt the miner in such a way that, never again will the present mine owners have a chance to work the mines. They will never be forgiven for what happened after 1926. The fact remains that they had ample opportunity to prove that free enterprise could do the job, when everything was in their favour, when the miners were crushed and their organisation beaten down. But they could not deliver the goods. All they did was to drive the people right down into the abyss, and it will be a very difficult job now to get people to go back into the mining industry.

A Conservative speaker followed with an entirely different view of the miners' attitude to the Bill. Lieut-Colonel Sir Cuthbert Headlam (Member for Newcastle-upon-Tyne, North) could not find 'signs of any enthusiasm for this Bill even in my own county of Durham'.

Sir Cuthbert, a magistrate in the county of Durham, who edited the *Army Quarterly* and was learned in the law, asked why it should be expected that the miners would be perfectly content to carry out their work in a better spirit simply because they had got rid of the private owners. 'When you come to think of it, what is the difference? Very likely the same men who have been employed in managing them for the last 20 years will be continuing to do so when the Bill is passed.' He concluded: 'What does it really matter to the miners whether they are employed as State servants or as servants of private owners?'

These two speeches are fair specimens of the way the debate was conducted by Members from the mining counties who could not but have some awareness of the industry and of those engaged in it. Then came two Members who had a still closer connection with coal, the one as miner, the other as mine-owner. The first was Charles Frederick Grey, a local preacher of Hetton-le-Hole, who sat for Durham. He introduced himself as follows: 'I was hewing in a Durham colliery as recently as June last year, and my experience embraces almost every activity in and around a mine. I have had the distressing and demoralising effect of working for 6s 6½d a day, and taking wages into a home which could not produce the minimum of necessities for a decent standard of existence.'

Replying to Sir Cuthbert Headlam, he said: 'It would amuse the miners to hear Rt Hon. Gentleman opposite speaking about the miners not wanting nationalisation. They want more than nationalisation of the mines. They seriously want nationalisation and the taking over of control of the welfare scheme. Much good has been done but much more could be done.'

He gave as an example diseases such as silicosis, which could be treated quickly and effectively if miners got frequent medical examination: and then discussed why output was low, saying; 'The blame is attributable to the owners. For years, they have treated the miner abominably. Low wages, long hours, miserable compensation, bad conditions, wretched death benefits, and virtual slavery were the lot of the miner. For years, the miner stood this, until it got to breaking point.'

But when miners 'realise that they are working for their country, and not for capitalist exploiters', the necessary tonnage would be reached and 'vastly exceeded'. He held strong opinions on compensation to owners. He thought about 'how much compensation they are to get . . . in terms of confiscation', and the less the owners got '. . . the better I shall like it'.

On personnel, his view was very bluntly stated: 'The mining industry under nationalisation must not be a happy hunting ground for well-paid-executives holding unconstructive sinecures. There is no need for a small army of experts. Officialdom must be kept in strict subjection and reduced to an absolute minimum.'

Colonel Clause Granville Lancaster, who had sat as Member for the Fylde division of Lancashire since 1938, opened the fourth hour of the debate and occupied nearly all of it. He had been educated at Eton and Sandhurst. Part of his army career had been in the Royal Horse Guards. As chairman of a colliery company he was directly interested; and indeed the half-dozen pits of his company, working the chief seams of the Nottinghamshire coalfield, had a payroll of nearly 6,000 miners and an output yearly of some 3 million tons. Colonel Lancaster assured the House that 'today I will subordinate my personal feelings in this matter' and said he would treat the subject with the impartiality it deserved. First he questioned 'the wisdom of so wholesale an experiment' as taking over the entire coal-mining industry; and cited examples from many countries of partial nationalisation to prove his contention.

The Colonel in his last argument said the Bill was a scheme for compensation and 'not a solution of the problems of this great industry'. All in the industry were agreed with the Reid Report, from which he quoted the 'great race of men' who were 'fit to rank with the greatest of Britain's industrial pioneers'. The Colonel concluded: 'The breed is still a good one. How good it is under proper leadership, the men of the 50th Division, the Sherwood Foresters and the Green Howards, the Lancashire Fusiliers and the South Wales Borderers, have demonstrated to the world.'

George Alfred Brown,* Member for Belper in the Derbyshire coalfield, believed 'industrial democracy must be present at every level in the industry . . . I have been down the pit only once, when I saw a 2ft 6in seam. The miners, being miners, insisted with great respect that I should go through that 2ft 6in seam. Having seen that seam, I am more than ever convinced that mining is not a job that is on all fours with any other job.'

He was followed by Tom Smith, Member for the Normanton division of Yorkshire. Born at Hemingfield, Barnsley, in 1886, he had a full career as an official of the Yorkshire Miners' Association and also as parliamentarian.† He had been MP for Pontefract 1922–4 and again in 1929–31, and then, through a by-election, for Normanton from 1933 onwards.

His speech, rich in fact and argument, ended as follows:

I have told the House many times that I am myself an example. My father always said I would never work in the pit whilst he did. I never did.

---

*George Brown, born September 1914, a ready and indefatigable speaker, was to climb rapidly up the ministerial ladder until he became Deputy Leader of the Parliamentary Labour Party in 1960. Defeated in a contest for the Leadership in 1963, he was later given a Life Peerage and sat in the House of Lords as Lord George-Brown. In March 1976 he announced that he had ceased to belong to the Labour Party.

†The offices he had held included Parliamentary Private Secretary to the Mines Department (1924, 1929–31), and then to David Grenfell, as Secretary for Mines (1940–2); and Joint Parliamentary Secretary to the Ministry of Fuel and Power (1942–5).

I went in at the age of 15½ when he died. What is true of me, is true of most of us . . . and under this Bill I believe the policy is going to be to eliminate the hard unnecessary labour, and get the coal at the coal face under the best possible means; to have decent roads to get that coal out; to have skip winding under the new development, and to get the coal to the top as soon as possible.

His constituents had sent a miners' representative to the House continuously for fifty-six years, and needed 'no converting to nationalisation', and so he said:

Just over 100 years ago now . . . this House passed a Bill to prevent women and young children working in pits . . . it was in 1874, that the miners of this country for the first time sent two men to this House, Alexander MacDonald and Thomas Burt, not for nationalisation but to ask for simple justice and for protection against accidents. We have moved a long way since then.

The third colonel in succession that evening to speak from the Opposition benches was the Member for East Grinstead, Ralph Stephenson Clarke. Colonel Clarke, educated at Eton and King's College, Cambridge, early disclosed his special interest, saying: 'The particular aspect to which I wish to devote my attention is the impact of the Bill on the consumer, the exporter, and the distributor – the consumer at home and abroad.' His views, he said, 'the result of many conversations with consumers, great and small, and with other distributors', did not favour the Bill.

There was in this debate a strange antiphonal alternation of Labour 'maidens' and Conservative colonels. This time the 'maiden' was Charles Rider Hobson of Wembley North, for twenty years a member of the Amalgamated Engineering Union. Born and brought up in a mining village, he knew 'something of the hazardous conditions'. He enlarged on this point saying:

No words used on the Labour side can be sufficiently harsh. On a dispassionate examination of the facts and figures, I marvel at the generosity of His Majesty's Government with regard to their compensation. In fact, I am inclined to think the mine-owners ought to be penalised for the inefficient manner in which they have administered this national asset, this real wealth of Britain.

These remarks were noted by the next speaker, James Scott Cumberland Reid (Member for Hillhead division of Glasgow), a former Solicitor-General for Scotland and Lord Advocate 1941–5. Reid said he had 'noticed in the past that the Socialist Party has spoken with two voices on this question' of compensation. He then dealt with the 'bad method, which is wrong in nearly every case' of a global sum, only to find out from interjections by Shinwell and another minister his own deep ignorance on the matter. Presumably to cover up his confusion this eminent Scots lawyer went into much detailed argumentation on the financial side of the Bill and at quite considerable length (he spoke from 8.47 pm to 9.43 pm).

The next speaker was the Chancellor of the Exchequer. The Rt Hon. Hugh Dalton (Eton and Cambridge) was ready for the fray. Dalton was large in figure; and even larger in voice. There was no diffidence whatever about Hugh. If there was anything to be known, he knew it, particularly on questions of economics and administration. Bluff and hearty, he was a classic 'back-slapper' who could also administer 'face-slapping' when he thought it would do his opponents a bit of good. So he began by taunting the Tories with feebleness ('I do not feel that the Opposition have got their hearts in this battle' were his opening words) and went on to show that they had been abandoned by their old allies, the Mining Association. Terms of reference had been agreed between the ministry and the Mining Association, who had 'accepted the principle of global sum as being reasonable' and had 'withdrawn their opposition to the principles of the Bill'.

They have declared they are prepared to facilitate what they say they regard as the inevitable transfer of this industry from private to public ownership. All this would suggest that they are sceptical as to the power of the Tory minority in this House, or of the Tory majority down the passage, to obstruct its passing into law; and, therefore, the Mining Association have given up the ghost.

Hugh Dalton's taunts brought a speech of some considerable asperity from George Edward Peter Thorneycroft, the Member

for Monmouth.* Tall and elegant, with all the polish afforded
by his schooldays at Eton, this ex-artilleryman, who was an
MP before he was 30, had for a time paraded along with
Hogg and a few others as one of a 'left Tory' group. He
raised first the question of reorganisation, and why proposals
for reduction of the number of production units, as set out in
the Reid Report, had never been carried, saying:

I will tell you why in my view that has not been done before. I think
there are two reasons. One was the obstruction which has come in the
past from what I could call the sullen resentment of the Mining Association corporations of any suggestion whatever for the reorganisation of
the industry. The second was what I might call the dogged conservatism
of the Mineworkers' Federation in reference to most ideas concerned
in new methods and new machinery.

Then he showed himself what seemed a sharp enough
resentment at the attitude of the Mining Association, saying:

So far as the Mining Association is concerned, they no longer trouble
us . . . Whatever the future of the industry, and whatever new forms of
energy may be devised as an alternative to the use of coal, the mine-owners
can rest content. They can sit back and draw their State income from
their inalienable bonds.

After saying that the Bill would make 'the miners' position
no better' and 'the consumers' position definitely worse',
Thorneycroft put the question: 'Why set up a State monopoly
at all?' and went on to say:

Mr Foot claims that his Report kept in reserve the best elements of private
enterprise. I suppose the Right Hon. Gentleman claims that his report
contains the best elements of Socialism. From the consumers' point of
view, there does not seem to be much to choose between them. They are
both monopolies. 'New Presbyter is but Old Priest writ large.'

George Daggar, who had been a miner's agent for eight
years and was now Member for Abertillery, a constituency

*Peter Thorneycroft was himself afterwards, during the year 1957, to be a short-dated
Chancellor of the Exchequer. His policy of dear money was to be the opposite extreme
to that of Dalton's chancellorship. By 1976 he (now in the House of Lords) had been
appointed to head the Conservative Central Office by the new Tory leader Margaret
Thatcher.

neighbouring on that of Monmouth, represented by the preceding speaker, rose at 10.54 and in the quarter of an hour before the debate and the House were adjourned he voiced anxiety lest sufficient use was not made of the skill and technical knowledge of the miners. He also answered some arguments of opponents, that the Bill would destroy personal freedom, saying:

The people I represent exist in virtue of the mines in my Division, and they knew little of freedom during the inter-war period. For 17 years the only freedom they had was to go to the Assistance Board. They were denied the freedom to work in order to maintain their own families.

I lived, as I have stated, in a Division that lost over 12,000 as a result of migration. The only freedom that they were able to exercise was to destroy family life, break up their homes, and go elsewhere. (29 January 1946)

Thus ended the first day's debate on the Second Reading.

8. THE SECOND DAY'S DEBATE

When on the next day the question was again proposed 'That the Bill be now read a second time', the first speaker was the previous Minister for Fuel and Power, Major Gwilym Lloyd-George, the Member for Pembroke who eighteen months earlier had appointed the Reid Committee. Asking what had the Labour Government done to start putting the recommendations of the Reid Report into effect, Major Lloyd-George was interrupted by Hugh Dalton rising to point out that in six months he himself had done nothing. The Rt Hon. and gallant Gentleman retorted first that he had had surveys made of each region, and then questioned the much-mentioned 'psychological effect of nationalisation', asking of the miners, '. . . . when the State takes over the mines what will the effect on him be?'

He will go to the same pit and get the same lamp from the same man; he will go into the same cage, will probably be lowered by the same man, and, when he gets to the bottom, he will, if he is in certain parts of the country, see the same expression on the face of the pony. He will see the same manager, the same deputy, the old roadway, the same coalface, and, on the Friday, he will probably be paid by the same man. But because the boss is different, it is said, it will make all the difference. (30 January 1946)

This speech had not only caused interruptions from the government front bench but had ruffled the Fuel and Power Ministry. An angry answer to it was given by W. Foster, Member for Wigan from 1942 onwards and Parliamentary Secretary to the ministry. Having started in the pit at 12 years of age, he spoke of his thirty years' work underground. His retort to Major Lloyd-George and to other opponents roused comment and caused a rise in temperature:

The Rt Hon. and gallant Gentleman never understood the industry and never understood the miners. Otherwise, he would have been able to prescribe remedies for dealing with the immediate problems. Instead, since we came into the Ministry we have not found any constructive suggestion or any constructive policy which had been put forward prior to our arrival.
Major Lloyd-George: I challenge that remark absolutely. A great deal of work had been done on the basis of the Reid Report and if the Hon. Gentleman will look in the archives of the Ministry he will find proof of this.
Mr Foster: I can assure the Rt Hon. and gallant Gentleman that whatever he did when he was at the Ministry we know all about it and it is as the result of knowing what he did that we found out what he had not done.

Squadron-Leader Emrys Owain Roberts, Member for Merioneth, spoke briefly; his speech lasted less than seven minutes. As a Liberal he supported the Bill, 'in so far as it gives an opportunity for the transfer to public ownership of the coal industry', but thought it would have been better to have separate coal boards for each nationality 'one for Wales, one for England and one for Scotland if they want it'.
Then came a maiden speaker, one of the many. This was David Griffiths, Member for the Rother Valley division of the West Riding of Yorkshire (a seat which even in the Labour 'recession' five years ahead he held by over 42,000 votes to less than 13,000 for the Conservative) and for seventeen years an official of the Hickleton Main Branch of the Yorkshire Miners' Association. In his speech he mentioned that 'as a

comparatively young man' he had had 'to work ten hours a day at a colliery for 1s.2d.'. Hence his contempt for the personages opposite without any such experience which he expressed as follows:

As a miner at the coal face, where I worked for 26 years, it was my practice, when I had heartburn, to get a little bit of coal and suck it. I am firmly convinced that, although I have heard more about coal and coal questions from Hon. Members opposite since I have been in this House, than ever I heard in the whole of my experience in the Mines, they could not, with all due deference to them, hew enough coal to cure my heartburn.

By the late afternoon the Tory Opposition had produced an elaborate amendment* to be moved by H. V. Raikes.

Henry Victor Albert Mackinnon Raikes (educated at Westminster School and Trinity College, Cambridge) Member for the Wavertree division of Liverpool, was a determined parliamentarian. His attempts to enter that institution had begun in 1924 at the age of 23, an age at which he was called to the Bar. After fifteen years in Parliament, Raikes was put in charge of a reasoned amendment which had, searchingly enough in its concentration upon matters omitted, exposed the bareness of the Bill. But his speech did little more than cover similar ground to that traversed by earlier Tory speakers.

David McAdam Eccles, born in 1904, educated at Winchester and New College, Oxford, begged to second the amendment. He was Member for the Chippenham division of Wiltshire. In his half-hour speech D. M. Eccles set out what

---

*This House declines to give a Second Reading to a Bill which, while setting up a State monopoly in the production of coal, suggests no immediate action to arrest the decline in the output of coal and the increase in its cost of production or to restore our export trade in coal to the levels reached under free enterprise;

contains no policy for the recruitment of labour to the Mines or for governing the relations between workers and managers on the one hand and the Coal Board and the Minister on the other hand;

offers no statutory safeguard to employees of the industry against being adversely affected by the change of ownership;

provides neither a fair method of compensation nor the opportunity to reinvest the proceeds of compensation in new productive enterprise;

fails to provide for the publication of adequate reports and accounts or their submission to parliamentary scrutiny;

and affords no real protection to the general public either as domestic and industrial consumers or as tax payers. (*Hansard*, Vol. 418, 30 January 1946) he regarded as 'the fundamental difference between the Socialist party and the Conservative party' on nationalisation:

On this side of the House, we see nothing which warrants a dramatic change in human nature that will suddenly make men and women want to serve unselfishly a State monopoly. Hon. Gentlemen on the other side of the House take a different view. I appreciate their difficulty. They would like to introduce Socialism into this country without the aid of military discipline, and in a society of free men and women that cannot be done.

Mr Skeffington-Lodge (Bedford): Does not the whole history of our war effort completely invalidate what the Hon. Gentleman has just said?

Mr Eccles: I do not know whether the Hon. Gentleman desires to perpetuate all the wartime controls on labour. I presume from his interjection that he does.

Mr Skeffington-Lodge: The point which I wanted to make is that the common weal can evoke just as much attention to duty and as much hard work as ever a capitalist proposition will be able to bring about.

Mr Eccles: That is where we differ. In my submission, common danger is something much more powerful as a stimulus than common weal. We shall see.

The next speaker was Margaret McCrorie Herbison, Member for North Lanark since 1945. Born 12 March 1907 and educated at Dykehead Public School in Shotts, at Bellshill Academy and at Glasgow University, she had been a teacher in the Glasgow schools before she became an MP: but she still retained the attributes of a schoolteacher; her habit of references to 'my miners' was reminiscent of the days when 'my pupils' was on her lips. Supporting the Bill, she referred to the high accident rate, the 'execrable wages' and 'intolerable' working conditions and then said:

I speak with some feeling on this matter. My father was a man who worked in the mines all his life, and whose body was wracked, bruised and torn through that work, while my brother had his lung pierced by an accident caused by a runaway hatch and lost a finger in the pit for which there was no adequate compensation. The tragedy is that these are only two of thousands who have suffered in this industry under private ownership.

She ended by insisting that 'Compensation must not be too high; it could not possibly be too low for owners who have taken huge profits from the blood, sweat and tears of our miners and their womenfolk.'

Thomas Frederick Hubbard had entered the House of Commons in 1944 at a by-election. The House was ready to listen to the maiden speech of the representative of Kirkcaldy, birthplace of Adam Smith who in the eighteenth century urged the ending of slavery in the Scottish pits. Hubbard, replying to the Member for Wavertree who 'spoke disparagingly of the men who came here many years ago, and who so often spoke about the hard times they had in the mines', praised those whom he held were famous men, saying:

I suggest that the Bill now before the House is a tribute to those who have come to this House and those who sent them. One thinks today of the great industrial leaders of the past, Arthur Cook and Herbert Smith, Tom Richardson and Tom Richards, and Scotland's own leader, Bob Smillie. It is a pity they are not here to see the results of their great labour. One must also think of those great present-day leaders of the mining industry such as we find in the persons of Will Lawther, Arthur Horner, Ebby Edwards and Abe Moffat, who comes from my own county of Fife. All of these have done so much to bring before the country the great need of the industry.

Roland Jennings had been Member for the Sedgefield division of Durham 1931–5: and then in 1939 at a by-election was once more seated, this time for the Hallam division of Sheffield. A chartered accountant in his fifty-second year, he was outspokenly opposed to the Bill. He feared lest: '. . . at a later date we bring disaster and bankruptcy not only to the coalmining industry, but to such industries as the iron and steel industries of Sheffield which may have to pay very heavily for one of their raw materials, namely, coal.' He expressed this view on the subject of prices:

I think the Minister should not have power to interfere with industrial or domestic selling prices.
Mr Gallacher: Suppose the Board decided to put an uneconomic price on the major industry and the Minister with his wider knowledge of the economic and political situation was of the opinion that that was undesirable. Would it not be good that he should have power to control the Board?
Mr Jennings: The Hon. Member has put a hypothetical case. There is

Shearer-loader at the coalface, Kellingley Colliery, Yorkshire

some substance in what he said, but there was some substance in what I said. Therefore I say that the Minister should not have authority at all.

William Thomas Paling, who had been a colliery check-weighman and a member of the West Riding County Council, had in 1945 entered Parliament as Member for Wentworth division of Yorkshire. He answered a number of criticisms. Finally he recorded his emphatic opinion that the compensation was overgenerous.

Clifford William Hudson Glossop, Member for the Howden-shire division of East Yorkshire (and with previous parliamentary experience from 1931 to 1935), began by saying that he could not claim the intimate knowledge of the mining industry of so many who had spoken in the debate. C. W. H. Glossop, educated at Harrow, a prominent agriculturalist (he was the unmarried President of the British Friesian Cattle Society) ended his remarks as follows:

For years the miners have been led to believe that if only the industry were nationalised, they would get jam today, tomorrow and every other day. I believe that when this Bill becomes an Act and its operations are seen in practice, the miners will realise that they have been deluded. I never decided with a clearer conscience to go into the Lobby to vote against a Bill because I believe the very objectives claimed for this Bill – betterment of the conditions of the miner – are not going to be fulfilled.

John Richard Thomas, born 9 March 1897, came of a Wrexham family in North Wales. His education was 'private'. He had been in practice since 1928 as a chartered accountant: and was now since 1945 Labour Member for Dover. He began:

It is indeed a great privilege to me to have the opportunity of supporting this Bill. It is a privilege for two reasons. The first is that I was born and bred in the colliery slums of North Wales, where we had bread, often no butter, but seldom did we have jam; and secondly, in my constituency they are the large majority of the mineworkers of Kent.

He said the industry should not be considered 'as a going concern but as a dying industry', and was afraid the mine-owners would be given too much. The word 'compensation' was a misnomer: 'We are not giving the mine-owners compensation. We are presenting them, whatever the amount may be, with what is, in fact, a gratuity . . .'

As 8 o'clock approached Harold Macmillan, since 1945 MP for Bromley,* rose to close the debate for the Opposition. Macmillan, having been a scholar at Eton and an exhibitioner at Balliol College, Oxford, had by 1919 become aide-de-camp to the ducal Governor-General of Canada and by 1920 he had·married Lady Dorothy Evelyn Cavendish, daughter of the 9th Duke of Devonshire. He had been thrice wounded during the war: and since 1925 had written half a dozen books. His was a skilful enough speech, in which he began by restating the technical and economic arguments in favour of ending the existing set-up; and then went on to ask a series of questions for the Lord President of the Council (Herbert Morrison) to answer. Of the Bill he said:

This is not syndicalism, Socialism or 'the mines for the miners.' Compare the Bills of 1924, 1936 and 1937. Under every one of those Bills, for which the Labour Party were responsible, the miners were to obtain a large measure of control at the centre, in the regions, and in the districts. By this Bill all they do is exchange one set of owners for another, and rather more remote owners – what I might call the 'nine bright shiners' of the Coal Board.

Harold Macmillan spoke of the recruitment to the armed forces of miners in 1939–40 as 'the one serious error' of Ernest Bevin 'in his handling of the labour situation'. He went on in his teasing and chaffing manner (which often gave an impression of supercilious scorn) to deal with other members of the government. Finally he summarised Conservative policy thus:

The recommendations of the Reid Report do not require this Bill, and we have the high authority of the author of the Report himself.
    The policy that should have been followed, which we put forward and which is still our policy, is the policy of compulsory amalgamations; the financing of the re-equipment by the industry itself through machinery provided by the State if necessary; a charter for the miners; the restoration of managerial responsibilities; a safeguard for the consumer through the competition between the reorganised, but proportionately much smaller groups in the industry.
    That was our policy and we stand by it.

*He had represented Stockton-on-Tees 1924–9 and 1931–45.

The Lord President of the Council (who was also Leader of the House) closed the debate for the government on the Second Reading; Herbert Morrison, now in his fifty-eighth year, had filled many offices in local and national government and was still with every prospect of succeeding in the end to the highest office of all. Morrison, contrasting with the previous speaker (the son of a policeman following the son-in-law of a duke), had yet something of the same self-confident manner. Indeed he always spoke with an air of self-confidence but was ever circumspect and eschewed any very violent attack on the aristocratic Tories. All his sharpness of speech was reserved for such as might stray from the fold. He began by saying that he would refuse to be provoked by Macmillan; and that the Opposition were reduced to asking a volley of questions because they did not know what line to take. Later he referred to 'the many quotations from a book which I published in 1933 called *Socialisation and Transport*, saying:

I am very grateful for the advertisement which this, if I may say so, excellent book has received. It is a great pity that it is now out of print . . .
There was an awful lot of controversy when it was published, especially from the Labour Party. I was denounced with great vigour in many quarters. The discussion went on, and now, having had all the bricks thrown at me, I see the doctrine preserved, and it is coming right in the end. Substantially, that book stands.

In this passage Morrison made reference to his success in having altered Labour Party policy on nationalisation (which had been a triumph over his one-time party leader George Lansbury) and in having defeated the rival doctrine of workers' participation, held for so long by a past generation of mine-workers and their leaders.

When the question was put, the Opposition amendment was defeated by 359 votes to 182 – 'a decided and emphatic majority'. The Bill had received its Second Reading.

The next stage in the process of passing a Bill through the House of Commons is its detailed consideration in Committee, clause by clause and indeed line by line. This is followed by the Report stage. Thereafter the Bill in its amended form comes up for the final stage, the Third Reading.

9. THE THIRD READING

Over a hundred days had elapsed since the House of Commons had given the Bill its Second Reading on 30 January and sent it to be dealt with in Committee clause by clause until the amended Bill could be reported back to the House on 15 May. Hard upon this came the Third Reading which began and ended on Monday 20 May. As was customary, it was the junior minister who begged to move 'That the Bill be now read the Third time'; but it was not the same junior minister as it had been a hundred days earlier. The veteran Lancashire miner William Foster of St Helens had been dropped. In his place was put forward one whom Chancellor of the Exchequer Dalton claimed as his protégé; and the House welcomed the young Hugh Gaitskell, CBE, as the new Parliamentary Secretary to the Ministry of Fuel and Power.

Hugh Todd Naylor Gaitskell, son of a member of the Indian Civil Service, born on 9 April 1906, was educated at Winchester and New College, Oxford, where he took first-class honours in philosophy, politics and economics. For some ten or twelve years thereafter he held a succession of minor university posts, until the 1939 outbreak of war (when he was 34 years old) presently transformed him into a temporary civil servant. In this capacity he became Principal Private Secretary to Hugh Dalton, then Minister of Economic Warfare, 1940–42; and afterwards became Principal Assistant Secretary in the Board of Trade, 1942–5. He had written a book on *Chartism*, published in 1929; and another on *Money and Everyday Life,* 1939. At the general election of 1945 he had stepped from the civil service into Parliament as Member for South Leeds. Now in less than a year he was a junior minister. Soon his aspiring spirit would be gratified with more and more important posts, until before he was 50 he was to graduate as Leader of the Labour Party. Gaitskell opened by saying that they had spent a lot of time on the Bill; with two days on the Second Reading, eighteen days discussing 250 amendments, three days in the Report stage dealing with 143 amendments and new clauses. He did 'not think that the Opposition can now claim that they have not had enough time to discuss this Bill'. A number of important changes had been made:

For example, as a result, I freely admit, of representations made from the other side of the House, the Minister now has specific powers to give directions to the National Coal Board if either of the Consumers' Councils should disclose a situation which merits a direction on his part to the Board. We have, again, the new Clause on patents – not a controversial matter but certainly a change of substance.

Other changes had dealt with interim income and restrictions on transfer of compensation stock; and he drew attention to two other important modifications:

We have a new Clause – an important one this – imposing upon the Minister the obligation to make regulations regarding pensions and gratuities, and finally we have the new Clause imposing upon the Board the obligation to enter into consultation with various appropriate organisations, so as to set up effective machinery for the settlement of disputes in the industry.

It was a conciliatory speech – as indeed it had to be, with so many faults of omission confessed.

Colonel Lancaster, the Member for Fylde, opened the Third Reading debate for the Opposition saying that he took it as 'a compliment to the coal industry that the Labour Government have selected one of their ablest Back Benchers to occupy this position at this juncture'.

Later he took up the argument, much used by government speakers, of the 'psychological advantage to be obtained from nationalisation', saying:

About 15 years ago, I had the opportunity of spending some months in the Russian coalfields, studying conditions there. They had embarked on Communism, so far as coal mining was concerned, with something of the same belief. They thought that there would be an immediate psychological reaction in their favour. There could have been no greater disillusionment.

They had to learn the long and painful lesson, which we all have to learn, that whether a man is a soldier or a coal miner, or anyone else, he will react precisely as circumstances warrant.

Whilst he proposed to vote against the Bill, nevertheless the Colonel ended with a sort of blessing:

The Minister and his colleagues will be responsible, in a short while, for the lives and the welfare of something like one million men and their families, and for nothing less than the foundation of the economic structure of this country. Men of goodwill in all parts of the House must wish them well. May they prove themselves worthy of their trust.

After these two opening speeches the debate completed its six-hour course without any particularly novel argument being adduced by any of the speakers. It gave an opportunity for rejoicing on one side and for gloomy forebodings on the other. Several mining Members built triumphal arches of oratory for the passage of the Bill: and the voice of the Opposition was muted.

Horace Edwin Holmes, born 30 March 1888, who after a long career as a trade union official (including twenty-four years on the Royston Urban District Council) had succeeded on the untimely death of George Griffiths as Member for Hemsworth in mid-winter, now made his maiden speech in which he said: 'I have nearly 50 years of mining experience behind me. I went into the collieries in 1901, and have been attached to them ever since in practical, technical and administrative direction.'

Sir Peter Bennett of Birmingham was the next speaker, from the standpoint of an industrialist – being Chairman of Joseph Lucas Ltd, and a director both of ICI and of Lloyds Bank as well as a past President of the Federation of British Industries. He was followed by Ronald MacKay, the Member for Hull, North-West. This industrialist of a younger generation (he was born on 3 September 1902) came from the Antipodes in 1934, took up the practice of law here as a solicitor and plunged into politics; he had written books in Australia on the *Industrial Arbitration Act,* and in Britain in 1940 on *Federal Europe.* Having held wartime appointments in the Ministry of Aircraft production, he was now the Managing Director of Tarran Industries Ltd. He devoted his speech to a refutation of the arguments put forward by Colonel Lancaster, mainly in the Second Reading debate, about coalmines in Australia.

Major Lloyd-George (Pembroke), the former Minister of Fuel and Power, argued that the Bill had not been given enough thought beforehand, as was shown by the omissions (e.g. no mention of conciliation machinery) that were only now made good. Then Tom Smith of Normanton, supporting the Bill, gave an historical survey. He was soon to resign his parliamentary seat in order to become Labour Director of the North-Eastern Division Coal Board.

Major Niall Malcolm Stewart Macpherson, Liberal-National Member for Dumfriesshire, had followed his father Sir Thomas Macpherson from education in Midlothian to Trinity College, Oxford. But whereas his father had a (mainly legal) career in the Indian Civil Service, the son, going in for business, trained with J. & J. Colman Ltd, the makers of mustard; and managed their Turkish branch 1933–5. While saying that 'Whatever Government came into power it was realised that reorganisation would have to take place', he held that this was not the best form of reorganisation; and put a somewhat awkward question: 'The miner might very well ask what is to be the position in regard to the Essential Work Order. The Order is supposed to be taken off whenever circumstances permit. Under this Bill, when will circumstances permit?'

Sir Arnold Babb Gridley, Member for Stockport since 1935, born 16 July 1878, President of the British Association of Chambers of Commerce, had been for many years engaged in the administration and direction of various electric supply and manufacturing undertakings at home and abroad, and during the War of Empires had been controller of Electric Power Supply at the Ministry of Munitions. He began by complimenting Hugh Gaitskell for 'a good parliamentary performance in opening the Debate today'. Sir Arnold showed himself adept enough at assembling quotations and discharging them upon the House: from the Reid Report; from *The Times*, which, he said, 'is by no means friendly to the Conservative position'; and from fellow MPs against the Bill.

William Gallacher, now in his eleventh year as Communist Member for West Fife, performed the feat of making a three-minute speech in support of the Bill – but with reservations. Gallacher, for many years Chairman of the Communist Party of Great Britain, had for over forty years been closely associated with miners as an agitator and as a champion of their rights. He said:

I just want to pay a tribute to the Minister and to touch on two Clauses in the Bill. My tribute to the Minister is for the way in which he has carried this Bill through its various stages. He has shown great skill, still greater patience and, in my opinion, highly commendable toleration.

Clause 10 is the one that I do not like. It allows of compensation to the coalowners. They should not have received any compensation; the most that they should have received was a life annuity . . .

The most important Clause in the Bill is Clause 43, which deals with the relations of the Board with the representatives of the miners. As has been pointed out time and time again, there will be no coal without the miners, and the better the miners are pleased, the more coal you will get. Therefore, I hope that one of the first actions on the part of the Board will be to come to an understanding with the representatives of the National Union of Mineworkers, and that the miners will get the five-day week, without a drop in pay, and the Miners' Charter.

It is to be noticed that no part of this Bill has received less discussion than that particular Clause.

In the Bill it will be found that provision is made for everybody connected with the industry except the miners. So I hope that in the future discussions on this matter the Miners' Charter will be granted at the earliest possible moment, and the miners thereby won over for this great new development of the mining industry, which is now to be run for the public good.

Once more, Roland Jennings, of Hallam, Sheffield, came in, to oppose the Bill, because in his opinion (he was a chartered accountant) 'it would seriously increase the cost of coal to the steel works in the constituency which I represent'.

Moved by the Jennings speech, especially on valuation, the next speaker, 55-year-old James Edward Glanville, Member for Consett since 1943, retorted strongly. He had come to the fore in the Durham coalfield as a fiery agitator. He said:

The Hon. Member for Hallam [Mr Jennings] talked about valuation. Although I am not committed to confiscation, I am sorely tempted to agree with the Hon. Member for West Fife [Mr Gallacher]. Let me say at once that these coal mines should be bought, not in order to provide an everlasting heritage for the owners, but for, as my Hon. Friend says, 'A decent price to get rid of them.'

He described the 'concern' of the Opposition for the members of the mining community as 'pathetic', adding, as one who had worked '40 years down in that "dark hole" . . .',

Fourteen or fifteen years ago in County Durham, as my friends there know well, we established what was known as a subsistence wage for miners – 6s.8½d. per day for men over 21. As soon as our young men reached the age of 21, they were sacked by the coalowners, and their juniors were promoted to save a paltry sum of about 4d. a shift. They chased the young men out of the mining industry for a few paltry coppers a day. The owners did not care where they went. Today, they are scattered in factories all over the country, and when Hon. Members opposite are short of coal they cry 'Where are the young miners?' It was the damnable policy pursued by the coalowners which chased these young men out of the coal industry. That is undeniable. That is the record of private enterprise in the coal mines.

As Glanville, victimised after 1926, looked across the floor of the House and listened to the Opposition's speeches expressing their concern for the welfare of miners under nationalisation, his indignation burst out, and led to a sharp exchange of class feeling from both benches. Recalling the aftermath of the miners' defeat in 1926 and his own victimisation, he said:

There is a certain pleasure in being victimised; it proves that you have been faithful and true to the class to which you belong, and it proves that you did not curry favour with the 'bosses'. We know what struggles and hardships are, and what is the lot in wages and bad conditions of the miners. Our fellows are today working in two foot seams, for low wages, lying on their sides in water and with water dripping on them. It is quite true that Hon. Gentlemen opposite know something of technical mining – but there is not a damned man among you who could hew a ton of coal.

This roused Earl Winterton, whose main distinction, apart from his length of limb and spare frame (which reminded some of the aforetime well-known music-hall tune 'The Human Hair-Pin'), had come to be that he had sat longer in the House for the same constituency (Horsham since 1904) than any other Member. The following interchange took place:

Earl Winterton: In the new regime of the House of Commons is the expression 'not a damned one of you opposite' permissible? Is that the new procedure of this House, Mr Speaker?

Mr Speaker: I did not hear the Hon. Member say that.

Earl Winterton: Yes, he did. He said it most distinctly – 'not a damned one of you opposite.' Is that modern procedure by Hon. Gentlemen opposite to be allowed in this House?

Mr Glanville: I do not think that you heard me say it, Mr Speaker, but

I did. I withdraw the expression at once, knowing full well that damnation is something that is waiting for them later on.

Mr Speaker: I do not think that is a proper withdrawal. The Hon. Member should withdraw it unreservedly.

Mr Glanville: I withdraw it altogether. I have kind feelings towards the Noble Lord, and I think he and I would make good friends. There is one word I want to say in conclusion. As a boy of 12 years of age I worked 10 hours a day in a coal mine for 1s.2d. a shift. We have improved beyond that now, but that was not through any kindness displayed by the coalowners. The story of this industry is the story of the most brutal industry on earth, because it reaches back to the days when women dragged the coal in baskets from the coal pit . . . That is the story of this industry, which is the most bloodstained of all our industries, and the most tyrannical, too.

Earl Winterton: On a point of Order. I have always understood from the Rulings given by your predecessors and by yourself, Mr Speaker, that the Third Reading of a Bill is concerned only with what is in the Bill and that it is on the Second Reading that Members can go back in the long history of an industry such as this, back almost to antediluvian times. The Hon. Gentleman is not making one reference to the Bill as it now stands.

Mr Speaker: On the Third Reading of a Bill like this it is very difficult not to avoid the background of the industry, but I hope Hon. Members will not transgress too much.

Mr Glanville: If I use an antediluvian argument it is only because the coalowners are antediluvian in their outlook and in this Bill we are modernising the industry. We come here with a new outlook on life. The men in the coalfields of this country will be highly pleased when they know that this Bill has gone on to the Statute Book.

He was quickly followed by Kenneth Pickthorn, whose contempt for the ordinary mortal, especially those on the Labour benches, was made evident by every quirk of his mouth and by the side-glances he threw at them as he addressed himself to Mr Speaker. The Member for Cambridge University, a constituency which was to disappear with all other university seats before the next general election, rose to put a few points about 'the effects of this Bill', not upon coal getting (which he said he was not very competent to comment upon) but 'upon Parliament', saying that it was a measure of first-class constitutional importance.

Charles Frederick Grey, the local preacher from Durham, who had spoken at length on the Second Reading, came once more into the debate. He uttered praise and thanksgiving to the minister. But he had one criticism, on compensation, of the minister:

He has made the mineowners very happy indeed; they certainly did not expect the handsome compensation which they are to receive. This aspect of the Bill is the only one on which I feel tempted to criticise my Right Hon. Friend. I would not have paid the owners one farthing; they have robbed and plundered long enough.

Major Peter Geoffrey Roberts, Member for the Ecclesall division of Sheffield spoke next. Born on 23 June 1912, the only son of a Norfolk baronet (Sir Samuel Roberts), Major Peter had followed his father from Harrow to Trinity College, Cambridge, and then into the practice of the law. But he was also a farmer (of 2,000 acres in Norfolk) and a director of capitalist companies such as Wombwell Main and the Barnsley District Coking Company. He ended by saying:

I shall vote against the Third Reading of the Bill, because I believe it is not the right way to deal with the industry . . .
But I see a ray of light, because when things become difficult, I think it will be possible for the Board to lease back the mines – not to sell them back, as one Hon. Member said – to individuals, possibly to the management, or the man, or a group of people who will get together, and on some basis of that kind to produce coal in an efficient manner.

David Johnstone Pryde, Member for Peebles and Southern Midlothian, was born on 3 March 1890. Detail of his career, as given (presumably on the best authority) in *Who's Who*, runs as follows:

Educ: Lesswade Secondary School, Scot. Labour College. Colliery clerk (2 years); entered mines; studied under John McLean, M.A., Private Tutor, Rev. William Nicholson, M.A.; meteoric career as miners' T.U. Official, 1921–33. Mid and East Lothian Miners and Nat. Union of Scot. Miners; filled every position in both political and industrial organisation; victimised for T.U. activities 1926. Entered Bonnyrig and Lesswade Town Council, 1938. Twice election agent to J. Westwood; contested (Lab.) South Midlothian, 1935.
Recreation: angler.

D. J. Pryde began his speech with the Mining Charter of the monks of Newbattle Abbey in 1210 AD and ended a rapid historical survey thus: 'I suggest to Hon. Members that they do not divide on this Bill but rather that they should do the opposite – take it to their bosoms and say, "Yes, we will come in behind the Government and will give to the country this great new coal charter after 736 years".'

But he did not lure the Tories to his way of thinking. Harold Davies, Member for Leek division of Staffordshire, also began historically, saying: 'I think this is the 55th Act of Parliament that has dealt with the mining industry since 1775.' Harold Davies had trained as a schoolmaster and tutor in adult education. In his seven-minute speech he answered innuendoes about absenteeism, recruitment and other matters:

To the grammar school to which I had the fortune to go, went boys up to the fifth and sixth forms with me . . . I came back to my area four or five years later and saw these boys, who had higher school certificates, walking the street. They were the flotsam and jetsam of the system of mine ownership in this country before this Bill.

Next spoke Sir Hugh Vere Huntly Duff Lucas-Tooth (born 13 January 1903, educated at Eton and Balliol) who had become the Member for the Isle of Ely at the age of 21. In his thirtieth year he was called to the Bar in Lincoln's Inn and twelve years later, having meantime become Lieut-Colonel of the Queen's Own Cameron Highlanders, he once more entered Parliament, this time in 1945 as MP for Hendon South. He said: 'I am satisfied that this Bill will not be to the benefit of the coalmining industry. I believe that it will not be the encouragement which it has been held out to be to the mining community. I shall have no hesitation, therefore, in going into the Lobby to vote against it.'

Emrys Hughes was a Welshman who for years had made his home in Scotland. There he was assistant editor of *Forward*, becoming full editor when Thomas Johnston retired. An out-and-out pacifist who never missed an opportunity of expressing his views, he succeeded Sandy Sloan as Member for South Ayrshire at the beginning of 1946. He made a short speech. In five minutes he first recalled the work of his wife's father, Keir Hardie, who had introduced the first Bill to nationalise the mines in 1893, fifty-three years before: 'Twenty years after that Bill of 1893, we had another Bill and, in refreshing my memory of Debates in 1913, I find we had then the same old arguments as have been trotted out by the Opposition this evening.'

Emrys Hughes dealt with compensation saying: 'I agree with the remarks of the Hon. Member for West Fife [Mr Gallacher] . . . He has been very generous to the coalowners in this Bill. The coalowners are very lucky indeed that they are going to be treated in this way, instead of having their compensation assessed by a board of miners and people who know the conditions in the industry' (20 May 1946).

10. LAST LAP IN THE COMMONS

After hours of debate on the Third Reading Harold Macmillan at 8.40 p.m. rose to say that nothing which had taken place during the Committee or Report stages had overcome the Opposition's objections or allayed their fears. The Bill still did not deal with the questions they regarded as vital:

They are, the decline in output, the increase in cost, the virtual dis-appearance of the export trade in coal, the recruitment of labour, the publication of adequate reports and accounts and their submission to effective Parliamentary scrutiny, and the protection of the public, both domestic and industrial, both as consumers and as taxpayers.

Macmillan then claimed credit for one important clause dealing with relations between management and workmen, saying:

While the Bill, as originally introduced contained – incredible as it may appear – no reference whatever to the industrial relations between managers and workmen, on the one hand, and the Coal Board and the Minister, upon the other, the Minister has wisely yielded to our plan. Clause 43, which was called by Hon. Members opposite the most important Clause in the Bill, and which did not even exist on Second Reading, now places upon the Board the duty of consultation with all appropriate organisations with a view to preserving and, we hope, strengthening the machinery for conciliation, consultation, and arbitration. After all, this is a most vital point. This is the very heart, the core, of the whole problem. These successes of the Opposition are, therefore, not inconsiderable.

Apart from the merits he claimed for the Opposition, Macmillan alleged many demerits of haste and carelessness in the work of the government in preparing the Bill for legislative enactment.

Macmillan showed himself a skilled debater in the ease with which on the one hand, as above, he airily stigmatised the 'mistakes' of the previous Leaders of his own Tory Party and so shrugged off responsibility for them; while on the other hand he sought to adopt arguments from left-wing members of the Labour Party. Thus Macmillan said:

First, let me take the human aspect, the psychological and emotional problem, which is the result of the chequered history of the industry. Will change of ownership of itself solve that? This Bill vests the ownership of all the colliery undertakings in a board of nine men – nine men not elected by, not even containing a single elected representative of, the mining community. It is not nationalisation in the old sense of the word.

I heard an echo from the old days from the Hon. Member for South Ayrshire [Emrys Hughes] who has just spoken. This is not Socialism; it is State capitalism. There is not too much participation by the mineworkers in the affairs of the industry; there is far too little. There is not too much syndicalism; there is none at all.

In the new ownership, the miners have no share except that of belonging to the general body of citizens – a kind of 'pay as you earn' share. To the men, the new owners will mean the Board. However gifted or eminent they may be, they will be more remote and more soulless than the old owners.

It was against a background first of speculation and then of resentful discussion about the members of the Board that Harold Macmillan now brought in the name of Lord Hyndley whom he described as 'a very distinguished and highly qualified industrialist', saying:

He has been Managing Director and Chairman, I understand, of Powell, Duffryn & Co., for many years and then chief adviser to the Minister of Fuel. He is now the Chairman of the Coal Board. He has been, in turn, capitalist, civil servant and commissar. All this is a very respectable and praiseworthy record, but from the human and dramatic point of view, after these long years of agitation, oratory and emotion, it is not very inspiring. As a climax it is a bit flat.

Mr Kirkwood: So you think.

Mr Macmillan: May not the miner, remembering Keir Hardie, Bob Smillie and Herbert Smith, and all those great figures of the old great days, and contemplating Lord Hyndley, echo Milton's words and say: 'New Presbyter is but old Priest writ large.'

To wind up the debate, the minister who had presented the Bill on First Reading now rose in his place on the Treasury Bench. Emanuel Shinwell began: 'The Right Hon. Gentleman the Member for Bromley [Mr Macmillan] has made a characteristic and lively speech to the House, following the many interesting and thoughtful discourses we have heard from him during the Debate.' These words were Shinwell's 'velvet paws'. For the Minister of Fuel and Power, like the patriarch Job, could say: 'Behold, my desire is that the Almighty would answer me, and that mine adversary had written a book.' For a book the Tory Leader had written, and a very good book too, in the opinion of those most devoted to his political advancement. It was called *The Middle Way;* in it Harold Macmillan had deserted the ranks of the defenders of private profit in coal and had come down on the side of state control. It was impossible for Shinwell not to mention that the Bill had the support of 'the considered opinions of the Right Hon. Gentleman himself in the past'; nor to let his claws out in a relatively mild scratching motion as follows:

The Right Hon. Gentleman described the matter in this language, and I beg of Hon. Members opposite, who have been loudly applauding him to take note. The Right Hon. Gentleman wrote: 'The State, it seems to me, should sweep away every obstacle to the reconstruction of the mining industry, and itself take over the power and responsibility of a rational exploitation of our coal resources. Through the efficient business management of a public utility concern, it could secure to the new industries a reliable and cheap supply of the raw materials they require, and gain for the workers in the mining industry the higher standard of life to which they are so justly entitled. This is an industry that has long passed out of the phase in which social purposes can best be served by private profit incentive.'

It is doubtful whether that is the path which leads to the leadership of the Tory Party, but 'other times, other manners.' There we must leave it.

Shinwell then argued that if the Opposition prided themselves on concessions, then it demonstrated 'my friendliness, my benevolence, my generosity and my willingness to compromise'; but, if 'I have made no concessions whatever', as

Harold Macmillan alleged, then 'the Opposition have no call to pride themselves on any achievement'.

The minister then selected characteristic phrases by Opposition speakers and held up their 'picturesque language' to derision. The Bill had been described as a 'frivolous piece of publicity' by Eden, and by another as 'very flimsy'. It was regarded as 'objectionable', as 'authoritative', as 'inadequate', as 'vague and ill-defined', and as 'a Socialist dream'. At this William Gallacher interjected: 'It gave Hon. Members opposite a nightmare!'

Shinwell continued saying that Gwilym Lloyd-George (a pale copy of his famous father) had spoken of 'buckpassing', of 'eyewash', and of 'a kind of swindle' and of a 'smash and grab raid'. He himself had been described by Macmillan as 'a witness who has something to conceal', and by others as a 'complete totalitarian dictator', convicted of 'stubbornness' and of 'obstinacy'. Such a collection of epithets, he remarked, 'denotes the extensive vocabulary of Hon. Members opposite – accompanied by a somewhat limited courtesy'. Shinwell's concluding words were:

We can afford to give the mineworkers the best conditions and the highest standard of wages, and we can minister to the needs of our national industry and afford to coal consumers coal regularly and at the cheapest possible price.

I am aware of the difficulties that beset the Ministry of Fuel and Power – I am under no illusion about the future – but I am proud to have had the distinction conferred on me, along with my colleagues at the Ministry and elsewhere, of being allowed to promote this great Bill in this House.

Then came the moment at 10 p.m. when the question was put: 'That the Bill be now read the third time' (20 May 1946).

CHAPTER VI

IN THE HOUSE OF LORDS

1. THE LAW AND THE CONSTITUTION

The law-making body of the United Kingdom is a trinity of Queen, Lords and Commons* anciently known as the Queen-in-Parliament – just as the executive body is the Queen-in-Council. The government of the country, as well as the enforcement of its laws, is carried on in the name of the queen who nominally possesses all power. But since by the British Constitution 'the Queen reigns but does not govern', all that is said or done by the queen has to be in accord with the decision – which is called 'the advice' – of the ministers, all of them members of the Privy Council. Thus the ministers are responsible for everything said or done by the queen or in her name and so are the real rulers of the country for the time being.

Thus it was the Prime Minister, the Lord President of the Council and the Chancellor of the Exchequer who, together with Sir Stafford Cripps, supported Emanuel Shinwell in presenting the Coal Industry Nationalisation Bill to the House of Commons. Indeed the new Parliament had opened in August 1945 with the speech from the throne promising nationalisation, uttered by the monarch in person but composed by the ministry.

The Bill, having passed the Commons Third Reading on 20 May 1946, went the next day to the House of Lords where there was little likelihood of its meeting with a rough reception. Nevertheless the miners who were following each detail of the legislative process, who knew of the disappointments suffered in the past and the mutilation of measures near to their heart by the unelected Lords Spiritual and Temporal, kept

*As seen in the time-honoured opening phrase of each Act of Parliament: 'Be it enacted by the Queen's most Excellent Majesty, by and with the advice and consent of the Lords Spiritual and Temporal, and Commons, in this present Parliament assembled and by the authority of the same as follows . . .'

a wary eye on the proceedings in the Upper House. Tradi-
tions of the miners' unions went back for over fifty years to
the time when Gladstone's proposed Home Rule for Ireland,
supported by the mining MPs, was completely destroyed by
the House of Lords. Hence it was that Gladstone made a
valedictory speech urging that the House of Lords 'must be
mended or ended'.

But in 1946 the Lords (their claws cut by the Parliament
Act of 1911) were not disposed to make trouble. Accordingly
when the Coal Industry Nationalisation Bill was 'brought
from the Commons' it was read the first time and sent for
printing.

On Tuesday 28 May 1946 'the House met at half-past two
of the clock, the Lord Chancellor on the Woolsack'; and after
prayers, the order of the day was for the Second Reading of
the Coal Industry Nationalisation Bill. The Lord Chancellor
(Lord Jowitt) rose and said:

My Lords, in rising to move that this Bill be read a second time, I
desire to make it quite plain to your Lordships that I do not do so as the
result of any doctrinaire preconception of what is the right solution for
this industry. I myself welcome the proposition that every question of
nationalisation must be considered and must be justified upon its own
merits.

This opening statement, as his hearers must have felt, was
fully in accord with the past political career of their chairman.*
The Lord Chancellor then went on to deal with the existing
situation, full of difficulties; and with the steps taken in the past
to surmount these difficulties. Lucidly he traced facts and

*William Allen Jowitt, knighted in 1929, raised to the peerage with a barony in 1945,
given a step up to a viscountcy in 1947 and to an earldom in 1951, was now 60 years
of age. Eldest son of the Rev. William Jowitt of Stevenage, he was educated at Marlborough and New College, Oxford, when he was called to the Bar, Middle Temple, in 1909.
He entered Parliament as Member for The Hartlepoole 1922–4, as a Liberal. He got in
again, this time for Labour, at Preston in 1929 and was immediately made Attorney-
General in the second MacDonald administration: and when on 24 August 1931 Ramsay
MacDonald left the Labour Party, Jowitt clung to his old chief and to the Attorney-
Generalship until September 1932, when he had to resign office as no constituency had
chosen him as their representative. His buoyant disposition brought him once more into
Parliament, this time (1939) again as a member of the Labour Party and an aspirant to
office. So, as Member for Ashton-under-Lyne 1939–45 he was successively Solicitor-General,
Paymaster-General, Minister without Portfolio (1942–4) and Minister of National Insurance
(1944–5). After the general election of 1945 he was made Lord Chancellor.

suggested remedies as given in the Reid Report as well as in earlier reports of committees and commissions back to the Sankey Commission in 1919. He said that he proposed to 'spend no time on destroying the idea of dual control'.

We had in the 1914–1918 period dual control, a control which amounted to little more than a guarantee of the profits of the companies, with practically no operational control. That system, we all agree, is a vicious system and must go. [Quoting the Reid Report on the subject he went on] We have tried output restrictions. We have tried price control. I myself bear a very heavy share of responsibility for that, in the 1930 Act, and I discovered, rather to my surprise, that I was quite popular, for the time being, with some of the coal-owners. But it has not succeeded.

Lord Jowitt then dealt with the history of amalgamation schemes not one of which had hatched out; he gave telling quotations from the Reorganisation Commission Reports (by Sir Ernest Gower, 'one of our ablest civil servants', its chairman) and concluded this portion of his opening speech:

I believe that amalgamations on any considerable scale are absolutely impossible under any system of private enterprise. What is the alternative? We hear a good deal about the establishment of a central authority, whether in the form recommended in the concluding chapter of the Reid Report, or in the weaker form of the declaration made during the time of the Caretaker Government by Major Lloyd-George, or in the cumbrous, complicated shape proposed by the Tory Reform Committee.

I say that to propose such a central authority, after ten years' completely abortive pre-war experience of the Reorganisation Commission (during which not one single compulsory amalgamation was carried through), is no more than to revert to the discarded and hopeless remedies of a bygone age . . . Even if you got these amalgamations you could not deal with the finance of the industry as a whole. And moreover you would do absolutely nothing to improve, or to give yourself a chance of improving labour relations.

Then Lord Jowitt passed to the offensive, referred to the Tory Party's amendment 'declining to give this Bill a Second Reading in another place', and finally explained some of the main provisions of the Bill.

For the Opposition, which far outnumbered the government

supporters, Lord Swinton* spoke first: 'Speaking for the Opposition, I accept the principle of this Bill, however much I doubt its wisdom. I am, however, going to accept the noble and learned Lord's challenge to put to him a number of what are, I hope, constructive suggestions.'

Speaking in place of the Liberal Leader Lord Samuel, Lord Isaacs † said at the outset 'we are prepared to give to this Bill our general support', and then criticised Lord Swinton, whose speech he described as 'a somewhat chastened challenge. It was less a fiery cross than a cross-examination.' The Liberal substitute Leader ended by saying:

Speaking for myself, I do not pretend that I shall greet the passing of this Bill with any particular outburst of ideological jubilation. Frankly, it runs counter to much that I have myself in the past deeply and sincerely believed. But I believe that now there is no longer any other way. This way is going to be uphill road, but the other ways lead only downhill, and I would rather, for myself, follow an uphill road with the chance of reaching the heights than a downhill road with the certainty of reaching the depths.

Lord Londonderry (Charles Stewart Henry Vane-Tempest-Stewart, 7th Marquess with a long roll of other titles including Viscount Castlereagh and Viscount Seaham), born 13 May 1878, educated at Eton and Royal Military College, Sandhurst, had been MP for Maidstone from 1906 until he succeeded his father in 1915. He had not only to look after the big family interests in the north of Ireland (Chancellor of Belfast University, HM Lieutenant Co. Down, Leader of the Senate – Government of Northern Ireland 1921–6 – and in Durham (Chancellor of Durham University, Lord Lieutenant of Co. Durham), but also had a hereditary interest as one of the

*Born 1884, and baptised Philip Lloyd Graeme, he assumed the name of Cunliffe-Lister at the age of 40, and finally was made 1st Viscount Swinton of Masham. His education was Winchester and University College, Oxford, and in 1908 he was called to the Bar. He sat in the House of Commons 1918–35 for the Hendon Division of Middlesex. He had been President of the Board of Trade 1922–3, 1924–9 and 1931; Secretary of State for the Colonies 1931–5; Secretary of State for Air 1935–8; Cabinet Minister resident in West Africa 1942–4; Minister for Civil Aviation 1944–5.

†Gerald Rufus Isaacs, 2nd Marquess of Reading, born 1889, educated at Rugby and Balliol, had been Chairman of the Central Valuation Board under the Coal Act of 1938 (and was soon to be chosen as Chairman of the Central Valuation Board and Panel of Arbitrators under the Coal Industry Nationalisation Act).

leading noblemen of the Conservative Party for which at the opening of each Parliament his metropolitan mansion, Londonderry House, had always been available, with the marchioness receiving the guests. As Secretary of State for Air 1931–5 he had defended the use of bombing aeroplanes to quell tribal risings in the North-West Frontier of India and in the Middle East.

But the noble marquess did not follow the example of his great-grandfather who opposed tooth-and-nail all such mines Bills. So far from seeking to reject the Bill, he would follow the lead of Lord Swinton in seeking to amend it.

There are very few families who have been closely associated with the coal industry for four generations as my family have been. I am sure that I may be allowed to say that I am proud of the experience of the Londonderry Collieries. That institution really dates from the beginning of 1828, when my great-grandfather made the harbour at Seaham and sank the pit at Seaham with no assistance whatsoever from anyone. My family has had no assistance – I am talking of the financial side – and I sank a pit in 1923, trying to follow the family tradition because as was natural I was deeply interested.

He drew a distinction between 'the socialist propaganda section' (the National Union of Mineworkers) and the miners themselves. That propaganda had brought 'continuous abuse of the owners personally'; but, he said: 'I am happy to think that in the Londonderry collieries, of which I have the honour to be the head, we have had a gratifying measure of loyalty and co-operation. We have had a lot of co-operation for generations. I must admit that I am told it does not exist everywhere else, but I do not believe that.'

Lord Lindsay of Birker, born 1879, educated at Glasgow University and University College, Oxford, from 1924 Master of Balliol and later Vice-Chancellor of Oxford University, before 1914 was one of the half-dozen academics in Britain known to hold socialist views. After translating Plato's *Republic* he wrote *Karl Marx's Capital* in 1925. But the Spanish Civil War of 1936–9 brought him into politics as a Popular Front candidate. So soon as C. R. Attlee took office, A. D. Lindsay was ennobled.

Lord Lindsay, after saying some kind words about the noble marquess, turned to the German-educated Professor

Lindemann whose hobnobbings with Prime Minister Churchill had brought him a peerage as Lord Cherwell of Oxford. Lord Cherwell a few days earlier had hinted that perhaps coal might be nationalised and, said Lord Lindsay:

. . . he ascribed that to the doings of agitators. I would pray such a very eminent scientist to apply the elementary principle of scientific induction to this problem. Why is it that agitators are so successful in coal and nothing like so successful in any other industry?
Lord Cherwell: Perhaps it is because the noble Lord himself appears to have visited the worst districts and spoken to the men there so often.
Lord Lindsay of Birker: That is a very nice and charming thing for the noble Lord, Lord Cherwell, to say. I might say that from other evidence, too, I am sure it was in existence long before I got there. I do not think that I am as good an agitator as all that.

This waspishness of the two old dons was not generally felt as a welcome addition to the atmosphere of the Upper Chamber. The next speaker, Viscount Stonehaven of Ury (born 1908, educated at Eton and the Royal School of Mines and succeeding to his father in 1941), was a civil engineer by profession. So naturally he made a number of technical comments on British mining.

Viscount Long of Wraxhall, born 1892, educated at Harrow, MP for the Westbury division of Wiltshire 1927–31, 'could not help but be impressed by the tribute which the noble Lord, Lord Lindsay, paid to my noble friend the Marquess of Londonderry'. He said: 'It brought back memories of a direct relation of mine, who was a pit-boy in Durham and who rose to be the great manager of collieries in the north, the late Sir George Elliott. I happened to be talking to my noble friend just now and he well remembered, somewhere in the eighties or the nineties, when this great pit-boy advocated the amalgamation of collieries.' Viscount Long was very sceptical indeed about the Bill, saying: 'The Bill creates a monopoly . . . In 1623 an Act was passed to abolish monopolies . . . yet, having had our freedom for over 300 years, we are, at this vital moment, granting once again vast monopoly, upon which I believe there can be no going back.'

The next speaker, Baron Balfour of Inchrye, born 1897, educated at Royal Naval College, Osborne, had sat in the

House of Commons for the Isle of Thanet 1929–45. Having held office (Parliamentary Under-Secretary of State for Air 1938–44; Minister resident in West Africa 1944–5), he was careful to state the fact that '. . . it is quite clear on all sides that the Government have got a mandate for this Bill. The Bill will not be challenged.'

At 5.51 the debate was adjourned and the House of Lords rose from their labours, which had occupied them fully for three hours and twenty-one minutes.

2. SECOND DAY IN THE LORDS

The next day (29 May 1946) the first speaker was Charles George Ammon (made Lord Ammon of Camberwell in 1944) who had spent twenty-four years in the post office service; had been Chairman of the London County Council; had held junior office in the Labour administrations of 1924 and 1929–31; and was now not only Captain of the Gentlemen-at-Arms but Government Chief Whip and Deputy Speaker of the House of Lords. Lord Ammon, author of *Christ and Labour*, had played a leading part in philanthropic and religious insitutions as President both of the Brotherhood Movement and of the Band of Hope. Lord Ammon set forth that there was instance after instance of opportunities missed, of the failure of the coal-owners to agree among themselves about amalgamation or other schemes of improvement of the industry. The strongest case for that had been made out by the Lord Londonderry, who gave the impression, 'like the Prophet Job, of a man rightfully conscious of his own integrity and his own goodness, who was puzzled and worried to know how these troubles had come upon him'.

He told us that he himself had approached his fellow coal-owners as far back as twenty years ago with the suggestion that they should co-operate in schemes of amalgamation, but that he was cold-shouldered and lost heart. He and his friends had to give up their proposed scheme and were unable to carry it forward. That is the reason, I venture to say, why no other Government would be able to take any better step to give a fair chance of getting the industry on the right lines than the step which has been taken.

Christopher John Henry Roper-Curzon, 19th Baron Teynham, born 1896, Captain RN (retired), would have preferred rationalisation to nationalisation: he too doubted 'that this Bill will improve the conditions of the industry, the welfare of the miners, or, what is more important, produce more coal'. He concluded that the industry would be 'slowly strangled by bureaucratic control'.

Francis James Rennell Rodd, 2nd Baron Rennell of Rodd, born 1895, educated at Eton and Balliol, in 1941 succeeded his father, who had helped in 1925 to form the strike-breaking body called the OMS for the purpose of defeating any attempt of transport and other workers to rally to the side of the mineworkers. Lord Rennell, a merchant banker, found very satisfactory two principles 'established in the Bill': 'The first is that the compensation value payable is payable on the enterprise of the colliery as a running concern.' The second cause for satisfaction was that 'compensation is payable in compensation stock, which is a charge on the Consolidation Fund'.

John Percival Davies, born 1885, educated at Sidcot, Bootham and Manchester, was, like the famous Frederick Engels, a cotton manufacturer with socialist views. Seven times he entered parliamentary contests as a Labour candidate; seven times he was defeated. Such a stalwart partisan seemed to Prime Minister Attlee to deserve recognition; and J. P. Davies that same year, 1946, had been raised to the peerage as Lord Darwen of Heys-in-Bowland. He said that there was no doubt that a great national asset of coal had not only been 'wastefully used' but 'wastefully exploited', and that only by the unification of the industry was it possible to save that waste. Commission after commission, inquiry after inquiry, all recommended some form of unification. He then referred to the effect he hoped it would have upon the conditions of life of the miner: he pointed out that the tendency had always been to govern the miner's wage by what the poorest mine could pay. In every mine there were three periods – the period of the sinking of the shaft, the period of maximum efficiency and the period of deteriorating returns. The miner's wage had largely been governed by what the poorest seams could pay in the period of decreasing returns. National owner-

ship would make it possible to level out the whole pro-
ductiveness of the industry so that a proper wage could be
paid to the miners throughout the industry.

Lord Hutchison of Montrose, born 1873, attained the rank
of major-general before he entered politics and banking. He
had been National Liberal MP for Kirkcaldy 1922–3; Liberal
MP for Montrose 1924–31; and then Liberal National 1931–2.
In the House of Commons he had been Liberal Chief
Whip from 1926 to 1930. In the House of Lords (his title was
created in 1932) he, after a time, held office as Paymaster-
General, 1935–8. He was Treasurer of the Liberal National
Organisation. He began by saying: 'My Lords, I would like
to introduce my remarks by pointing out that I am interested
in coal through the Fife Coal Company, and I speak as an
interested man. The Fife Coal Company produced Sir Charles
Reid. He was with us all his life in the mines, and was
our chief engineer. All who are interested in coal have read
the Reid Report. His son Dr Reid is now our chief engineer . . .'
His speech ended with these words:

Many of us on this side of the House do not like this Bill. Personally I
hate it. It was a great wrench to have one's interests taken away from one –
interests which were not only one's own interests but one's father's.
That is much more so in the case of the noble Marquess, Lord Londonderry,
than in my own case. It is a great wrench to be taken away from all
that and away from the men you have known all your life. However, I
wish you well and I hope that the scheme will be a success. May I
say that if we owners can help you by consultation or in any other way
we are at your beck and call whenever you want us?

Viscount Ridley (Matthew White Ridley) born 1903, educated at Eton, owned about 10,200 acres in Northumberland,
of whose county council he was Chairman. He felt that it was a
Bill which 'mostly due to past history, has become inevitable';
but he was troubled about how it would work, and in particular
about the closing of pits, which was 'bound to lead to a great
deal of dissatisfaction and unhappiness'.

Lt-Col Charles Ian Kerr,* created Lord Teviot in 1940, had
been Chairman since that year of the Liberal National Party.

*Born 1874, MP for Montrose Burghs 1932–40, Chief Whip of his party 1937–9 and
Controller of HM Household 1939–40.

'I am aware from personal experience of the dangers of mining, and I have always had since those days when I was an actual practical miner, a great feeling of affection for all those who work underground.'

Lord Teviot was very critical of 'the experiment', which he hoped would not prove a failure.

The next speaker was a famous figure, 'Evans of the Broke', who like Nansen and Shackleton earlier had for a couple of generations been an idol of schoolchildren for his prowess, as well, of course, as being the recipient of multitudinous honours from many societies and governments. Admiral Edward Ratcliffe Garth Russell Evans, born 1881, had been entered for the navy at an early age, and had become a sub-lieutenant in 1900. The peaks of his career were Antarctic exploration (he was second in command of the British Antarctic Expedition at the age of 28 and commanded and brought back the expedition after the death of Captain Scott in 1913) and naval actions in the 1914–18 War. He commanded HMS *Broke* in 1917 when that ship with HMS *Swift* engaged and defeated six German destroyers. Thereafter he had been Commander-in-Chief of the Royal Australia Navy 1929–31, on the Africa station 1933–5 and at the Nore 1935–9. He was the London Regional Commissioner for Civil Defence throughout the six years of the war. Now in the Upper House, which he had entered as Lord Mountevans of Chelsea in 1945, he supported the Bill in a vigorous speech:

My Lords, because I come from mining stock in the Rhondda – not very profitable – and later have been connected with Lancashire, I have always taken a lively interest in the miner. I am proud to count among my friends Will Lawther, who has just presented the Miners' Charter, Jack Lawson, Ebby Edwards, the late Herbert Smith of Barnsley, Arthur Horner and Joe Hall.

The admiral told how he had visited the coalfields during the critical months of the war, and declared that victory quite largely had depended upon coal output between June and September 1941. 'A race against time', he had told the miners:

I remember likening their dangerous work to that of the Merchant Service, particularly the firemen, and I asked them to sink their

differences with managements and with their unions for the sake of democratic freedom. I told them that it did not matter whether they were
Communists or Conservatives, adding that I was neither. What I said in
the course of my many addresses was that one day soldiers and sailors
and airmen would be able to tell the miners that their help had saved
the nation. That, my Lords, is the truth.

He had learned a lot through the production 'blitz' in the
mines, and had brought to the attention of Lord Woolton,
as Minister of Food, that their supplies of food at work
should be adequate:

I pointed out that the munitions industries had unfair advantages over
the mineworkers, in being better paid and better fed – the latter advantage due perhaps to canteens. But I also pointed out to him that
bureaucracy had been partly responsible for delays in coal distribution,
for miners know, as well as I do, how bureaucracy has thwarted
them. As recently as February this year members of the Women's
Royal Naval Service in this country were getting better meat and sugar
rations than the miners.

Then he dealt with the strike troubles of two years earlier,
which he said had been precipitated by a 'Government mistake
– not this Government's mistake, but the late Government's
mistake, one of the most ghastly mistakes ever made'. He
recalled that after owners and miners had agreed that certain
allowances should be made, the Mines Department had told
the miners' leaders it could not be allowed. He added: 'All
this is remembered by the miners, as well as all the sarcasm,
and the calling of the miners "traitors" when they went on
strike. We should remember what we owe to the miners.'

Lord Llewellin* did not think much of the Bill: he fore-
saw many dangers and he ended by saying: 'Although we do
not like it, we wish it well.'

The Minister of Civil Aviation (Lord Winster of Wither-
slack) spoke next. Reginald Thomas Herbert Fletcher, soon to
be made Governor of Cyprus, born 1885, sat in 1924 as

---

*John Jestyn Llewellin, born 1893, educated at Eton and University College, Oxford, was
called to the Bar in 1921. He sat for the Uxbridge division of Middlesex 1929–45, held
junior office continuously from 1931 to 1942 and then senior office in a rapid series of posts
ending as Minister of Food 1943–5. He was created Baron Llewellin of Upton in 1945.

Liberal MP for Basingstoke (Hampshire). By 1929 he had joined the Labour Party. He was MP for Nuneaton (Warwickshire) 1935–41. In 1942 he was ennobled and in 1945 became Minister of Civil Aviation. Winding up the Second Reading debate for the government, Lord Winster deprecated the language of Lord Llewellin complaining that 'the noble Lord said that the Board would "pup". I suggest that "proliferate" is rather a pleasanter word than "pup"?'

After Lord Winster's speech, the Bill was then read a second time and 'committed to a Committee of the whole House'.

3. THE BILL IN COMMITTEE

Three weeks after the Second Reading had passed through the House of Lords without a division, the Lord Chancellor moved 'That the House do now resolve itself into Committee'. The chair was taken by the Earl of Drogheda.*

An amendment to Clause 1, stressing the importance of the export trade in coal 'not mentioned in the Bill at all', was moved by Lord Teynham.

The Lord Chancellor (Lord Jowitt) said that 'I find myself in agreement with the noble Lord's observations' on the importance of the export trade, but disagreed with the proposed wording of the amendment; the amendment was, by leave, withdrawn. But the next amendment to the first clause of the Bill was pushed to a division. It laid down the duty of the Board to make supplies available 'in such quantities and at such prices as may seem to them best calculated to further the public interest'. To this Viscount Swinton moved that the following words should be added: 'without giving any undue or unreasonable preference or advantage to or in favour of any particular person or company or any particular class of trade, business, manufacture or industry.'

Claiming that it would 'provide a safeguard for the consumer

---

*Charles Ponsonby Moore, 10th Earl of Drogheda, born 1884, educated at Eton and Trinity College, Cambridge, served in the Foreign Office from 1907 to 1918, then in the Irish Guards, had in the second war been 1940–5 in the Ministry of Economic Warfare, latterly becoming its director-general.

– industrial, domestic or whoever he may be', Lord Swinton said it was the sort of safeguard which Parliament had always insisted upon whenever a monopoly of a substantial kind was being created.

He was supported by Lord Maugham* who said: 'I do not think that anybody, until the advent to power of this Government, has ever thought it could be right to give to a monopolistic body designed for the production of something absolutely necessary, both for industrial and domestic purposes, the right to discriminate as between the people to whom the goods produced are to be sold.'

The Lord Chancellor in reply said that the practice of the coal industry before the war had been to differentiate according to the use to which the coal was to be put:

There was and there has been for years one rate for domestic consumers, another rate for railways, another rate if the coal was to be used by the steel industry or according to whether it was to be sent by rail, by road or by ship, coastwise or shipped for export. All those matters have in the past been the practice of the coal industry.

I am not saying it is desirable that those practices should go on; that is obviously a matter which the Coal Board themselves ought to determine as a matter of high policy and not as a result of a more or less casual decision by putting words into this clause which sets out their function . . .

I cannot accept this amendment, though I will draft something between now and the Report stage.

This 'something', he indicated, would remove all fears of dishonest practices. Lord Swinton said that he could not accept this 'very limited offer' and must press his amendment.

The Earl of Perth,† a representative peer of Scotland

---

*Frederick Herbert, first Viscount Maugham of Hartsfield, born in 1866, educated at Dover College and Trinity Hall, Cambridge, a barrister of Lincoln's Inn in 1890, a Chancery Judge in 1928, a Lord Justice of Appeal in 1934, a Lord of Appeal in Ordinary (with a life peerage) 1935–41, was 1938–9 Lord Chancellor: he was elder brother of the dramatic writer and novelist Somerset Maugham.

†James Eric Drummond, born 1876, educated at Eton, served in the Foreign Office (often as private secretary to successive ministers). From 1919 to 1933 was Secretary-General of the League of Nations (created in the Treaty of Versailles 1919) and British Ambassador to Italy 1933–9. He succeeded his half-brother in 1937 becoming 16th Earl of Perth and 12th Viscount Strathallan. He was also Baron Drummond (1686); Lord Drummond of Gilston (1685); Lord Drummond of Rickleton and Castlemaine (1686); Hereditary Thane of Lennox and Hereditary Steward of Menteith and Strathearn.

since 1941, and from 1946 Deputy Leader of the Liberal Party, said:

My original intention was to support the amendment which has been moved because in my view it afforded a safeguard against an undue encroachment by the State on what I may call the inherent right of the individual. That is a good Liberal principle which I fully support. But I do feel, having received the Lord Chancellor's assurance, that I no longer wish to support the amendment.

Their Lordships divided: Contents, 54; Not-Contents, 28.

The division thus insisted upon and carried by Tory peers against Labour and Liberal votes may be easily recognised. It was the parliamentary process known as 'showing their teeth'. But it must be said that, teeth thus once shown, there were no further divisions called during the three long summer afternoons that the House of Lords sat in Committee upon the Coal Industry Nationalisation Bill.

The next amendment moved came from the Labour side, from one who had been a member of the Fabian Society since 1917, Baron Marley of Marley in Sussex.* Lord Marley brought forward an amendment to add to the duties of the National Coal Board participation (with a levy of up to 6d per ton) in scientific research both in the getting and treatment of coal and also in safety and health of mineworkers.

He was supported by Lord Barnby. †

The Minister of Civil Aviation, Lord Winster, thanked the mover and seconder of the amendment, which, however, being 'somewhat inappropriate in its form and meaning', the government could not accept. The amendment was, by leave, withdrawn.

---

*Dudley Leigh Aman, born 1884, educated at Marlborough and at Greenwich Royal Naval College, entered the Royal Marine Artillery in 1902. 'He retired from Service at his own request in 1920 to devote himself to service with the Labour Party.' Between 1922 and 1929 he five times contested very difficult seats such as Petersfield, Thanet and Faversham. Undaunted, he went up against these Tory strongholds in south-east England but without success. So he was given a barony in 1930 and the same year was made Lord-in-Waiting to the king and finally for a few months Under-Secretary of State for War.

†Francis Vernon Willey, 2nd Baron Barnby, born 1884, educated at Eton and Magdalen College, Oxford, served in the 1914–18 War as Colonel of the Sherwood Rangers before he was made Controller of Wool Supplies in 1916. From 1918 to 1922 he had been Member for South Bradford and from 1919 to 1933 Master of Fox Hounds of the Blankney Hunt in Lincolnshire.

4. LORD CECIL'S AMENDMENT

Now came one of these curious examples of the working of the British parliamentary system by which the normal machine-like precision grinding and cutting of the two-party system is from time to time thrown temporarily out of gear. The reduction of the status of Members of Parliament to cogs in the machine of the two-party system was a process which had gone on for several generations ever since Sir Robert Peel a century earlier had split the Tory Party on the issue of protection versus free trade. With each passing decade it became more and more difficult for any Member to assert himself or the interests of his constituents or of the people generally against the intensifying pressure of the party machine. A Member of either House of Parliament must have not only much prestige of achievement or position but also strong convictions matched with a fearless disposition before he could effectively break through the ordinary processes and patterns of this two-party tradition. Thus, more than once, as in the case of Lord Henry Bentinck in the 1910–18 Parliament, it was someone with the prestige attaching in Britain to aristocratic position who could intervene. On this occasion it was Viscount Cecil of Chelwood who rose to move, as an amendment to Clause 1 of the Bill, that the Board should have the duty to secure 'the recognition of the right of those employed in any mine to be consulted as to its working'. This proposal, as the saying is, put the cat amongst the pigeons; Viscount Cecil of Chelwood, better known for long in many capacities as Lord Robert Cecil, was now in his eighty-second year. In addition to his own experiences, he belonged to what was probably the most political family of the British land-owning class; for the Cecils had first come into political prominence as servants of the Tudor monarchs, King Henry VIII and his daughter Elizabeth, 400 years ago.

Edgar Algernon Robert Cecil was the third son of the third Marquess of Salisbury, thrice Prime Minister in the late nineteenth century, to whom he had for a time been private secretary. After Eton and University College, Oxford, and a distinguished career at the Bar (Inner Temple), he had entered Parliament in 1906. He became a foremost debater for the Conservative Party, held a series of offices in the coalition governments of the First World War and then in the Conservative administrations from 1923 to 1927. He was a member of the Cabinet in 1927 and a keen partisan of disarmament. When the Tripartite Naval Conference of Britain, Japan and the USA collapsed at Geneva in complete and utter failure in August 1927, Lord Robert Cecil as he then was immediately resigned from that Conservative Cabinet whose part responsibility for the breakdown he had the best means of knowing. Thereafter he devoted himself to works of peace; recognised by the gift in 1937 of the Nobel Peace Prize. From 1923 to 1945 he was Honorary President of the League of Nations Union and thereafter was made Life President of the United Nations' Association. But Lord Cecil's zeal for the prevention of war and the establishment of a lasting peace went far beyond that of the other holders of these somewhat dubious marks of recognition. He knew the limitations too of the semi-official bodies of which he was president: and he knew the Foreign Office from within and was aware of what a former Leader of the Labour Party had called its 'queer subversive mentality'. So he gave his support freely to every unofficial body that fought for peace, without consideration of previous party allegiance. For him, as for few others, peace came far before party. These associations of his later life had brought him second thoughts on many questions, including that of control of industry. Hence his amendment.

It had not been proposed to make any changes in the principles of employment, and no right was given to the workers to be consulted about the management, 'or even to be told about its prospects', he pointed out.

Their position will remain as the sellers of their labour to their employers who will in future be the State and not private individuals, and when they have received their wages the transaction, so far as they are concerned, will be complete.

No doubt the Coal Board will be answerable for its conduct of the industry to Parliament, and Parliament will be responsible to the electors. So far as the miners are electors, they will have that satisfaction, but that cannot extend of course – nobody pretends in all the discussions I

The National Coal Board 1946 in session at Whitehall. Left to right: Professor Sir Charles Ellis, T. E. B. Young, Ebby Edwards, Sir Arthur Street (Deputy-Chairman), Lord Hyndley (Chairman), Sir Walter Citrine, Sir Charles Reid, L. H. H. Lowe and J. C. Gridley

Map showing NCB Divisions

have heard on this Bill that it can extend – to what I may call the details of the management in each pit. Moreover, so far as the control exists – control by the electors that is – it will obviously have to be shared by all the other electors, so that the miners will have no special rights in the matter.

He was not opposed to the Bill, but he had doubts as to whether by itself it would achieve all that was expected, which was why he had put down the amendment.

In the debate on the Second Reading Lord Cecil had been 'struck with the unanimity' of all speakers about 'the cause of the present difficulties in the industry' – the 'appalling absence of goodwill', the 'bitterness', the 'complete barrier between the capitalist employer and the manual worker'. He said:

In such a state of things, the wonder is that the industry has gone on as well as it has gone on. But even so, in the fifty or sixty years – I am sorry I have to put it in that way – of my public life, I cannot remember any prolonged period when unrest in the coalfields was not a matter of anxiety to every Government in turn, and it was not altogether assuaged by the tremendous danger of two world wars. I venture to remind your Lordships of this (and I am only, of course, saying what all of you know quite well) because it seems to me the really urgent problem that we have to solve in this matter.

He could not believe that buying out the coal-owners would prove a complete remedy: 'I cannot help feeling that the fundamental difficulty is that the miner feels himself powerless to correct evils of which he is the conscious victim, and therefore, not unnaturally, rejects all responsibility for the consequences.'

The Marquess of Londonderry, also formerly a member of Conservative Cabinets, and himself perhaps more responsible in the public eye than any other for the breakdown of disarmament conferences, at once rose to challenge some of the remarks of Lord Cecil, claiming that it was 'apparent', that he had 'not made a very close personal study of a mining district'.

But now backing came from the Lord Archbishop of York, saying: 'Mechanisation no doubt has brought very great advantages to the country, but in a large number of cases it has meant that the worker has lost a great deal of initiative and responsibility. The man who gives his life to any industry is anxious to feel that he has some real active part in it. He does not claim that the men should decide the technical matters.'

Dr Garbett may have been, probably was, unaware that his statement repeated in almost the same words a famous sentence in Marx's *Capital*, written eighty years earlier. He ended his brief speech with the plea: 'Therefore let the Government make it quite plain that this consultation is going to be regarded as the principle.'

Then Lord Cranborne spoke very briefly 'to support what has been said by my noble relative Lord Cecil in the eloquent speech he has just made'. The labourer would be equally unhappy if employed by 'a far more remote employer, the State'. What he wanted was to feel that 'in some manner' he was employing himself, getting 'a fair share of the rewards of his labour', and knowing all that was happening – so far as anyone could – in his industry.

Lord Strabolgi, an ex-naval officer, took a different view, saying:

Where you have an industry, nationalised or privately owned, you must have that sometimes unpopular word 'discipline'. If you lay down as a condition that the management in the mines must consult the miners as to the working of the mines, that is on highly technical matters affecting their own and everyone else's safety, then you are suggesting something that may be dangerous and even mischievous. Therefore, I say that these words in this Amendment are most unfortunate.

The way to restore good relations between managements and pitmen would be to 'have a wide and easy avenue or ladder of promotion for the miner's well-educated young son to get his technical qualifications and rise to the highest position on his merits' (18 June 1946).

Lord Elibank for the Liberal Party was 'very largely in agreement with the noble Lord who has just sat down'.

But the Lord Chancellor was as suave as could be. He suggested that Clause 1 was the wrong place for such an amendment which could be better considered under Clause 43; and when it came to that he would with the collaboration of Lord Cecil try to find some words to express their feelings. Lord Cecil agreed.

Clause 1 as amended was then agreed to after two hours and forty-five minutes of discussion. There were sixty more clauses to be discussed. But the Lords managed to get through them all in the next two days. The Bill had passed through Committee.

5. REPORT STAGE IN THE LORDS

A fortnight later, on Tuesday 2 July, the Coal Industry Nationalisation Bill entered the Report stage. After amendments had been reported, then on Clause 1 *(Establishment of National Coal Board and functions thereof)* the Lord Chancellor moved an amendment in subsection 1(c) to take the place of the words which had been inserted in Committee against the wishes of the government by other words which would meet their Lordships' wishes on the 'avoidance of any undue or unreasonable preference or advantage' by the NCB in their duty of 'making supplies of coal available'. Honours were even: the Lords had divided against the government; the Lords now graciously accepted without a division the government's rewording of the amendment. All this took a quarter of an hour.

The next business was still on Clause 1. The Lord Chancellor moved an amendment which he said was intended to give effect to Viscount Cecil's proposal for giving workers the right to be consulted about the management of the industry. The wording of the amendment, in subsection 4 to Clause 1, was that the Board should avail themselves of '(b) the benefit of the practical knowledge and experience of such persons in the organisation and conduct of the activities in which they are employed'. In doing so, he expressed at some length his feeling that the House was 'indebted to the noble Viscount, Lord Cecil of Chelwood, for raising this matter'. He said that he had 'found myself on reflection, as I very often do, coming to the conclusion that he was right and that I was wrong'. He concluded his praise in these words: 'In principle I entirely agree, as I said on the last occasion, with what the noble Lord then said. I think the most important and most difficult task that this new Coal Board will have will be to get these relationships right.'

It was just before three o'clock that he proposed the new paragraph. Lord Cecil replied that he was 'honestly extremely grateful to the noble and learned Lord for the great trouble he has taken and for the great effort he has made to deal with the point I raised'. He hoped, therefore, that the Lord Chancellor would 'not mind if I venture to make one or two verbal criticisms'. Then Lord Cecil, after stating his preference for the word 'operations' over the word 'activities', said:

There is one other point in which he does disagree and always has disagreed with me. I quite recognise that he does not like to say that these men shall have a right which is to be recognised. I quite realise that there is a disagreement of that kind, but I am not much afraid of it.

If you say to a man, 'You have got a right to do these things; we are going to recognise it, and you must show you are worthy of the exercise of that right', I cannot help thinking that that is the kind of way you will get at their minds better than you will if you say, 'We are anxious to see what you have got to say from that point of view'.

He did not want to stress the question of right, if it were thought to be going too far. But he could not believe it would shock a Labour Government as a whole: 'On the other question, of activities and operations, I do very earnestly ask him to say whether he cannot move one step further in my direction.' After the Lord Chancellor said he would see what the parliamentary draftsman would think about the last point, the amendment was agreed to. Clause 1 had passed the Report stage.

It took between three and four hours for the sixty other clauses.

That same day, after what was for them a late sitting (they did not rise until nearly seven o'clock), the Lords dealt with all the other clauses and schedules and so finished the Report stage. In the main the suavity of the Lord Chancellor was potent with their lordships. But there was still a clash to come over an amendment to enlarge, not the amount, but the scope, of compensation for former owners; finally the amendment was not pressed, though it received support from the veteran Liberal Leader, Lord Samuel. Earlier the leaders of the Tory Party in the Lords had made clear their reluctance to force amendments into the Bill by divisions on a proposal that, in nominating for the two consumers' councils, the minister should consult bodies representative of various interests. Viscount Cranborne said: 'I believe that this is an eminently democratic proposal. I should have thought that this would have appealed to noble Lords opposite. Indeed, I thought we had won our point on Committee stage. I am sure I never heard such a sympathetic reception given to any other Amendment as was given by the noble and learned Lord, the Lord Chancellor.'

Then there occurred a passage which, if it could not be described as the cut and thrust habitual amongst commoners, nevertheless represented gentlemanly gibes at the Lord Chancellor's earlier changes in allegiance, although not going so far as to trouble the depths:

I have a faint suspicion that the noble and learned Lord is perhaps rather more sympathetic to the proposal than is the Minister. I do not know whether that is so. The noble and learned Lord, the Lord Chancellor, has an admirable Liberal past. The Minister, so far as I know, has not. It may be a reversion to his earlier views—
Lord Strabolgi: Admirable, or Liberal?
Viscount Cranborne: He has both, I am sure. At any rate, I do regard this as what may be called a Liberal proposal. I do not want to press the Amendment to a Division – we do not wish to press any Amendments to a Division if it can be avoided – but unless the Government are prepared to modify their view, I am afraid we have no option.
The Secretary of State for Dominion Affairs [Viscount Addison]: My Lords, we desire to be accommodating. Perhaps the noble Lord will let us report the discussion again to the Minister and we will consider whether on Third Reading we cannot meet the point. (2 July 1946)

Yet at the very end a breeze had blown up suddenly. Lord Winster, who had much the same capacity for ruffling their Lordships' feelings as the Lord Chancellor had for soothing them, put forward a government amendment to Clause 31 about the form of the Board's annual accounts. There was an hour's discussion before 'their Lordships divided: Contents 55, Not-Contents 158 and the Amendment was disagreed to accordingly'.

6. THIRD READING IN THE LORDS

'My Lords, I beg to move that this Bill be now read a third time,' began Lord Jowitt. After four minutes of mutual compliments, the Lord Chancellor thanking their Lordships for their collaboration and the spokesmen of the Tory and Liberal parties thanking the Lord Chancellor (for his 'fullest collaboration', for being 'throughout a model of reasonableness and conciliation'), the Bill was read a third time, with the amendments. Then the Lord Chancellor moved the Amendment on consultation, gracefully substituting the word 'operations' for 'activities'. In doing so, he said: 'My Lords, the noble Viscount, Lord Cecil of Chelwood, has told me that he is unable to be present to-day, but he has expressed his gratitude for this Amendment, and I am very glad to be able to meet the wishes of one for whose judgment all quarters of the House have a profound regard' (4 July 1946). Thus Clause 1 reached its final form in the House of Lords, after this much disputation over the niceties of meaning of these two words that the English tongue had borrowed from a French or rather a Latin source.

All was now plain sailing. It seemed the Bill would go through in less than half an hour. But there came a little snag or obstacle which the Lord Chancellor, moving an amendment to Clause 31 *(Board's accounts and audit thereof)*, had himself placed in the fairway of the Bill's progress. He said: 'My Lords, here I must reveal another of my faults.' In drafting the amendment he had not noticed that he had left out the words 'in conformity with the best commercial standards'. This caused some consternation; for it appeared that their Standing Orders made it impossible to move a handwritten amendment to an amendment. The Lord Chancellor had hit upon the solution: they should now duly pass the wording which all knew to be wrong, and get it put right 'when this Bill goes back to another place'. He went on to explain that in the House of Commons all would be put right: 'When the Chancellor of the Exchequer reads my remark (if he does me the honour of reading my remarks) that this is a mere mistake for which I am responsible, I cannot think there will be the slightest difficulty in his inserting these words again which, as I say, he did authorise me to insert at an earlier stage.'

This statement caused a certain amount of constitutional surprise amongst their Lordships. The Tory spokesman, Viscount Swinton, began: 'My Lords, I am glad we can end on so cheerful and harmonious a note,' and concluded: 'I thought we could do anything in this House, but I have now discovered there is one thing we cannot do: we cannot, on Third Reading, do what we would all like to do, which no doubt is a very wise restraint upon our natural and even rational desires.' The ripples caused by the point of order from 'the noble and learned Lord on the Woolsack' did not die down immediately. They gave occasion for the Marquess of Salisbury to plunge into an explanation of parliamentary procedure in the Upper House which swelled into a eulogy of that body. Lord Salisbury said: 'My Lords, perhaps your Lordships will allow me to say one word upon the point of order which has arisen with regard to this Amendment. I share with my noble friend who has just sat down the feeling of reluctance which we all have when we think we could put a thing right but find we are not allowed to do it. If only there could be a little concession made to enable us to use our judgment, then why should we not do it?'

But many years of experience had made it a settled practice not to insert an amendment on the Third Reading, without its being circulated, and with full notice. He then expatiated upon the merits of the practice:

After all it is a wonderful thing that our Bills get through Parliament in any shape which a reasonable man can understand. They are the subject of frightful struggles in both Houses of Parliament – perhaps not a violent struggle in your Lordships' House, but sometimes a violent struggle in another place. Every sort of Amendment is inserted, some of them with notice, some of them without notice, some for a good reason and some for a very bad reason. They come to your Lordships' House to be discussed. We take a lot of trouble about them, and we have built up a number of safeguards in order that, if possible, the Bill should ultimately emerge as an Act of Parliament in a reasonable and proper form.

After continuing in this strain at some length, he began to draw to a conclusion: 'I am a very senior member of the

House and I have, in my recollection, known struggles over this subject before, but this practice is what has emerged after the struggle, and we have affirmed it.'

'I am a very senior member of the House' – the claim was certainly warranted in the case of James Edward Hubert Gascoyne-Cecil, now in his eighty-fifth year. He had been a Member of Parliament for over sixty years; first in the Commons, where he sat every year from 1885 to 1903; and then, on the death of his father, in the Lords which he led from 1925 to 1929. He had held office in Tory governments, first from 1900 to 1905, including the Presidency of the Board of Trade, and then from 1922 to 1929, including the office of Lord President of the Council. He had not the scope of his father, the Marquess who was thrice Prime Minister; nor had he ever shone in debate like his younger brothers Lord Hugh and Lord Robert or like his Prime Minister cousin Earl Balfour; but he had an extremely high opinion of the House of Lords, which he believed was shared by king and Commons. He said:

Is it not wonderful how we manage things in the House of Lords? We have nobody to control us; we are masters of our own procedure and of our own order. And in this connection we carry out our duties, I think, very appropriately, and I believe to the great admiration of all who observe us. It is accordingly an immense responsibility that lies upon us not to make mistakes by ignoring the teachings of experience in our procedure. Therefore, I felt very glad when I heard the Lord Chancellor explain that he could not alter his amendment without notice.

No doubt this will be put right in the House of Commons, but I thought your Lordships would forgive me if I said one word to show why it was an important matter.

The House of Lords, having shown some animation in vindicating its venerable practice, accepted an amendment consequential to the last alteration in Clause 1, and the Lord Chancellor was finally able to say: 'My Lords, I beg to move that the Bill do now pass.' On Question, the Bill was passed, with the amendments, and returned to the Commons.

The Bill to nationalise the coal industry was over the hurdle of the Lords, with a large number of considerable amendments.

7. BACK IN THE COMMONS

The legislative process can speed up towards the end of a Bill's passage through Parliament. As soon as the Bill had been amended and read a third time in the Lords, it was back in the Commons, where the Minister of Fuel and Power proposed 'That the Lords' Amendments be now considered' and intimated that acceptance of them was desirable. Captain Crookshank, main spokesman for the Tory benches, said: 'Here we are with 15 pages of amendments, and if it is not unprecedented,* it must be years since we had such an enormous number of Amendments sent down from another place. For that, the Government ought to be exceedingly grateful' (10 July 1946). He claimed that Tory arguments had now 'come back to us in the form of Government Amendments introduced in another place'. Then came the first Lords'· Amendment to Clause 1 *(Establishment of National Coal Board and functions thereof)*, referring to avoiding 'undue or unreasonable preference' for one type of consumer over another. Shinwell moved: 'That this House doth agree with the Lords in the said Amendment.' Harold Macmillan rose to improve the occasion:

This question of discrimination was one of the major issues discussed and debated at length in Committee, and, at every point, the Right Hon. Gentleman, in varying moods, sometimes, with his well-known light humour, and, sometimes, in his more bitter and sarcastic manner, resisted every attempt of my Hon. Friends and myself to introduce this conception that there should not be discrimination between similar classes of users.

Fortunately, what we were unable to achieve has been achieved in another place.

Whether from natural traditionalism, which is part of the old Labour movement, or from greater deference to another place, those words which, when they came from common mouths, fell despised, were when they came from noble lips, gladly received.

After these jeering remarks and some consequent reflections on the work of the Second Chamber, usually referred to as

---

*It was, however, by no means unprecedented, as was stated an hour later by Mr Bowles, the Member for Nuneaton, who instanced a recent Conservative Bill which came back from the Lords with twenty-five pages of amendments.

'another place', Shinwell introduced the amendment framed to meet Lord Cecil's request, about the Board using the 'benefit of the practical knowledge and experience of such persons in the organisation and conduct of the operations in which they are employed'. After once more moving 'That this House doth agree with the Lords', Shinwell explained the government's attitude to it:

It was represented to us that, although the Board was empowered to seek the establishment of joint machinery for the purposes of considering terms and conditions of employment, and, indeed, all matters pertaining to the welfare of the industry, further consultation might be necessary on the organisation and conduct of the Board's operations, and that individuals might be brought in.

The minister, in this a faithful follower of Herbert Morrison, did not conceal his lack of enthusiasm for the amendment.

It is not very easy to see how this would be possible administratively, but, at any rate, it is worth a trial. It is very desirable that the fullest measure of co-operation and collaboration should emerge and, therefore, we have accepted this proposal.

Thereupon Harold Macmillan welcomed the amendment, as 'of considerable importance' and said:

Under pressure from the Opposition, there was introduced at a late stage in the Committee, a Clause dealing with conciliation in general, and the setting up of appropriate machinery for the consultation of those engaged in the industry.

It was a curious and, indeed, remarkable omission from one of the first great nationalising Bills, that from start to finish not the slightest reference was made to the people engaged in operating the pits. I have studied with some care the Debates on this Clause in another place, and I think we are indebted to a very respected figure in our national life, Lord Cecil of Chelwood, who first raised this question.

Thereafter all the other amendments were dealt with and the debate ended, as in the Lords, with mutual compliments between Harold Macmillan and Emanuel Shinwell.

One week later the Bill went back again to the Lords to consider the amendment duly made by the Commons to correct the Lord Chancellor's drafting lapse which the machinery of the Upper House had been powerless to adjust. So it was recorded:

'Moved, That this House doth agree with the Commons in the said Amendment. *(The Lord Chancellor)*

On Question, Motion agreed to. (House of Lords *Hansard*, Vol. 142, 11 July 1946)

All was now put right, and the last stage had been reached. So on the next day, Friday 12 July, 'the House met at eleven of the clock. The Lord Chancellor on the Woolsack'. Two Bills were introduced on first reading: and then the House 'adjourned during pleasure'. When the House resumed a Royal Commission announced that a baker's dozen of Bills (including that on Coal Industry Nationalisation) had received the Royal Assent.

The Bill had become an Act of Parliament. Coal Industry Nationalisation had become the law of the land.

CHAPTER VII

THE END OF PRIVATE OWNERSHIP

I. THE NEW EMPLOYER

With the nationalising Act of Parliament passed on 12 July 1946, there began the full-scale preparation for taking over the industry. There had been many changes of ownership in the seven centuries of coal mining in Great Britain, but this was the biggest change of all. It was the prelude to a most thorough-going if not a final transformation of the industry itself. Instead of 800 or more separate colliery companies, with their directors running into several thousand, there were now nine men in whom all or nearly all was to be vested. These nine would have under them other men and other committees organised in areas and divisions: but the full responsibility rested on nine men alone.

As appointed by the Minister of Fuel and Power on 15 July 1946, the members of the Board were:

Lord Hyndley, Chairman
Sir Arthur Street, Deputy Chairman
Lord Citrine, Manpower and Welfare Member
Mr Ebby Edwards, Labour Relations Member
Sir Charles Ellis, Scientific Member
Mr J. C. Gridley, Marketing Member
Mr L. H. H. Lowe, Finance Member
Sir Charles Reid, Production Member
Mr T. E. B. Young, Production Member

Of the six executive departments in the charge of Board members, two were thus held by men well known to every trade unionist in the industry: the Secretary for twenty years of the Trades Union Congress, embracing over 9 million organised workers; and the first Secretary of the National Union of Mineworkers, who had before that been Secretary of the Miners' Federation of Great Britain for a longer period than any other since the 1914–18 War. Ebby Edwards had been very reluctant, thrice telegraphing 'NO' to the urgent request of the Minister of Fuel and Power. Ebby Edwards, indeed, had been 'conscripted' for the post by a decision of the NUM Executive Committee in February 1946, in response to an appeal from the government.

Under the National Board the coalfields were grouped into eight divisions, each with its divisional board, and forty-eight areas, each with its area committee. The six departments of the NCB were represented at divisional and area headquarters. For this alone there were therefore several hundred new posts to be filled: and in their first report the Board stated: 'In making appointments to the Divisional Boards the National Coal Board were able to draw on the assistance and advice of responsible bodies within the industry. The National Union of Mineworkers, for example, assisted by releasing those of their officials whom the Board wished to appoint as Divisional Labour Directors' (NCB 1946).

But there were some leading trade unionists, who, in spite of pressure from both ministry and trade union colleagues, decided that the interests of the mineworkers would be best served if they remained as servants of the union, lower though the remuneration might be. If there were any of the new rulers of the industry who had thought to rely for an easy passage on universalising the old saying of 'poacher turned gamekeeper', they had to swallow a few disappointments – but not so very many. No question, however, arose at any point of non-co-operation. On the contrary, there was the most cordial and welcoming attitude towards the new employer amongst union officials and elected committees. For example, at the Bridlington annual conference in the last week of June 1946, the following resolution was passed:

That, in view of the early Nationalisation of the Coal Mining Industry, it be an instruction to the National Coal Board, as soon as the Bill is passed and becomes law, to organise Area meetings in all areas of the Union, to which should be invited both the workmen and the management in order to bring before them their joint responsibility under the new ownership, and to seek their full co-operation in safety, efficiency and production, and to stress the need for a new industrial morality to secure friendly discipline in the industry. (NUM 1946)

Similar expressions of goodwill, with no dissentient voice, could be heard right throughout the year 1946, and were to reach their climax of expectation in its last month.

The nine members of the National Coal Board might wish to devolve as much responsibility as possible on to the shoulders of the divisional boards. But the divisional boards were not a legal entity; the National Board was: everything had to be done in its name. All delegations of responsibility to lower bodies had to be by deliberate acts, which had to be timed to allow for development of lower organisations and their functions.

Any consideration of what had been laid upon the Board by the Act, its duties, its purposes and policy aims, must lead to an understanding of how vast were these undertakings and how gigantic the task of the new organisation for the industry. The twenty-three district associations of coal-owners had conducted the district selling schemes set up under the Coal Mines Act of 1930; now the district associations were gone but the functions and staff of the schemes would pass to the Board. The Coal Commission, set up by the Coal Act of 1938, nationalising coal deposits 'was to use its power of granting leases in such a way as to promote "the interests, efficiency, and better organisation of the coal-mining industry" . . . On the vesting date the coal deposits and the other assets of the Commission, together with the service contracts of its employees were to pass to the Board' (NCB, 1946).

Since the dual control set-up in 1942 the industry had been under the operational control of the government, exercised by the Ministry of Fuel and Power through a controller-general in London and eight regional controllers in the coalfields.

The Coal Charges Account, which during the five years of its existence had had to be subsidised by the Exchequer to the extent of £27.5 million, was to be wound up, and after nationalisation the Board was to run the industry without subsidy.*

*The *National Coal Board Annual Report* of 1946, paragraph 10, states:
There had been in operation – also since 1942 – the Coal Charges Account, a financial instrument designed to keep up the industry's output during the emergency. Rises in

The Coal Industry Nationalisation Act transferred to the Board the obligations of colliery companies and others towards existing pensioners and preserved the superannuation expectations of all members of the industry's staffs, whether their expectations of benefit were based on right or on long-standing custom. There were some 200 superannuation schemes in the industry and many more arrangements based on a customary practice. Benefits varied from company to company. Many companies not only did not have superannuation schemes but did not pay pensions under customary practice. Where there were schemes, the classes of employee eligible also varied from company to company. Most schemes in the industry covered all office staff and also colliery officials down to the grade of 'deputy' or the equivalent.

Regulations were made by the minister towards the end of 1946 empowering the Board to take over existing schemes or parts of schemes and to set up a scheme of their own with the minister's approval.

After all these and other such immediate problems had found a solution, there remained the intractable problem created by seven centuries of separate coalfields, each within its borders exhibiting a wide variety of fuels that came under the common name of coal, each with a labour force that had grown up from feudal days in many generations with differing conditions and different wage levels and different customs, even with different names for the same grade of labour.

2. STRUCTURE OF THE INDUSTRY

The National Coal Board, whose members had been meeting as an organising committee for a dozen weeks or so after

production costs had been reflected in price increases, but these in themselves did not mean solvency for the less profitable undertakings which, without special assistance, would have gone out of production.

All colliery companies were required to pay into the Account a flat rate levy on each ton of coal produced. They drew varying sums to recover what they paid out on wage additions, guaranteed wage payments, etc. By this means, the burden of increased costs resulting from the war was spread. In addition, colliery companies drew sums which varied from district to district in order to make up a 'standard credit balance' laid down for each district. In short, the low-cost districts had to subsidise the high-cost districts. Payments were also made out of the account to keep solvent 'necessitous undertakings' – companies for which the ordinary drawings on the Account were insufficient.

their names had been announced in Parliament, were formally appointed on Monday 15 July, three days after the Act received the Royal Assent. Immediately they asked for a meeting with the NUM National Executive Committee which was then held on Tuesday 23 July 1946.

The Chairman of the National Coal Board pointed out that the first task of the Board was to establish the machinery under which the industry would require to be administered; the Board had decided that the industry should be divided into eight divisions as follows:

(1) Scotland
(2) Northern (Durham, Northumberland and Cumberland)
(3) North-Eastern (Yorkshire)
(4) North-Western (Lancashire, Cheshire and North Wales)
(5) East Midlands (North Derbyshire, Nottinghamshire, South Derbyshire and Leicester)
(6) West Midlands (North Staffordshire, South Staffordshire, Shropshire, Cannock Chase and Warwickshire)
(7) South-Western (South Wales, Forest of Dean, Bristol and Somerset)
(8) Kent

In each division there would be a board which, with the exception of the scientific director, was likely to take a similar form to that of the National Board. There would be a chairman, deputy chairman, director of production, director of labour, director of finance and a director of marketing.*

The Chairman said that although the Board would not take over control before vesting date, they were ready to do anything which would help deal with the very serious position in the industry. For their part, the Union representatives asked if discussions could begin on such matters as the five-day week and payment for statutory holidays. A joint subcommittee was

---

*In these original eight divisions there were some 950 mines directly operated. But there were nearly half as many again which were to be operated, under licence from the National Coal Board, by private concerns employing not more than thirty workers underground. There were 481 small mines of this kind out of a total of 1,431 mines in the whole country. In the licences issued by the Board there were certain stipulations, such as that: 'All agreements between the Board and the National Union of Mineworkers, regulating wages and conditions of service and the settlement of disputes, should be binding upon the operators of small mines' (NCB, 1946).

appointed to plan the campaign for joint area conferences, a proposal from the union which the Board welcomed.

The mineworkers' representatives were not ill satisfied with this first meeting and preliminary discussion; and when they met by themselves a month later they passed the following resolution:

That we welcome the Coal Industry Nationalisation Act, 1946, which provides for the transfer of the coalmining and ancillary industries from private to public ownership, and place on record our appreciation of the action of the Labour Government in so speedily implementing its election pledge.

We recognise that this is but the first step towards the ideal for which we have striven so long, and further that the industry can only be so re-organised as to offer satisfactory conditions of employment providing there is the fullest co-operation on the part of all employed therein. We, therefore, urge all members of the Union to recognise the necessity of breaking with the past and accepting their responsibilities with a view to ensuring the reorganisation of the industry and the success of the new system of ownership. (22 August 1946)

In their belief, they were off to a fair start.

Meantime, at the NEC meeting of 18 July 1946, Ebby Edwards said the present meeting would be the last that he would attend as Secretary.

So the minutes of that meeting were signed for the last time by Ebby Edwards. He had been MFGB Secretary for nearly fifteen years, NUM Secretary for eighteen months. All his life had been been devoted to the coal industry, first as a miner and then as a miners' agent or official. He was now in his sixty-second year. But he was not to be severed from the industry for several more years.

Meanwhile the ballot vote for his successor had been in progress during the latter half of July. The organisation of the counting and transference of the votes, undertaken by the Proportional Representation Society, was completed by 20 August, the report was submitted and the National Executive Committee minute of 22 August runs: 'That the Report be received and that Mr A. L. Horner be duly appointed as Secretary of the Union, such appointment to date as from 1 September 1946.'*

*See Appendix A to this chapter.

3. MANY NEGOTIATIONS

An immense amount of negotiation had to be carried through before Vesting Day, both by the National Coal Board and by the Union. But what day would be fixed as Vesting Day? In October 1946, the Minister of Fuel and Power consulted the Board about this, and asked if they would be willing to take over on 1 January 1947. The Board saw 'the administrative dangers of an early vesting date and the psychological dangers of a later one'. Under heavy pressure* they chose the early date which the minister then announced on 18 November 1946.

This done, the need for agreements on industrial relations became urgent, so that the miners' leaders were very busy in the last months and weeks of 1946. In their annual report of May 1947, the National Executive Committee stated:

We have indeed been fortunate in that we have had the advantage of being able to negotiate with people who, being concerned with the wellbeing of the industry, have demonstrated a willingness to satisfy, wherever possible, the just and proper claims of our people . . . Our association with the National Coal Board is not merely an association arising from periodical meetings, at which we, as your representatives, advance claims on your behalf only to find such claims invariably opposed by the Board as the employer, but there is, as it was intended by the Government there should be, the closest collaboration between the Board and our representatives . . . Our action in organising the Production Campaign in the Autumn of 1945, which led, for the first time in years, to a reversal of the downward trend in production and a steady, although insufficient, improvement in output, made it possible for us to assure the Board that the dictum of the colliery owners that improved conditions inevitably lead to decreased effort on the part of the workmen and a consequent loss of output, is without foundation and completely unjustified.

By an agreement signed on 5 December 1946 by the nine

---

*Reporting to a special conference, General Secretary Horner said that it had been no easy matter to get Vesting Date fixed for 1 January 1947. The National Coal Board had been very hesitant:
They have informed us, and we know that what they have said is true, that they are far from ready to completely take over the industry and to carry it on as it is intended ultimately to be carried on under the new regime . . . We have to ask you to bear in mind that this day – 1 January 1947 – has been pressed for by your Executive, and that it would have been postponed had it not been for the pressure of the Executive. (20 December 1946)

members of the NCB and twenty-seven members of the NEC, the Board and the Union set down their wish to adopt, with modifications, the national conciliation scheme established by an agreement of 25 May 1943. That existing machinery consisted of a Joint National Negotiating Committee and a National Reference Tribunal. The National Tribunal's awards, binding on both sides, amounted to compulsory arbitration (resisted for over half a century by the Miners' Federation and conceded only in the national emergency of the anti-fascist war). But already there had been a year of peace. Nevertheless, so greatly did they rely on the goodwill of the new employer, and on the continuing accommodating spirit of the government, that the sanction of resort to strike action (regarded as the birthright of a trade union) was quietly given up at the very inception of the new industrial relations.

The negotiation of a pit conciliation scheme which had not been part of 'the 1943 Agreement' was completed by the end of the year, and the agreement was signed on 1 January 1947. The procedure embodied in the agreement was this. If an issue arose between the men and the colliery official concerned, the matter was to be discussed at a 'pit meeting', followed, if there were still no agreement, by discussion at a meeting of a district disputes committee, consisting of representatives of the union and of the divisional board. Finally, if need be, the dispute was to be referred to an umpire.

A time limit was prescribed for each stage. Once it had been decided either by the colliery manager or by the Union lodge that a pit meeting was required, it had to be held within five days. If a second meeting was required it must be held within four days of the first meeting. If, after fourteen days from the time when the pit meeting was requested, settlement had not been reached, the question had to be submitted to the district disputes committee.

4. WAGES AND CONDITIONS OF EMPLOYMENT

By the National Wages Agreement of 1944, no applications

for wage increases, whether national, district or at an individual pit, could be made until the end of June 1948, except that an increase in piece rates could be claimed at a pit if a change in mining conditions had taken place. The Board and the Union agreed that collective agreements made between the Miners' Federation of Great Britain and the Mining Association of Great Britain and between constituent associations of both should continue – with modifications – after the Vesting Date; but the 1944 National Wages Agreement was modified in two ways. First, the ban on wage claims at collieries was removed – but not until six months after effective pit conciliation machinery had been agreed (this meant 1 July 1947). Secondly, national questions could be discussed in the following order of priority: payment for statutory holidays, guaranteed wage and the five-day week.

Lastly, outside wages and conditions of employment were many other matters of concern to both sides, such as the efficiency of the industry, safety, health and welfare. A National Consultative Council was set up, consisting of representatives of the Board, the National Union of Mineworkers, the National Association of Colliery Managers and the Deputies' Federation. The Council held their first meeting towards the end of November 1946, and immediately set about the establishment of consultative machinery in the coalfields.

5. SPECIAL CONFERENCE OF 20 DECEMBER 1946

Chairman Will Lawther introduced the business of what would be described as 'the last conference held before the curtain was rung down on the coalowners'. The delegates had already in their hands a resolution, to be moved by the General Secretary on behalf of the National Executive Committee and seconded by the Vice-President, in the course of which it was stated: 'Having considered the report of the National Executive Committee, the Conference approves the steps which have been taken by the Committee with a view to the claims of the Union as embodied in the "Miners' Charter" being implemented.'

The conference endorsed the action of the Committee in agreeing to a continuance of the conciliation machinery as adopted by the parties in 'the 1943 Agreement'; the carry-over of all arrangements in relation to wages and conditions of employment in the industry, subject to the amendments of Clauses 3 and 4 of the April 1944 Agreement; the commencement of early negotiations in regard to a new wages structure for the industry on the understanding that any new agreement so negotiated would become operative as from the date of agreement; and an arrangement in respect to payments for statutory holidays.

The conference also noted with approval the efforts made by the Committee to bring about an organised five-day working week in the industry and endorsed the arrangement made with the National Coal Board that the change would be introduced on the first Monday in May. Finally, in its long resolution, the conference instructed the National Executive Committee 'to press forward the claim of the Union in regard to Trade Union membership'.

Moving the National Committee's resolution, General Secretary Horner stated that: 'We have found both in the Coal Board and in governmental circles a readiness to accept all the twelve points in the Charter in principle. It now becomes a practical question as to how it is to be worked out.'

Enumerating the items of the Charter, Horner paused for a moment on item 7, the guaranteed wage, which 'came into our lives by reason of the introduction of the Essential Work Order'. He said:

The Essential Work Order has gone, and the Executive has retained the guaranteed wage for all time in this industry, and it will in future be part of our ordinary wages structure . . . Never again will workmen present themselves at collieries to be sent home without pay; never again will workmen in the mining industry be told, 'Your services are not required', and the employer escape the obligation to pay wages for that day.

I remember Arthur Cook used to say, 'When the pits stop, the employers have to feed the horses, but they don't have to feed the men.' The time has come when we can say to this Conference and the coalfield, 'A workman in this industry, if he is capable and available for work, shall for ever be entitled to a full week's wages if he is available for work during his normal working hours.'

Then he told of the conciliation schemes and about the National Agreement of April 1944; of the need for a new wages structure and the organisation of such grades as clerks and officials; then of the five-day week, statutory holidays and other matters in the resolution. In conclusion, Horner said:

I hope, therefore, that there will be an appreciation throughout the industry that things have changed, and when you put the flags up on vesting day – when the flags go over the pits for the National Coal Board – it does mean something different. It is a tremendous change . . . It is not a change in name; it is a change that gives us the possibility of realising things we have only dared dream about for years and years and years.

They had got a start with something concrete: unconditional payment for holidays and a pledge of a five-day week with six days' pay. But Horner emphasised that the secret of their success would lie in the productive capacity of the industry. He was emphatic that from Vesting Day they would have a different and entirely new responsibility:

It is quite clear, too, that in relation to us the Coal Board is an employer, but a different kind of employer – an employer with whom we share certain responsibilities, yet in the last analysis this National Union of Mineworkers remains a free and independent organisation whose main concern is the advancement and protection of the interests of its members.

We must take a long view, because the advancement of our members' interests lies not in sneaking victories from coalowners, but in establishing a firm and highly productive industry out of which these things can come and continue to come for ever and ever. That is a different role for our members.

Yet again he stressed the view that the 'day of agitation' in campaigning for those things was nearly finished; and that: 'The task in future is to use the best means we know to fight Mother Nature and to drag the coal out of her bosom. The future that lies before us is tremendous. The pits are ours. We can say what can be done with them.'

This very full programmatic address of the General Secretary left little enough scope for debate after questions had been asked and answered. This speech, with its high and indeed exalted tone, was not out of tune with the lively anticipations that thronged the minds of the delegates who were in a mood of high optimism. After all, they were on the threshold of the

Promised Land. Like the Israelites of old, their fathers had spent forty years in the wilderness since Robert Smillie, advocating coalmines nationalisation in 1906, had set them on their march with the words: 'We must establish a Labour Government in Great Britain before our interests will be safeguarded as they ought to be' (R. Page Arnot, *The Miners: Years of Struggle*, Allen & Unwin, 1953, pp. 129–30).

That day on the threshold they could not bring into their reckoning what struggles there might be within the Promised Land, with the Canaanites and with the Philistines, not to speak of the formidable Hittites. Least of all could they bethink them that one day the Assyrian would come down like a wolf on the fold.

In the brief debate that followed, the discontent referred to by the General Secretary was outspokenly expressed by Will Arthur of South Wales. On the question of 'Fullest co-operation with the Coal Board' he said: '. . . there are factors that have crept into the situation which are tending to destroy the confidence of the miner in the new administration'. Then he said that out of eight district nominations for general managers or production officers there were six Powell Duffryn agents: and up to three weeks earlier the chief production agent for the district was one of the Powell Duffryn men. The South Wales Area had sent in a resolution of protest against these nominations. Will Arthur said:

I am very concerned, as Mr Horner is, with the general effect of a breakdown in this organisation. What do we find? First we have a General from India who is absolutely ignorant of mining conditions. We have had in South Wales other men who were ignorant of mining. Our last Controller was a Judge who had spent most of his life in India. As Production Officer for South Wales I had the unhappy experience of meeting that gentleman across the table, and it was pitiful to try to negotiate matters of importance affecting production with a man who did not know what he was talking about. Now we have got another General from India.*

*General Sir Alfred Godwin-Austen (1889–1963) came of a distinguished military family including Lieutenant-Colonel Godwin-Austen (1884–1923) after whom was named the second highest mountain in the Himalayas (Mount Godwin-Austen, also designated K2, in the Karakoram Range). After service in the 1914–18 War at Gallipoli and in Mesopotamia he commanded the 14th Infantry Brigade in the Palestine Rebellion 1938–9. In the six-year war 1939–45 he served in East Africa, Abyssinia and Libya; and, after a spell in the War Office 1943–5, became Quartermaster-General of the India Command at New Delhi, thence appointed Chairman, South Western Division of the National Coal Board 1946–8.

The resolution was carried unanimously. So was the pit conciliation scheme as amended by the Executive Committee. So were the alterations to rules: of these perhaps the most important was the addition of a group No. 3, representing mainly colliery officials. On this Horner explained that the National Federation of Colliery Officials and Staffs had decided by a ballot vote of 7,000 to 600 to enter the NUM as a group, and they would expect all lodge officials to help in organising clerks and officials. They had told the Board that their aim was to have everybody below the grade of undermanager in the NUM:

The new organisation of the Coal Board will not require the employer to keep the clerk away from us for fear he will tell us his master's secrets; it will not require that we shall be afraid of the clerk knowing what is going on in our meetings. Those days are gone and finished. These men are necessary men; they are workers who have the right to exist and be organised side by side with the other workers in the industry.

Finally, after these resolutions had been passed, Horner rose to tell the delegates of the setting up of the National Consultative Council: and of similar bodies for the divisions and for the pits, saying that the old pit production committees, with their strictly limited powers, would be replaced:

That Pit Consultative Committee will be entitled to know every plan that is pending for that pit, to discuss such plans, to discuss all the measures necessary to implement them, and generally to ensure that the health, welfare and safety of the men of the pit are safeguarded.

This is not some kind of thing that is given you *ex gratia*. This is a right you have under the Act of Parliament, and we want you to pay as much attention as possible in this machinery to this phase of raising the status of the men, because it is here where you get the status and complete right of intervention on all matters affecting the industry, quite apart from wages and conditions.

Then the Chairman closed an historic special conference, saying: 'We feel that what the Secretary said earlier in the Conference is a true indication of the spirit of the men of the coalfield – with less man-power this year from May onward there has been a continual increase in output, and we are confident that that will be the spirit of our men in 1947.'

Twelve days later the new flag was to fly over the collieries of the United Kingdom.

APPENDICES TO CHAPTER VII

Appendix A

NATIONAL UNION OF MINEWORKERS
ELECTION OF SECRETARY, AUGUST, 1946

TO THE EXECUTIVE,
   NATIONAL UNION OF MINEWORKERS.

Gentlemen,

   We have the honour to submit to you a Report declaring the result of the election of Secretary of the National Union of Mineworkers, the counting of the votes in which was undertaken, at your request, by the Proportional Representation Society.

METHOD OF ELECTION. – The election took place under the single transferable vote system.

ASSESSORS. – Assessors appointed by the National Union of Mineworkers were present during the period of the counting of the votes. The counting took place at St. George's Hall, Westminster Bridge Road.

PAPERS RETURNED BY THE DISTRICT. – The total number of used papers returned by the Districts was 430,472. A statement showing the number of used papers returned by each District separately is given in Annexe I to this Report.

INVALID PAPERS. – Of the used papers returned, 10,823 were rejected, after consultation with the Assessors, as invalid. The general principle followed in deciding upon irregularly marked papers was to accept all papers in which the intention of the voter was reasonably clear. The main causes of rejection were the marking of ballot papers with two or more crosses, instead of figures, or the showing of first preferences, by means of the figure 1, against the names of two or more candidates. It is to be observed that the papers rejected constitute only 2.5 per cent of the total poll.

ANALYSIS OF FIRST PREFERENCES. – The valid ballot papers were sorted according to the first preferences, i.e., the figure '1' set opposite to the name of a candidate, with the following result:–

Names of Candidates	*First Preference*
Horner, A. L.	226,605
Jones, W. E.	167,074
Standing, J.	25,970
TOTAL	419,649

RESULT. – A. L. HORNER, of South Wales, is elected Secretary of the National Union of Mineworkers.

STAFF EMPLOYED. – The Staff consisted of Mr. George Humphreys, who acted as Returning Officer for the Proportional Representation Society, and 20 clerks available for such occasional work.

Trusting that the conduct of the election meets with your approval,
I have the honour to be,
For the
PROPORTIONAL REPRESENTATION SOCIETY
(Signed) George Humphreys,
Returning Officer.

Annexe I

NATIONAL UNION OF MINEWORKERS
ELECTION OF SECRETARY, AUGUST, 1946

Voting Papers returned by Districts:

	Valid Papers	*Invalid Papers*	*Total Papers Returned*
Cokemen	2,670	18	2,688
Cumberland	4,034	99	4,133
Derbyshire	18,271	563	18,834
Durham	62,462	2,301	64,763
Kent	2,823	127	2,950
Lancashire	23,030	605	23,635
Leicester	2,070	43	2,113
Midlands	26,712	631	27,343
Northumberland	26,649	885	27,534
North Wales	4,954	237	5,191
Nottingham	18,563	900	19,463
Scotland	35,412	669	36,081
Somerset	1,629	48	1,677
South Derbyshire	3,870	89	3,959
South Wales	82,168	1,591	83,759

Yorkshire	74,724	1,947	76,671
Group I	15,433	45	15,478
Group II	7,172	12	7,184
Power group	7,003	13	7,016
TOTALS	419,649	10,823	430,472

Appendix B

THE STATE OF THE INDUSTRY UNDER PRIVATE ENTERPRISE

(Excerpt from the First Annual Report of the National Coal Board)

44. Between the two world wars the history of the coal industry had been a tale of struggle with depression and shrinking markets. In 1913 – the heyday of the British coal trade – the industry produced 287 million tons, of which 94 million tons were exported or shipped as bunkers. During the first world war, overseas markets were lost and a spur was given to the development of foreign coalfields. After the war, currency difficulties and the impoverishment of many coal-importing countries contributed further to the decline in the coal trade. Competition in export markets (much of it directly or indirectly subsidised) was particularly strong from Germany and later from Poland. By the time of the trade depression in the early 1930s, output had shrunk to little more than 200 million tons, and exports to 50 million tons. As the industry's capacity was then far greater than the demand for its output, there was intense competition between in-dividual collieries and between whole coalfields. The ex-porting coalfields turned to the home trade to recoup themselves. Prices slumped, wages were cut, men were laid off and technical progress was arrested. Inter-district competition was reduced – first in the Midland coalfield by a voluntary arrangement between owners, and later by the Statutory Schemes established under the 1930 Coal Mines Act. The general recovery of trade in the late 1930s increased the demand for coal at home and abroad, but despite material improvements in some coalfields the industry as a whole could

hardly have been called prosperous. Before the outbreak of the second world war the technical standard of most of the collieries fell far short of American and Continental standards. Most revealing of the industry's lack of progress between the wars is a comparison between the change in output per man shift in Britain and other countries. Between 1913 and 1938, for example, the British output per man shift was increased by only 13 per cent. In America during the same period, it was increased by nearly 40 per cent, and in Germany and Poland by about 60 per cent.

45. During the 1939–45 war the industry deteriorated further. Much of the equipment of the mines became badly worn. Many miners went into the Forces. Output fell to 175 million tons in 1945, and exports and bunkers to a mere 8 million tons. In 1946 the industry's labour force had shrunk to about 690,000 – less than it had been at any time for fifty years. Of this total, 50,000 men were over 60 years of age, 300,000 were over 40 and 15,000 were 'Bevin Boys', conscripted during the war and due for release within two years. Absenteeism at the coal face was nearly 20 per cent, and output per man shift (all workers) was about 1.03 tons, compared with an average of 1.16 tons in the year just before the war. Yet, with the industry at this low ebb, British coal was most urgently needed both at home and abroad.

46. The finances of the industry were artificial. The Coal Charges Account subsidised high-cost districts – in particular, Cumberland, South Wales, Kent, Forest of Dean and Durham – at the expense of the others, and of the Exchequer. (NCB, 15 July to 31 December 1946)

INDEX OF NAMES

GENERAL INDEX